Power and Global Econ

What is the relationship between states' economic power and their formal political power in multilateral economic institutions? Why do we see variation in states' formal political power across economic institutions of the same era? In this book Ayse Kaya examines these crucial under-explored questions, drawing on multiple theoretical traditions within International Relations to advance a new approach of "adjusted power." She explains how the economic shifts of our time, marked by the rise of Brazil, Russia, India, China, and other emerging economies, have affected and will impact key multilateral economic institutions. Through detailed contemporary and historical analyses of the International Monetary Fund, the World Bank, the G20, and the International Trade Organization, Kaya shows that the institutional setting mediates the significance of the underlying distribution of economic power across states. The book presents both case studies and key statistics.

Ayse Kaya is an assistant professor of political science at Swarthmore College.

Power and Global Economic Institutions

Ayse Kaya

Swarthmore College

CAMBRIDGE
UNIVERSITY PRESS

CAMBRIDGE
UNIVERSITY PRESS

University Printing House, Cambridge CB2 8BS, United Kingdom

One Liberty Plaza, 20th Floor, New York, NY 10006, USA

477 Williamstown Road, Port Melbourne, VIC 3207, Australia

4843/24, 2nd Floor, Ansari Road, Daryaganj, Delhi - 110002, India

79 Anson Road, #06-04/06, Singapore 079906

Cambridge University Press is part of the University of Cambridge.

It furthers the University's mission by disseminating knowledge in the pursuit of education, learning and research at the highest international levels of excellence.

www.cambridge.org
Information on this title: www.cambridge.org/9781107544062

First published 2015
First paperback edition 2017

A catalogue record for this publication is available from the British Library

Library of Congress Cataloging in Publication data
Kaya, Ayse.
Power and global economic institutions / Ayse Kaya, Swarthmore College.
   pages   cm
ISBN 978-1-107-12094-5 (hardback)
1. Institutional economics.   2. Power (Social sciences)
3. International relations.   I. Title.
HB99.5.K39   2015
330–dc23

2015021265

ISBN 978-1-107-12094-5 Hardback
ISBN 978-1-107-54406-2 Paperback

To Andrew

With love and gratitude, always

Contents

List of figures and tables

Figures

Tables

Acknowledgments

During my long relationship with this book, I have had the privilege of receiving help from others.

My first expression of gratitude goes to John Haslam at Cambridge University Press and the anonymous reviewers. Haslam's interest in the project was critical. And, the two outstanding reviewers helped invaluably in getting the manuscript to its current form.

I am immensely grateful to the following Swarthmore colleagues for all their substantive input to this project as well as their words of wisdom and encouragement: Rachel Buurma, Philip Jefferson, Keith Reeves, Jim Kurth, Dominic Tierney, Rick Valelly, Stephen Golub, Ellen Magenheim, Mike Reay, and Lynne Schofield.

I benefitted greatly from the kindness of others to whom I remain thankful. Clint Pinehardt and the rest of the University of Texas at Dallas Political Science Department gave useful comments on Chapter 3 during my presentation there. Clint also provided feedback for Chapter 4, as did Irfan Nooruddin. Christopher Kilby also generously commented on a version of Chapter 3. I also thank Orfeo Fioretos and Anne Holthoefer for comments on drafts of Chapter 4. Columbia University's Committee on Global Thought (CGT) provided stimulating feedback on the book project as a whole during my presentation there. I thank Katharina Pistor especially; co-teaching as a postdoc at CGT with her and Michael Doyle remains an important experience. I benefitted from numerous presentations at ISA, APSA, and MPSA conferences.

I had great research assistants, who have all graduated from Swarthmore: Caleb Jones, James Mao, Paul Shortell, and Spencer Topf. All the students especially in my International Political Economy seminars facilitated critical conversations that showed intellectual maturity beyond their years. My friend Robin F. Matthews helped get the references and the format in shape.

I made a number of trips to Washington, DC, to talk to World Bank and IMF officials as well as insiders from other relevant organizations.

While I promised to keep them anonymous, I thank them all for the generosity of their time and input.

Two great scholars from my alma mater deserve special mention: Joel Krieger was a wise counsel throughout the project, and Craig Murphy, despite never having had me as a student, provided extensive comments on Chapters 1 and 2 more than once – his comments were integral to the growth of the project.

I felt the two following friends were always on my team and provided great help on this book (more than a few times!): Geoffrey Herrera, whose knowledge of I(i)nternational R(r)elations has always impressed me, and Asli Leblebicioglu, who is a wonderful economist and a patient one at answering all my statistical questions.

I feel bad not dedicating this book to my parents, who – a lifetime ago – let their eighteen-year-old leave Istanbul for college in the United States and have since then made many trips to help me. I promise them the next book. I could not have completed this project without Andrew Orloff.

1 Introduction

Tectonic shifts in the global economy have come to dominate today's public discussions on international politics.[1] The two largest changes are the rise of the large emerging economies, often narrowly defined as the BRICs (Brazil, Russia, India, and China), and, thanks in part to this rise, the potential loss of US hegemony. Indeed, at the time of the writing of this book, due to the rapid economic ascent of the emerging market economies, as well as US military (mis)adventures in Iraq and Afghanistan, both scholarly and public deliberations have increasingly turned away from the discussion of "US unipolarity" to assessing whether the multilateral order the US actors and their allies crafted at the end of World War II is resistant and flexible enough to survive the rising states.[2] At the end of the Cold War, scholars were racing to find the right phrase to mark the unprecedented world where the USA would stand alone as a superpower ("the end of history" versus the "clash of civilizations," for instance).[3]

Today scholarly and public discussions are instead trying to understand the implications of the rise of the BRICs and other emerging economies for the multilateral order, including its institutions such as the International Monetary Fund (IMF) and the World Bank. Since their inception near the end of the war, a handful of rich countries led by the USA have dominated these multilateral economic institutions. Although this asymmetric control over the institutions has long been controversial, it has become even more contentious as large emerging markets have increased their importance for global trade and financial flows over the past several decades, while the governance of the institutions has remained largely static, with the exception of some changes in

---

[1] For recent scholarly works on this topic, see, e.g., Beeson (2009); Hurrell (2008); Kahler (2013); Layne (2009 and 2012); MacDonald and Parent (2011); Schweller and Pu (2011).

[2] See, for instance, Brooks and Wohlforth (2009); Chin (2010); Ikenberry (2008); Ikenberry and Wright (2008); Mearsheimer (2001).

[3] Fukuyama (1992) ("the end of history"); Huntington (1993) ("the clash of civilizations").

2008–2010. In this context, questions about whether there is a "crisis" in the US-crafted multilateral order and whether this multilateral system will be able to continue to integrate the rising states, as opposed to being challenged by them, infuse public and scholarly discussions.[4] These discussions have only intensified with the 2008 global financial and economic crisis since this crisis emanated, unlike earlier crises of the late twentieth century, not from the developing world, but from the most advanced financial system in the world – the USA.

Underlying these various considerations is a question about the relationship between economic power and political power. Ultimately, questions about China's economic rise, for instance, hinge upon the extent to which China translates such economic power into political influence in the international order. Similarly, debates about the US-led multilateral political-economic order need to ultimately address the question of how the rising powers' economic prowess will affect governance through multilateral institutions. Undoubtedly, this is a multifaceted topic that scholars have approached from different angles, exploring for instance whether China is a "revisionist" state, whether the USA retains the legitimacy to revamp the existing multilateral economic institutions, or the extent to which the rising states would like to reform prevalent institutional rules. Yet, less has been said about the fundamental issue that forms the common thread in these various discussions: the association between economic power and states' political power in multilateral institutions.

This book examines this crucial issue by asking the following question: What is the relationship between states' economic power and their formal political power in multilateral economic institutions? This question raises others: Why do we see the same states possess different levels of formal political power in different multilateral economic institutions of the same era? For instance, when the USA and its allies created the IMF and the World Bank, they endowed these institutions with weighted voting, namely asymmetric representation of the member states, but they created the world trade organization of the time, the International Trade Organization (ITO), with equal voting. What explains this variation in members' formal political power across different institutions? Further, the IMF and the World Bank underwent shifts in members' formal political power in 2008–2010.[5] Contemporary accounts of these shifts have been lumped together and riddled with normative assessments (for

---

[4] Birdsall and Fukuyama (2011); Kahler (2013); Odell (2009); Voeten (2004).

[5] Voting in both institutions consists of two components – basic votes, which are distributed to member states equally, and quota (IMF) or subscription (World Bank) votes, which indicate the member's shares in the organization, which are in turn calculated by the

instance, while some considered the rising states to have increased their formal significance in the institution significantly, others have dismissed the changes as tangential). Yet, as this book shows, the 2008–2010 changes in these institutions enhanced the representation of the economically rising states at differing degrees: states, such as Brazil, China, and India, were able to translate their increasing economic power into greater formal political power relatively more in the IMF, but they were not as successful in the World Bank. Again, what explains the differences across the two institutions?[6]

Although the discipline of International Relations has long wrestled with the association between states' economic power and their political power within multilateral institutions, it still does not provide clear answers to these questions.[7] On one hand, power-based accounts of various kinds suggest that multilateral institutions will reflect the shifts in the underlying distribution of economic power, particularly the rise of certain states (e.g., Brooks and Wohlforth 2009; Gilpin 1981; Kirshner 2010; Layne 2012, p. 211; Schweller and Priess 1997). Robert Gilpin in his influential 1981 book *War and Change* has now famously argued that as the distribution of power changes, the rising states will fashion the international system, including its institutions, in accordance with their interests. Recent power-based perspectives not just rearticulate the notion that economic power and political power in institutions go hand in hand, but they also marvel at the gap between the two, namely while the distribution of economic power in the world has changed, the global institutions have not caught up with this change. Here, Brooks and Wohlforth (2009, p. 49) put it succinctly: "no one sitting down to design the perfect global framework for the twenty-first century would come up with anything like the current one . . . The existing architecture is a relic of preoccupations and power relationships of the middle of the last century." The authors emphasize that when these institutions were created at

member's relative economic weight and other economic variables. The latter component is more important in determining a member state's total voting power.

[6] Throughout the book, I use the G20 as a reference point for the large advanced economies that are on a relative basis economically declining, but nonetheless remain institutionally dominant ("the declining states") and the large emerging markets, which are the economically rising states ("rising states"). The book examines three different categories of states in discussing the low-income countries: (1) The Sub-Saharan African states (minus South Africa); (2) the UN classification of Least Developed Countries (LDCs); (3) the World Bank's classification of low-income countries.

[7] As Simmons and Martin (2002, p. 194) define, institutions denote implicit or explicit and effective or ineffective rules governing international behavior. The usage of the term institution here, as elsewhere in the discipline of International Relations, is broad and includes both formal and informal institutions (Koremenos et al. 2001a, 2001b; Simmons and Martin 2002).

the end of the war, they manifested the then distribution of power and because that distribution has changed today, these institutions are out of synch with the times. Overall, power-based perspectives suggest institutions (should) reflect the asymmetries in inter-state power.[8]

Yet, other perspectives disagree with this predominantly power-based analysis of the relationship between states' economic power and their formal political power in institutions. Randall Stone (2011, p. 18) emphasizes that weak states tend to receive "a share of formal power that is out of proportion to their resources" in multilateral economic institutions, so as to encourage their participation in these rules-based frameworks that the powerful states otherwise dominate. Stone's argument, thus, suggests that the relatively weak (judged by relative economic standing) will possess more formal political power in institutions than we might expect them to do just based on their importance to the global economy. In a different theoretical and empirical context, John Ikenberry (2000) makes a similar argument. He explains that in order to establish long-lasting institutional arrangements, just as the USA prudently did at the end of the war, powerful states signal "restraint" within multilateral institutions. Restraint means the dominant states do not grab all the political power they can, but rather agree to terms in institutions that do not necessarily mirror their economic and military resources. Both Stone and Ikenberry suggest that the distribution of inter-state economic power would not be reflected in institutions as asymmetries in members' formal political power; rather, the leading states would voluntarily tame these asymmetries (for different reasons).

These influential perspectives offer opposing processes, but the same outcome for how the distribution of formal political power in institutions will change when some states increase their economic (and military) power.[9] From the relatively more power-based approach, because institutions risk being relegated to the dustbin of history if they fail to update themselves with the changing distribution of power, the American actors should realize the unpalatable future for the existing multilateral

---

[8] Here and elsewhere, I do not use the term asymmetry in a normatively loaded manner – I do not suggest symmetry is desirable, nor asymmetry is undesirable. Rather, it simply provides another way for me to refer to a distribution of power, where some states have more than others.

[9] Economic power denotes economic resources, which can be assessed with reliance on widely accepted indicators, including the size of a state's economy, its record of economic growth, its participation in international trade relations (through imports and exports), and its participation in financial transactions (either as a recipient of investment or a source of it). The early debates between realists and liberals (e.g., Keohane and Nye 1977) regarding the importance of military versus economic power have lost prominence over time, as important realist approaches have focused solely on economic power (e.g., Drezner 2007; Grieco 1990; Krasner 1985; Viner 1948).

institutions (that they have created and dominated) and update them to reflect the changed and changing inter-state power relations. From the more institutionalist perspective, the US actors might realize that the continuation of these institutions, and their acceptability to a range of shareholders and stakeholders, demands the recognition of others' power and the continued signaling of "restraint." Once again, the outcome would be the Americans and their allies agree to enhance the formal political power of the rising states within the institutions.

From an even more intensely institutionalist perspective, one that sees multilateral institutions as solutions to collective action problems, through the provision of better information and hence the strengthening of monitoring and enforcement, how the distribution of economic power relates to the institutional setting remains unclear. As Robert Keohane's (1984) seminal work has argued, and the work following it has suggested, institutions are there to sustain cooperation "after hegemony," or at the very least despite the vagaries in the hegemon's influence. Based on this kind of an institutionalist perspective, institutions isolate the effects of power and create stable sites for interaction.[10] Yet, such an approach does not tell us enough about how institutions fare when the distribution of power shifts.

This book contends that existing approaches leave out key aspects of the relationship between economic power and formal political power in multilateral economic institutions. Importantly, while existing works focus on either power or institutions as distinct realms, we must examine their intersection as well.[11]

As the preceding synopsis of the literature reveals, there are three crucial (inter-related though distinct) issues that the existing perspectives overlook. First, the prevailing literatures do not focus adequately on the differences across institutions (of the same period) as to how the distribution of economic power manifests itself in the institutions. Going back to my earlier point, why did the institutional settings of the IMF and the World Bank, even though they are the twin international financial institutions in the literature, address the rise of large emerging economies differently in the 2008–2010 changes to members' formal political power? This variation is key to understanding how the rising states affect the multilateral order. It is also crucial to unpacking exactly how institutional settings interfere with power dynamics because without explaining how the distribution of power manifests itself differently across different

[10] Lake (1993, p. 465) notes that Keohane "goes further to suggest that states may be able to construct regimes to facilitate cooperation even in the absence of a single leader."
[11] While Stone (2011) is an exception here, his work focuses on "informal governance."

multilateral institutions, one cannot begin to tell a story regarding the importance of institutions in impacting power dynamics.

Second, based on the literature it is puzzling as to why there is a "lag" between the changes in the distribution of economic power and the distribution of political power in multilateral economic institutions (e.g., the Brooks and Wohlforth quote above). While power-based perspectives identify this lag as an important feature to study, they do not analyze either how the lag comes into existence or how it is overcome (e.g., Schweller and Priess 1997). By the same token, from an institutionalist perspective, the issue is similarly unclear, even though the institutionalist literature points to the presence of a discrepancy between institutions and power dynamics as a source for crisis in the system (e.g., Ikenberry 2012). If the preeminent economic power showed "restraint," as these accounts suggest, it is unclear as to why when that state is in relative decline, namely there are other rising states in the system, there would necessarily be a significant lag between the institutions and the distribution of power. Regardless, neither perspective focuses on analyzing the factors that contribute to the outcome of institutions outliving power dynamics.

Third, even the institutionalist literature does not tell us how exactly institutions matter to power dynamics (e.g., Krasner 1991).[12] It seems basic to say that institutions affect power dynamics, but once one starts digging into the question of how institutions moderate the inter-state distribution of power, one gets stuck in important but well-rehearsed answers. For instance, we know that states can set aside concerns for short-term gains and cooperate under the shadow of the future that institutions create. In this sense, we know that power does not blind state actors to creating a rules-based order that will serve their long-term interest. However, the institutionalist literature does not tell us how exactly institutions moderate or mediate inter-state power asymmetries. While part of this literature refers to asymmetries among states as an important factor to examine in multilateral institutions, it does not provide systematic and clear answers to the question of how the inter-state distribution of power relates to members' formal political power in institutions (e.g., Koremenos et al. 2001a, 2001b). Overall, prevalent literatures that focus on institutions and power treat these phenomena as separate realms, but leave their intersection under-analyzed.

This book not only borrows from, but also expands upon, these existing perspectives as well as others to show that the institutional setting

---

[12] Krasner, though, shows the opposite: how power might matter to institutional dynamics, not the other way around.

determines the significance of the underlying distribution of economic power. Institutions sometimes provide a relatively strong manifestation of the inter-state distribution of economic power, while at other times they mitigate that distribution. Taking the rise of China as an example, some institutional settings will be relatively more responsive to China's increasing importance in the global economy, while other institutional settings will be more immune to this shift in the inter-state distribution of economic power. Just as a dial on a sound system would adjust the volume, the institution adjusts the importance of inter-state asymmetries in economic power. The institution affects both how and how fast the shifts in the distribution of economic power manifest themselves as changes in member states' formal political power. For the remainder of the book, as shorthand, I refer to the book's analytical framework as the adjusted power approach.[13]

The book argues that institutional settings adjust power in three primary ways. First, the institutionally dominant states' core interpretation of the purposes and functions of multilateral institutions impacts their preferences toward the distribution of formal political power within these institutions.[14] Different states might have different interpretations of which (public) goods the institutions should provide, or they might have different priorities regarding the provision of various goods that the institution intends to supply. For instance, should the World Bank serve the poorest states only, or should it continue to serve the middle-income countries also? In turn, these interpretations influence states' attitudes toward the distribution of political power within institutions. Further, conflicts between different states' conceptualizations of institutional priorities can shape institutional outcomes, including the distribution of members' formal political power.[15]

Second, how members fund an institution, particularly the degree and the nature of state funding, affects the importance of the underlying inter-state distribution of economic power for the institutional context. For instance, the World Bank's non-concessional lending arm – the International Bank for Reconstruction and Development (IBRD) – raises money on international capital markets through its issuance of triple-A

---

[13] I do not argue this distribution of power can be precisely determined, but its general contours – where different states roughly sit in the hierarchy of economic importance – can be ascertained.

[14] The answer to which states are formally the dominant states within institutions is historically contingent. In the 2008–2010 period, there is little dispute the G5, or the G7 states, stand as the institutionally dominant states, with the USA as the leading state (e.g., Copelovitch 2010).

[15] These points do not suggest there are infinite possibilities in the way in which a state might interpret the key purposes of an institution.

rated bonds.[16] In contrast, the IMF does not have the ability to raise funds in a similar manner. How does this difference across the two institutions play into members' calculations about financial burden sharing? And, how does burden sharing relate to the relationship between the inter-state distribution of economic power and the distribution of formal political power in multilateral economic institutions? For instance, the nature of the institution's funding might create an "institutional logic" for asymmetries in formal political power.

Third, institutions mediate the importance of the inter-state distribution of economic power through institutional rules and conventions. Simply, institutional conventions denote well-established procedures and specific interpretations of rules for certain actions. Among the many conventions a single institution may embody, of interest here are those that concern formal political power, including the procedures for altering it. Reasonably, these existing rules and conventions determine the parameters, if not the content, of how members alter formal political power in the institution. Particularly, such rules may, more often than not, be a source for "incremental change" as opposed to more big-bang alterations (e.g., Pierson 2004; Thelen and Mahoney 2010).

Given that the literature currently lacks an integrative theory/approach to the inter-relationship between distribution of economic power and political power within multilateral institutions, the book aims to begin filling this gap. As the preceding discussions make clear, variation across institutions as to how power asymmetries manifest themselves is central to the adjusted power approach. For instance, all else being equal, in some institutional settings, the institutionally dominant states that are in relative economic decline will be more willing to enhance the position of the rising states, while in other settings they might be more reluctant. This point also helps explain the "lag" between the changes in the distribution of economic power and shifts in members' formal political power in multilateral economic institutions. While the argument that "institutions adjust power" may *prima facie* seem obvious, existing works, including the influential ones discussed above, have said less about the intersection of power and institutions and more about power *or* institutions as separate realms.

The book ultimately connects distinct literatures within International Relations. Analyses about the examination of multilateral economic institutions and the relative rise and decline of certain states generally remain separate within the discipline, though these matters are related. In recent years, scholars have produced theoretically diverse work on

---

[16] Non-concessional means the loans are at market interest rates.

multilateral economic institutions, with a particular focus on the World Bank and the IMF.[17] The design, the structure, as well as the inner-workings of institutions constitute the core of this literature. These works, by and large, remain analytically separate from another prolific line of research and thinking within International Relations that focuses on the rise and decline of influential states. This line of research, essentially, examines whether existing multilateral frameworks can accommodate the rising states, and the extent to which these states seek accommodation within it as opposed to challenging it. For instance, John Ikenberry (2008) have argued that the current multilateral political-economic system remains historically unique in the extent and the quality of its institutional formation with numerous "points of access" for the rising states; therefore, arguing for the peaceful rise of China. Others, such as Iain Johnston (2008), have shown that China can be socialized into international institutions, suggesting thereby that such socialization will likely lessen the chances for system-wide change. Yet, other approaches argue for the reform of multilateral institutions to perpetuate the projection of US power globally (e.g., Brooks and Wohlforth 2009; Ikenberry and Wright 2008). While this literature on rising states provides a macro-picture of the multilateral economic institutional context, it does not engage extensively with the detailed workings of multilateral economic institutions (and the corresponding literature).[18] Ultimately any understanding of the peaceful (or not) rise of economic powers, as well as their behavior within a specific institutional context, demands an analysis that combines the two literatures.

The book's focus on formal political power constitutes a critical dimension in the analysis of both multilateral economic institutions and how the rising states will impact these institutions. Formal political power, here, denotes a state's voice within an institution, as expressed by the rules and procedures of that institution. Two main components comprise formal political power – states' voting rights in the institution and states' representation in the constituent organs of the institution.[19] Formal political power helps explain "control" within an institution, and control remains one of the most fundamental aspects of understanding the design and function of institutions (e.g., Koremenos et al. 2001a, 2001b). Formal

---

[17] For instance, see Chwieroth (2010); Copelovitch (2010); Moschella (2010); Stone (2011); Weaver (2008); Woods (2006).

[18] Johnston's book, in terms of its focus on specific institutions, is an exception here, but his examples are drawn from the security realm.

[19] Formal political power exists in both relatively formal and informal institutions. Formal institutions rely more extensively on written documents and domestic ratification procedures than informal institutions, which rely less on codification (Lipson 1991; Chapter 7).

political power thus illustrates the "outer structural constraint" within which the institution work (Woods 2006, p. 4).[20]

Member states pay close attention to their formal political power within institutions. For instance, as one expert notes regarding the IMF, states have "a keen awareness that any change in the quota structure [which determines voting power] might affect their proportionate influence over the Fund's decision-taking and their ranking vis-à-vis other members" (Lister 1984, p. 76; see also Woods 2000). In the 1990s, Japan's efforts to enhance its position to the second largest shareholder in the IMF was marked by both Japanese insistence on this ranking and the British and French sensitivity to being surpassed by Japan (Rapkin et al. 1997). Due to a similar concern for rankings, since 1990, the UK and France have requested to tie their voting power in the IMF.[21] Formal political power is, similarly, sensitive in the World Bank. In fact, during changes to shareholding (thus voting power) the Bank permits members to exercise their "preemptive right." In cases where only a certain group of members stand to benefit from gains to their shares, the non-beneficiary members can preemptively increase their own shares so as to preserve their ranking in the institution.

Formal political power also tends to be a source of "prestige among peers" or even national pride, which again explains member states' close scrutiny of it (Boughton 2001, p. 857; see also Chapter 4).[22] For instance, in the 1980s, China's request to increase its capital subscription in the World Bank intended to bring its position, particularly voting power, in the institution "to a size which would be representative of China's position among nations" (IMF 1987, p. 11). Further emphasizing the importance of formal position in the institution from a ranking and prestige perspective, twenty-one members of the institution exercised their preemptive rights for the sake of the maintenance of their relative position in response to China's request.

Given the various ways in which formal political power matters, domestic ratification agencies that appropriate the funds to multilateral institutions, such as the US Congress, tend to closely scrutinize members' institutional standing (Lavelle 2011; Chapters 4, 5). For instance, a US Senate Committee report that analyzed the multilateral financial institutions from 2003 to 2010 puts it simply: "U.S. voting shares

---

[20] While it may not be sufficient to analyze formal political power, it is necessary.

[21] Officially, since the Ninth General Review (1990), they have requested to have the same quota in the institution, which means they hold the same voting power.

[22] For a general discussion of states' concerns with their relative positions in international institutions due to concerns about prestige, among other aims, see Lake (2013); Ikenberry and Wright (2008).

and veto authority should be maintained [in the IMF and the World Bank]" and that the position of the USA "helps maintain domestic support for the institution" (US Senate 2010, p. 4). The importance of formal political power for domestic ratification bodies compounds the importance of analyzing it (e.g., Putnam 1988; see also Chapter 3).

Even when members do not resort to formal procedures, formal political power impacts outcomes. For instance, the IMF and the World Bank's Executive Boards tend to reach decisions by consensus. However, consensus does not mean equal input. Rather, consensus suggests "a position supported by executive directors having sufficient votes to carry the question if a vote were taken" (Gold 1972, p. 198). And, "[a]t no time has the avoidance of voting connoted a dismissal of interest in voting power" in the two international financial institutions (p. 216; see also Boughton 2001, e.g., p. xxi). Regarding consensus in the IMF, Pauly (1997, p. 113) similarly notes: "everyone knows the way votes would come out if they had to be taken."[23] In short, formal political power is a critical factor in explaining both the (re)design of institutions and how they function.

In addition to exploring a critical dimension of institutional design and functioning, this book explores several empirical puzzles that the literature has largely ignored. In Chapter 3, I use an original dataset to analyze IMF quota changes over 1965–2010, showing US influence over these quota adjustments.[24] The literature has not systematically studied the determinants of IMF quotas, which on paper appear to be reasonably clear, as there is a quota formula with a number of economic indicators. The actual determinants of a member's quota, however, deserve discussion. For one, there were numerous formulae until 2008, and there was lack of transparency regarding which formula was used for which country. Further, the member states politically negotiate the actual quotas. Room for such political negotiation raises questions about whether the institutionally dominant states can exert informal influence. While scholars have explored US informal influence over matters where member states have delegated tasks to the IMF staff, such as loans, US influence over quota adjustments has not yet been studied. Chapter 3's finding that political-economic proximity to the USA enhances a member's quota shift is, thus, significant.

---

[23] By the same token, the voting equality at the World Trade Organization, where decisions are made by consensus, has also been consequential, particularly for the launching of new rounds (e.g., Steinberg 2002).

[24] IMF quotas determine members' maximum financial contributions to the institutions and thereby the bulk of their voting power. See also footnote 5.

Another relatively under-explored question the book examines is the origins of the multilateral trading system and the failed International Trade Organization (ITO). Chapter 4 probes why the US actors and their interlocutors created the multilateral trading system with voting equality, unlike the weighted voting system in the IMF and the World Bank. As the preeminent economic power at the creation of all three institutions, why did the USA agree to voting equality in the trade institution? This question has received little attention in the literature.

Finally, there is still very little scholarly analysis of the 2008–2010 changes in members' formal political power in the IMF, the World Bank, and the upgrade of the G20.[25] Among these changes, in 2008 the IMF revised its formula for determining member states' financial contributions (and thus the bulk of their voting power) within the institution, and for the first time moved to a single formula for all members. In 2010, the World Bank, also for the first time in its history, generated its own formula for determining members' shares, parting with its tradition of mostly relying on the IMF quota formula. These 2008–2010 shifts in the IMF and the World Bank constitute, disputably, the most extensive changes to the rules and conventions governing formal political power.[26]

To my knowledge, this is the first book on these recent shifts in formal political power at these multilateral economic institutions. While some might argue that a link between the rise of large emerging economies and the 2008–2010 changes at these three multilateral economic institutions (IMF, World Bank, G20) is self-evident, the nature of that link and how it differs across the three institutions demands detailed analysis. It also provides a great opportunity to explore the relationship between economic and political power. Further, the nascent literature that exists on these 2008–2010 shifts does not provide a cross-institutional, comparative analysis of the kind this book provides.[27] The detailed analysis of these changes contributes significantly not just to the analysis of how shifts in the inter-state economic power affect multilateral economic institutions, but also to charting the trajectory of these institutions.

Leading scholars have identified a need for the kind of analysis this book provides in order to advance our understanding of international political economic relations. For instance, Robert Keohane (2009, p. 34)

---

[25] Exceptions include: Kaya (2012); Lesage et al. (2013); Wade (2011); Woods (2010). The transition from the G7 to the G20 has produced an extensive literature, but I argue this literature has generally not studied the G20's institutional features comprehensively (Chapter 7).

[26] At the time of writing, some members are still in the process of implementing some of these agreed-upon reforms.

[27] While Wade (2011) talks about both the IMF and the World Bank, he does not analyze them in a comparative manner.

has noted that the discipline of international political economy (IPE) is "remarkably reluctant to focus on major changes taking place in world politics," such as the impressive economic development happening in China and its wider repercussions for international political economy (see also Mosley and Singer 2009). And he is not alone among prominent International Relations scholars critiquing IPE's increasing distance from crucial events unfolding in the global economy (e.g., Aggarwal 2010; Cohen 2010). The book's focus on the 2008–2010 shifts in members' formal political power in central multilateral economic institutions addresses these calls.[28] Another line of recent criticism comes from Drezner and McNamara (2013, p. 156), who identify the sidelining of power as one of the critical shortcomings of the current literature: "By bracketing the international elements of the political economy, and by excluding power and social dynamics in favor of economic analysis of preferences, conventional IPE has severely limited our ability to understand and interpret both the political sources and impact of phenomena." This book, in contrast, centralizes the study of institutional design and its adaptation in the face of a (changing) distribution of economic power.

The methods and sources

In focusing on the distribution of formal political power in multilateral economic institutions, and how that distribution relates to the underlying distribution of economic power, I use both case study methodology and quantitative approaches.

First, the cases chosen allow for a comprehensive examination of the relationship between the inter-state distribution of economic power and member states' formal political power in the most critical multilateral economic institutions. The two historical cases focus on the IMF, the World Bank, and the International Trade Organization (ITO) – the three integral multilateral economic institutions created at the end of the war.[29] These cases provide an examination of the core question in a direct way: why were these institutions planned with different rules for member state representation? The two international financial institutions embodied weighted voting, while the ITO embraced voting equality. While the origins of these institutions and the US leadership in creating them has been a prevalent concern in the literature, existing works have not

---

[28] Mosley and Singer (2009) specifically call for an analysis of the 2008–2010 changes in the economic institutions studied in this book.

[29] I analyze the IMF and the World Bank together. The ITO is a failed institution, but the surviving trade institution, the General Agreements on Tariffs and Trade, was planned as a part of the ITO (Chapter 4).

adequately analyzed the US actors' expressed preferences regarding the distribution of formal political power in these institutions and the relevant inter-state negotiations on them.

The three contemporary cases constitute the most prominent cases of shifts to member states' formal political power in multilateral economic institutions – the IMF, the World Bank, and the G20.[30] Analyzing the instances of adjustments to member states' formal political power is necessary to being able to ascertain the inter-relationship between shifts in inter-state economic power and states' formal political power at multi-lateral economic institutions.[31] These cases are particularly suited to the purposes of this book, as they reveal institutional responses to the relative economic decline of the institutionally dominant members (the large advanced economies) and the rise of large emerging economies, which has been occurring over the last several decades (e.g., Canuto and Lin 2010; Layne 2009; Chapter 5). Examining the variation between the economic shifts, on one hand, and their institutional implications for formal political power, on the other, directly facilitates the core purpose of this book.

As these points suggest, *within each time period*, the inter-state distribution of economic power can be treated as the same across institutions. Put differently, within each period, the analysis "controls for" the distribution of economic power in understanding why that distribution manifests itself in varying degrees across different institutions.

First, beyond providing an analysis of the adjusted power approach in different time periods, the inclusion of both historical and contemporary cases enriches the analysis of the relationship between economic and political power. Understanding the historical background in formal poli-tical asymmetries enables a more comprehensive analysis of the relation-ship of states' economic power and their formal political power in multilateral economic institutions. The historical cases also permit the exploration of some theoretical propositions in depth by tracing actual events. As an example, while a strand of the rational choice literature on

[30] Beyond centrality of the IMF and the World Bank to the governance of the global economy (e.g., Drezner 2012), they are the only financial institutions that boast nearly universal membership. The G20 case is prominent because it led to the sidelining of the G7, another central governing body, and facilitated reform of other institutions, particu-larly the Financial Stability Forum (FSB).

[31] Here, if the dependent variable was "reform" or "change," then selecting based on the dependent variable might have been a concern, but the dependent variable is the dis-tribution of formal political power in multilateral economic institutions, and the central aim is to analyze how shifts in them relate to changes in the underlying distribution of economic power.

multilateral institutions, the rational design theory, identifies voting rules as a key dimension of institutional design, it leaves it under-analyzed (Koremenos et al. 2001a, 2001b; see Chapter 2).[32]

Second, the cases chosen allow the analysis to be focused on a distinct number of select variables because the institutions under study are economic inter-governmental organizations. Put differently, focusing on similar institutions reduces the potential pitfalls of having to consider the impact of variables that would stem from analyzing different types of institutions. For example, the Financial Stability Board (FSB) also experienced changes to members' formal political power during the 2008–2010 period, but this change to the FSB resulted directly from the changes to the G20 and, importantly, the FSB is *not* a "substantial inter-governmental organization" and has non-state actors as members (Griffith-Jones et al. 2010, p. 7; Chapter 7). While extensions to this book could examine more institutions, here investigating the shifts in members' formal political power only in central economic inter-governmental institutions avoids other methodological issues that could arise from examining inter-governmental versus hybrid institutions.

Third, while the G20, which constitutes the focus of the final case study, is a relatively informal inter-governmental institution in comparison to the other institutions examined, its inclusion in the book serves a critical purpose beyond analyzing crucial shifts in the current global economic order. Although the 2008–2010 shifts in members' formal political power in the IMF and the World Bank were long-drawn-out processes and have been relatively contentious, a number of rich country leaders upgraded the existing G20 from being a marginal forum for finance ministers to a central forum for heads of state in 2008 without demand from the rising states (Kirton 2011). This ease with which the rich countries extended their club contrasts with the frictions in the IMF and the World Bank. Probing the reasons for this difference and whether the adjusted power approach's central claim (that institutional settings adjust the importance of the changes in the distribution of economic power) stands in the case of the G20 strengthens the analysis.[33] Overall, the case studies, as commonly used in the literature, provide an

---

[32] Koremenos et al. (2001b, p. 1060) analyze the distribution of voting in an institution as a dependent variable labeled as "control" and state frankly that their "findings on control ... are sparse, so we do not claim much for them."

[33] While the G20 is an informal institution and the IMF and the World Bank are formal institutions, the core variables of analysis are applicable to the G20 (see footnotes 7 and 19). Also, just as not all formal institutions are the same, not all informal institutions are the same either, which again motivates a focus on the institutional features of the G20.

opportunity to explore the extent to which the evidence meets the expectations of the book's analytical framework, the adjusted power approach (e.g., Drezner 2007; Odell 2001; Stone 2011).

In addition to case studies, the book also quantitatively investigates the determinants of formal political power. Particularly, Chapter 3 analyzes shifts in member states' quotas in the IMF between 1965 and 2010, upon which the contemporary cases examining the 2008–2010 period elaborate (Chapters 5 and 6). The quantitative examination of IMF quotas also helps explain how individual (member state) positions have changed within the IMF, while the rest of the book focuses on meta-trends, marked by the relative economic decline and rise of certain states. Since IMF quota shifts have traditionally influenced members' shares in the World Bank, Chapter 3's discussions also provide a window into Bank share adjustments.[34] Aside from the explanatory statistics in Chapter 3, throughout, the book relies on descriptive data, most of which I collected for this study.

The book utilizes a range of documents in addition to scholarly books and articles, including archival material on the IMF, the World Bank, and the International Trade Organization (ITO) and other official documents, including transcripts of Board meetings and speeches from these institutions. The reliance on original documents allows the book to provide a close-up of actors' preferences (as they were expressed) and traces events in detail.[35] The book also benefitted from a select number of anonymous interviews with current or former IMF and World Bank officials. Although I do not use the evidence from the interviews on their own, they nonetheless contributed to confirming (or otherwise) some of the points I make regarding the 2008–2010 changes to members' formal political power in the IMF and the World Bank as well as the G20.

Plan of the rest of the book

The next chapter (Chapter 2) outlines the theoretical framework of the book – the adjusted power approach. While this approach extrapolates from existing theories, such as variants of realism and institutionalism, the chapter also identifies how the content and expectations of the theory differ significantly from these existing approaches.

---

[34] Unfortunately, I could not formulate a complete dataset of shareholding changes in the Bank.

[35] One of Elster's (1989, 2000) main criticisms of rational choice is its avoidance of in-depth analysis and assuming rational action based on outcomes. Process tracing of this kind is thus important in avoiding *post hoc ergo propter hoc* reasoning.

Chapter 3 begins the historical analysis of the relationship between the inter-state distribution of economic power and members' formal political power within the institutions. It demonstrates that the IMF and the World Bank ended up with weighted voting largely because of the US designers' and their interlocutors' belief that this system of voting would best fit the institutions' intended functions and purposes. The Chapter also details the rules and conventions regarding the changes in members' formal political power specifically focusing on IMF quota (thus voting power) adjustments. The manner in which the member states negotiate these adjustments provides an opportunity for the institutionally dominant state(s) to exert influence. To explore whether or not this potential for influence has indeed materialized, the chapter examines members' quota increases in 1965–2010. The evidence demonstrates that an increase in the member state's volume of bilateral trade with the USA boosts the increases a member receives to its quota. Overall, Chapter 3 outlines the origins of formal political asymmetries within the IMF and the World Bank and sheds light onto the determinants of individual member quotas.

Chapter 4 provides a follow-up to Chapter 3 in asking why the multilateral trading system was created with voting equality, when the two international financial institutions preceding it were not. As the chapter shows, the voting differences across the three institutions cannot be dismissed easily because the US officials floated a proposal for weighted voting during the inter-state negotiations on the ITO. In explaining voting equality at the ITO, two immediate answers deeply rooted in International Relations literatures come to mind: (1) the trading institution was created three years after the financial institutions, when the Cold War was beginning, which raises questions about whether the onset of the Cold War had something to do with voting equality; (2) the USA had to signal "restraint" by relying on voting equality. Differing from these explanations, the chapter argues that the voting equality in the multilateral trading system can primarily be explained with reference to the US designers' conceptualization of the institution. Interestingly, contrary to the expectations of "two-level games," the US negotiators pursued their vision, even when domestically key groups, which would ratify the ITO agreement, contested that vision. In the end, the chapter researches a relatively under-analyzed issue on formal political asymmetries within multilateral economic institutions, while providing support for the adjusted power approach and engaging with alternative theoretical expectations.

Chapter 5 begins with a descriptive analysis of the rise of large emerging economies in the last three to four decades, which provides the necessary background to the contemporary cases of the book (Prologue to Chapter 5). I label the large emerging economies as "the rising states" and the large advanced economies as institutionally dominant but (relatively) economically "declining states," though the discussions pay attention to discrepancies within these groups as well as to the poorest states.

After this prelude to the contemporary cases, Chapter 5 proceeds to analyze the 2008–2010 shifts in the member states' formal political power in the IMF. These changes were more extensive in redistributing formal political power away from the institutionally dominant but economically declining states (the large advanced economies) to the rising states (the large emerging markets) than earlier reform plans had suggested. A number of institutional factors, underlined by the adjusted power approach, help explain this outcome of relatively extensive "accommodation." Importantly, the declining states considered increases in the rising states' formal political power as essential for more effective surveillance of these countries' economies as well as their greater involvement in burden-sharing the financing of the institution. The manner in which the member states fund the IMF affected the content as well as the timing of the 2008–2010 changes. The institution relies heavily on state financing, whether through quotas or loans, with little ability to raise capital on its own. Further, the chapter shows that existing institutional conventions on the adjustment of formal political power help understand the process of change and its incremental nature.

Chapter 6 examines the 2008–2010 shifts to member states' formal political power in the World Bank. Both in comparison to earlier reform discussions at the Bank and in comparison to the IMF, these shifts were relatively less extensive in distributing formal political power toward the rising states. This outcome of "limited accommodation" can partially be explained with reference to the tensions between the rising and the declining states regarding the role the latter (should) play in the provision of the institution's intended global good of economic development. Specifically, the former would like to see the Bank as serving increasingly only its poorest members, thereby discouraging the rising states from relying on the institution's non-concessional resources. In this context, greater position enhancement by the rising states would only increase the ease with which these members could rely on the IBRD's relatively inexpensive loans. Further, for various reasons, the burden-sharing rationale was relatively muted at the World Bank. At the same time, the Bank's institutional conventions, particularly its tradition of following IMF shifts in quota, limited the possibilities for change in the Bank as well as affecting the nature of the shifts in members' formal political power. Finally, even though the Bank's mission is multilateral economic development, and thus low-income countries play a crucial role in whether or not the Bank succeeds in its mission, the low-income countries made only minor gains through the 2008–2010 reforms. This last point further supports the adjusted power approach's contention that a mere focus on institutional purposes would not adequately help explain the 2008–2010 changes, just as a sole emphasis on power dynamics among core states would not suffice either.

Chapter 7 examines the 2008 upgrade of the G20, which seemingly poses a puzzle to the adjusted power approach. While much of the book, particularly the 2008–2010 shifts in the IMF and the World Bank, show that the declining states' accommodation of the rising states was a contentious process, where the declining states aimed for limited accommodation at varying degrees, the G20 case does not display the same level of contention. In the case of the G20, in 2008, a number of leaders from the large advanced economies extended their club to the rising states by upgrading an existing forum (G20 gatherings of finance ministers to G20 summits of heads of state) and consolidated this upgrade by subsequently relying on the revamped G20. Further, the G20 relies on relatively egalitarian decision-making procedures, giving its members equal formal political power. Hence, the accommodation in this case can be identified as both discretionary and extensive. Why was accommodation relatively more contentious in the IMF and the World Bank, but discretionary and extensive in the G20? The chapter argues that the core institutional features and functions of the G20 as an informal, "delegatory" institution explain the different nature of accommodation in the G20. The G20 delegates tasks to other institutions and does not itself execute on them. This particular informality, in turn, makes differentials in states' formal political power within the institution relatively less important, contributing to the understanding of the nature of the declining states' accommodation.

Chapter 8 concludes by discussing the broad implications of the book, further locating it vis-à-vis existing arguments and frameworks. It highlights the relevance of the book for understanding the governance of the global economy through multilateral economic institutions. For instance, the book shows the difficulty in narrowing the perceived gap between the shifts in the distribution of inter-state economic power and the members' formal political power in multilateral economic institutions. Even a crisis that is perceived to be monumental, such as the 2008 global economic crisis, did not alter existing institutional practices to the point of allowing radical change. Rather, the institutions adjusted the importance of the crisis, just as they mediated the significance of the underlying distribution of economic power. At the same time, the book's discussions of the 2008–2010 shifts in formal political power demonstrate the tensions between the key actors – the economically rising and declining states – that remain under-addressed. In this respect, the concluding chapter shows that while the 2008–2010 changes reveal the revival of the existing multilateral institutions, they also elucidate their potential sources of weakness.

2 Conceptualizing political asymmetries in multilateral economic institutions

This chapter elaborates on the theoretical discussions in Chapter 1 with a view to advancing the adjusted power approach. Specifically, it derives a number of propositions that the rest of the book explores regarding the inter-relationship between states' formal political power in multilateral economic institutions and the inter-state distribution of economic power. No integrative theory on the relationship between inter-state economic asymmetries and formal political asymmetries within institutions exists, which is a gap this book intends to fill. Existing theories help explain inter-state power dynamics among states *or* institutional cooperation, but they leave the intersection of power and institutions under-analyzed.

Particularly, two primary issues that help explain the intersection of power and institutions get sidelined in existing debates. The existing literature does not discuss variation in how the distribution of economic power relates to the distribution of formal political power within multilateral economic institutions. Nor does it adequately analyze how the shifts in the inter-state distribution of economic power would affect members' formal political power within institutions, which constitutes a critical feature of the design and functioning of multilateral institutions (see Chapter 1).

Variation in the relationship between economic power and formal political power Power-based analyses, particularly a variety of realist approaches, claim that the underlying inter-state asymmetries in economic power get replicated in multilateral economic institutions (Brooks and Wohlforth 2009; Gilpin 1981; Kirshner 2010; Schweller and Priess 1997). For instance, Gilpin (1981, p. 9) argues that "those actors who benefit most from a change in the social system and who gain the power to affect such change will seek to alter the system in ways that favor their interests." Specifically, "a rising state attempts to change the rules governing the international system" (p. 186). The expectation here, then, is that as the distribution of economic power among states shifts, so will the distribution of formal political power within institutions.

Recapturing the perspective of Gilpin and other classic-tending realists, Kirshner (2010, p. 65) articulates the logic of institutional structures following changing power asymmetries succinctly: there is "the need to acknowledge power: both the reality of the power of others and the necessary limitations of one's own."[1] If institutions replicate underlying asymmetries in inter-state economic power, there is little room for variation in the distribution of formal political power across multilateral economic institutions.

In contrast, within institutionalist accounts and their offshoots, it is difficult to tell how power and institutions interact.[2] The institutionalist school essentially suggests that as rules-based platforms for multilateral cooperation, institutions create a different universe of inter-state interaction, where reputational worries in iterative games, predictability achieved through information-sharing, and greater trust in compliance reign in the place of power. As the surfacing of power asymmetries within institutional contexts might hamper that very cooperation, this school of thought puts faith in the ability of states to tame those asymmetries.

Even though a part of the institutionalist literature signals the importance of power asymmetries among states, it does not advance a systematic treatment of the implications of those asymmetries for institutional design. In putting forward a detailed analysis of the "rational design of institutions" (RDT), Koremenos, Lipson, and Snidal (2001a, 2001b) have identified five key features of institutions – membership rules, scope of issues covered, centralization of tasks, rules for controlling the institution (voting rights in particular), and the flexibility of arrangements.[3] Four overarching issues explain these dependent variables: distribution problems (the fact that there are multiple outcomes that would be Pareto-efficient), enforcement issues, the number of actors involved, and uncertainty (both about the world and about state

---

[1] The realist school has, by and large, moved beyond the discussion of "do institutions matter?" (Brooks and Wohlforth 2009; Drezner 2007; Jervis 1999; Krasner 1983; Schweller and Priess 1997; an exception is Mearsheimer 1994/1995). And, realists and institutionalists have converged, in some respects, on their analyses of institutions. An important area of disagreement concerns the extent to which institutions can constrain great powers. While institutionalists believe institutions can constrain great powers, realists disagree (e.g., Keohane 1998; Jervis 1999).

[2] Krasner's (1991) criticism that the institutionalist accounts are commensurate with multiple equilibria in institutions (different outcomes that would satisfy the pursuit of mutually beneficial goals through institutional frameworks) and his argument that the choice of equilibrium hinges upon power dynamics stem partially from this ambiguity in institutionalist works.

[3] I use Koremenos et al. (2001a, 2001b) given their extensive articulation of design features and the vast literature they inspired (see, e.g., Koremenos 2005; Reinhardt and Kucik 2008; Thompson 2010).

preferences). The relationship between these specific dependent and independent variables is what gives the RDT project its "unique identifier" because the rational choice approaches broadly share RDT's core premise that institutions result from intentional pursuits.[4] Put differently, the assessment of RDT should lie not in whether states purposefully create institutions to pursue goals, but rather in the said connections between various design features (dependent variables) and underlying collective action barriers (the explanatory factors).[5]

RDT leaves power under-analyzed, as the theory's architects and others also note, despite emphasizing that "the distribution of actors' capabilities" should be accounted for in understanding institutions (Koremenos et al. 2001a, p. 778; Duffield 2003). As Duffield (2003, p. 417) points out, RDT "devote[s] only one paragraph . . . to a discussion of the implications of the actors' capabilities . . . they offer little or no discussion of the types of capabilities that matter or the circumstances under which these capabilities may influence institutional choices." In discussing "control," which includes members' formal political power within an institution, RDT foresees "asymmetry of control increas[ing] with asymmetry among contributors" (p. 791). While this point seems to suggest that power differentials influence institutional design, the authors' notion of asymmetry does not necessarily pertain to power differentials. They explain the reasoning behind the aforementioned conjecture as "an intuition that an actor's control over an institution relates to the actor's importance to the institution" (p. 792). What that importance is, however, remains indeterminate. It is plausible that a poor state might be relatively more important than a great economic power for an institution that aims to engender global poverty reduction (an example here would be the World Bank).

This indeterminacy ("importance" to an institution could mean anything) is not a light criticism. From a methodological perspective, if one can define "importance to an institution" in any way that one likes, the theory does not elucidate much and is relatively vulnerable to retro-fitting (i.e., fitting the empirical examples to the theoretical framework). Others agree with this point. Duffield (2003, p. 416) writes that further "disaggregation [in RDT's theoretical framework] should have been attempted to ensure adequate conceptualization of the variables and to facilitate subsequent evaluation of the framework." Indeed, Koremenos et al. (2001b, p. 1057) acknowledge this issue: "[t]he danger . . . is that

---

[4] Koremenos et al. (2001a, p. 22; 2001b, p. 1051) agree with this point.
[5] Again, the authors themselves underscore this point when they emphasize "[o]urs is *a* rational design framework, not *the* framework" (Koremenos et al. 2001b, p. 1053, emphasis original).

models will be modified to fit the data" given generality. In any case, specifically on control, which includes voting rights, the authors emphasize their "findings on control . . . are sparse, so we do not claim too much for them" (p. 1060). Overall, the architects of RDT themselves emphasize that "'power' needs to be analyzed more fully and explicitly" (2001b, p. 1054).

In sum, institutionalist accounts seem to suggest that power is subordinated to the gains from cooperation in institutions, and that while power dynamics and asymmetries are not immaterial, the institutionalist accounts do not tell us how exactly these factors matter (see also Ikenberry 2000; Keohane 1984; Chapter 1).

Relationship between the shifts in inter-state economic power and formal political power   At the same time, neither the realist nor the institutionalist school provides an explanation regarding how the shifts in the distribution of economic power affect the distribution of formal political power in multilateral economic institutions. Going back to the Gilpin and Kirshner quotes above, both authors suggest that rising powers, thanks to their increasing prestige and/or capacities, stand in a position to alter institutions in accordance with their interests. However, that assumption remains debatable. As Brooks and Wohlforth (2009) note, while institutions should reflect underlying asymmetries in inter-state economic power, they often fail to do so (see Chapter 1). There is, thus, a "lag" between the shift in the distribution of economic power and the changes in the distribution of political power within multilateral institutions (Schweller and Priess 1997). In other words, institutions are sticky when it comes to asymmetries as well.[6] Yet, these power-based accounts do not systematically explore the roots of that stickiness.

The institutionalist accounts are equally unclear on this point, though for different reasons. Here, it is worth distinguishing among different institutionalist perspectives.

Some accounts centralize the notion that great powers willingly constrain themselves in institutional contexts in order to "lock in" a system that is both favorable to their interests and is stable and legitimate (acceptable) (e.g., Goldstein and Gowa 2002; Ikenberry 2000). In this respect, the leading states compromise at the creation of the multilateral economic institutions. These accounts, however, also emphasize that the distribution of formal political power does indeed need to be modified as the distribution of economic power changes. Ikenberry (2012, p. 6), for

---

[6] For example, from different perspectives Goldstein (1988) and Pierson (2004).

instance, diagnoses a "crisis" in the contemporary multilateral order and finds that the "crisis stems from the fact that the underlying foundations of the old order have been transformed." He then lists "shifts in power" as one of the major reasons for the changes in the underlying foundation. The implication of this point is lucid – institutions need updating to catch up with the times. Yet, institutional approaches cannot easily explain – within their frameworks at least – as to why shifts in the inter-state distribution of power would necessitate such change.[7] More importantly, they do not tell us enough about the process of institutional updating as well as the reasons as to why the distribution of formal political power in institutions outlives the underlying shifts in inter-state economic power. One obvious reason is that the leading states within multilateral institutions resist change that disadvantages them, but this point itself raises questions about the extent of restraint or compromise that exists in the first place.

Similarly, RDT also does not clarify how and why institutions should respond to change in the inter-state distribution of power and why there is institutional stickiness on the distribution of formal political power (a critical design feature) remains unclear. As I discuss in the upcoming parts of the book, while this framework is appealing in suggesting that state actors deliberate about institutional design choices, the theory does not offer any clues as to how the shifts in the distribution of power would relate to institutional change. As just discussed, the role of power relations for institutional design outcomes remains unclear within the theory because institutional (re)design focuses on "connections between specific cooperation problems and their institutional solutions" (Koremenos et al. 2001b, p. 1051; italics removed). Change in institutional features, in this framework, does not result from shifts in inter-state power dynamics, but rather from changes in collective action problems. While this point is reasonable, for the theory to tell us more about how inter-state power dynamics matter, it would have to connect the collective action problems central to its analysis (enforcement, distribution, and uncertainty) to shifting power dynamics, which it fails to do. For instance, the theory does not suggest about why China was not able to translate its economic power into political power as much in the World Bank as it was in the IMF in 2008–2010 (see Chapters 5 and 6).

---

[7] Even though Brooks and Wohlforth (2009) and Ikenberry (2000) put forward different perspectives regarding the relationship between the distribution of economic power and the distribution of formal political power in global economic institutions, their policy recommendations converge (see Brooks et al. 2012). While this convergence could stem from a similarity in the authors' normative leanings, this said piece is highly empirical.

In short, existing theories inform the analysis greatly in terms of either power *or* institutions, but not the intersection of the two. I do not dispute the usefulness of these frameworks, but rather I suggest that they do not adequately explain the relationship between the inter-state distribution of economic power and member states' formal political power in multilateral economic institutions. Having further expanded upon why and where there is a contribution to be made, I now turn to outlining the adjusted power approach and its propositions that the book's cases empirically analyze.

The adjusted power approach

When the US actors and their allies created the three post-war multilateral economic institutions at the end of the war, they enshrined them with different rules for voting and member state representation. In other words, the then underlying distribution of economic power among states manifested itself differently across the three multilateral economic organizations. And, as this book will show, when the IMF and the World Bank instituted changes to members' formal political power in 2008–2010, the underlying distribution of economic power had different implications for members' standing in the two institutions. For instance, the large emerging economies, which have experienced high levels of economic growth in the last several decades or more, made greater gains to their formal political power in the IMF than in the World Bank. What explains the variation in the extent to which, and the manner in which, the distribution of economic power (in a period) surfaces in multilateral economic institutions?

The adjusted power approach advanced in this book argues that the importance of the distribution of economic power remains contingent upon the institutional setting. In this respect, institutions act as volume dials that will determine how loudly or quietly the distribution of economic power will play out in their frameworks. More precisely, institutions affect both the nature and the speed with which changes in the distribution of economic power manifest themselves as shifts in political power.

According to this approach, the extent to which the rising states enhance their formal position within these institutions ("position enhancement") will hinge on the interaction of three key factors: (a) the declining states' conceptualization of the rising states' role in the functions and purposes they prioritize for the institution; (b) the financial burden-sharing arrangements within the institution, and how these burden-sharing arrangements relate to "a"; (c) the existing rules and conventions of institutions regarding the governance and adjustment of formal political asymmetries.[8] Put differently, these three key factors will determine the extent to which the declining states tend toward "accommodation," which here denotes the declining states' concessions to increases in the rising states' formal political power.

The interactions among these variables demand a case-by-case analysis, but, based on the adjusted power approach, the following propositions can be made for a period, such as the current one, where a shift in the distribution of economic power is underway (Chapters 1 and 5). The more the declining states consider the rising states crucial for the fulfilment of the functions and purposes of the institution in accordance with their expectations from the institution, the greater the declining states' tendency for "accommodation," *ceteris paribus*. The greater the state funding of an institution, the greater the declining state's tendency for accommodation, as long as this burden-sharing motivation does not conflict with the declining states' aims regarding the functions and purposes of institutions. Finally, existing rules and conventions regarding the governance and adjustment of formal political power limit the possibilities available for shifts in formal political power. In other words, there is path dependency (e.g., Fioretos 2011; Pierson 2004; Thelen and Mahoney 2010).

While the point that institutional settings adjust the importance of the inter-state distribution of economic power applies to the creation of the institutions as well as the question of whether or not and how they change in the face of a changing distribution of economic power, the latter is a greater concern in this book. Looking at the creation of the institutions, the expectation is that the specific conceptualization of the dominant state(s) and the financing of the institutions will constitute the key explanatory variables. And in these historical cases, naturally, my aim will be more to delineate the institutional rules and conventions pertaining to the adjustment of formal political asymmetries than to assess how actual changes get filtered through the institutions (which becomes a question as institutions mature). In contrast, the contemporary cases will illustrate the issue of how institutions filter the shifts in the inter-state distribution of economic power, as it is a pertinent question that continues to demand an answer from the literature.

---

[8] There are different usages of economic hegemony available in the literature; here the concept refers to the least demanding of these definitions: "a country whose market power ... significantly exceeds that of all rivals," where market power denotes "sufficient size in the relevant market to influence prices and quantities" (Eichengreen 1987). For alternatives, see Keohane (1984, p. 34); Mearsheimer (2001, p. 40).

Let us consider the contemporary period, which has been marked by the rise of large emerging economies (the "rising states") and the relative economic decline of the large advanced economies that remain institutionally dominant in multilateral economic institutions (the "declining states"). How will this shift in the distribution of economic power manifest itself in multilateral economic institutions? The rest of the chapter addresses this question, moving from a discussion of assumptions to making propositions.

Assumptions   Three basic assumptions will guide the rest of the analysis. First, the relationship between the distribution of formal political power within multilateral economic institutions and the underlying distribution of economic power hinges significantly upon the behavior of the institutionally dominant or leading states, who are also willing to take the leadership position. This point is relatively non-contentious, and the rest of the book substantiates it. Undeniably, the United States' consent and willingness for change in existing multilateral economic institutions matters significantly today. This chapter will, nonetheless, discuss how the preferences of non-leading states interact with the position of the leading states.

Second, while the rest of the analysis refers to states as having certain inclinations or exhibiting certain behavior toward formal political asymmetries within institutions, there is no assumption here that states are unitary actors. Rather, the analysis in the rest of the book focuses on key actors, such as the US international negotiators and their beliefs and arguments, about institutional design, and redesign. Nonetheless, the analysis reasonably assumes that by the time state actors represent their position internationally (i.e., to their interlocutors on the international realm), they will have settled on a position that can be regarded as that state's position (see, e.g., Drezner 2007). Hence, the rest of the analysis will refer to states as having preferences toward asymmetries, which is a shorthand for state actors' preferences that have been hashed out through domestic and foreign discussions prior to presentation on the international realm.

Third, the book assumes rationality in actors in a basic way.[9] Despite definitional disagreements, scholars converge on rational action exhibiting the following characteristics: utility maximization, rank-ordered and transitive preferences, and decision-making under uncertainty (expected utility) (Green and Shapiro 1994). The book interprets state actors as goal-oriented with rank-ordered preferences, but it does not assume that

---

[9] For both critical and endorsing discussions of rational choice theory, see Cox (2004); Elster (1989/2007); Ferejohn (2004); Green and Shapiro (1994); Ostrom (1991); Shepsle (2006).

rationality always reigns, nor does it assume that states are able to process every piece of relevant information before having a general sense of their goals and update the information as it changes. This non-*homo economicus* conceptualization of state actors foresees these actors as struggling to juggle various goals they face during institutional design and exhibiting partial updating of preferences in the face of changed evidence and circumstances. It also assumes that rational behavior coexists with non-rational behavior, in which actors either follow old patterns of doing things or selectively update information. While the point that actors in real life are not textbook idealized versions of rationality is important, it does not lead to the abandonment of the conceptualization of actors as primarily goal-oriented creatures.[10] In any case, because the book provides detailed analyses of state actors' positions and the changes in them, the notion that state actors are goal-oriented is not merely an assumption, but a point that the book's evidence corroborates.[11] With these three assumptions in mind, I now turn to deriving the propositions that will guide the empirical analyses in the book.

To accommodate or not to accommodate?

Given the adjusted power approach argues that the extent of the institutionally dominant but economically declining states' accommodation of the rising states (i.e., giving the rising states more formal political power) will hinge upon key institutional features, it is worth analyzing first why accommodation is a reasonable strategy as well as why the declining states might wish to limit the extent of accommodation, even when they concede it. By extension, the extent to which the tension between accommodation and limited accommodation will resolve in favor of one or the other also depends on institutional features.

Accommodation as a reasonable strategy   Accommodation under which the declining states agree to increases in the rising states' formal political power will likely be a dominant strategy for a number of reasons. Notably, declining states are not declined states, but rather the leading states within institutions that have experienced relative losses to their economic power (see also Chapter 5). First, from a cost-benefit analysis, the declining states' costs of maintaining their institutional positions have increased due to the relative decline in their economic positions (Gilpin

---

[10] Keohane (1984, Chapter 7) offers a detailed discussion of how state actors do not behave like *homo econonomicus*, but can nonetheless be interpreted as rational actors.

[11] Elster (1989) identifies context-assumed preferences as one of rational choice theory's major shortcomings.

1981; Kirshner 2010; MacDonald and Parent 2011). Relative decline puts both greater domestic scrutiny and greater constraint on the declining states' multilateral financial commitments. These commitments need not be large to intensify the domestic debate about how scarce resources should be allocated.[12] The change in cost-benefit analysis may encourage accommodation, as the declining states seek to share the burden of maintaining the institutions with the rising states. If decline coincides with shrinkage in their economic resources at home, such as through an economic crisis, then their multilateral commitments come under even greater pressure (for evidence see Lavelle 2011).

Second, because allowing the rising states to increase their formal political power would facilitate the institutions' continuation, accommodation is a rational cost to bear. A couple of assumptions underlie this perspective. Increasing the formal political power of rising states would likely lessen these states' existing or potential grievances against the institution, thereby enhancing the legitimacy (acceptability) of the institution in the eyes of others (e.g., Ikenberry and Wright 2008). More critically, because existing multilateral economic institutions reflect the power dynamics present at their creation, the increased legitimacy of the institution would benefit the rising states. For instance, today's institutions contain rules and policies that the United States, as their leading creator, has generally found preferable and conducive to its interests (e.g., from different perspectives, Ikenberry 2000; Brooks and Wohlforth 2009). In this regard, the United States would prefer change *within* the institutions to a change *of* the institutions – it would prefer the continuation of existing institutions.

Accommodation of the rising states could, thus, contribute to the maintenance of a rules-based order that, on the whole, benefits the declining states. Institutional frameworks constrain the rising states within an existing rules-based framework that privileges the hegemon and its allies (e.g., Ikenberry 2009). The declining states can "bind" the rising states in institutional settings under which "a state seeks to exert some control over another state's policies by incorporating it in a web of institutional arrangements" (Schweller and Priess 1997, p. 9).[13] The more the rising states can be brought into the framework of existing institutions and made to participate in these institutions, the more their actions can be controlled. And, assuming that the rising states are less

---

[12] Interviews confirmed this point.

[13] A different interpretation of this point is that through accommodation, the declining states might want to limit the gains rising states pursue. Adding the point about current institutions reflecting the interests of their creators (declining states) relatively more to the point about "binding," the notion of wanting to check or limit the rising states' gains also emerges as a possible rationale.

interested in, and therefore less bound by, institutions where their voice is stymied, the declining states have a rational reason to accommodate the rising states. Overall, *declining states tend to consent to some level of "accommodation" of the rising states.*

Tendency for limited accommodation during decline While the declining states face incentives for accommodation, they will also face countervailing incentives for limited accommodation. This pressure for limited accommodation has a number of plausible sources.

One possible reason for limited accommodation comes from the declining states' losses in relative informal political power in the multilateral economic institutions. Stone (2011) argues that the greater a state's informal political power, the more inclined that state will be to give higher formal political power to weaker states. According to Stone, informal power depends on structural power, which depends on alternatives a state has outside of an institution. He puts it this way: "[weaker states] are willing to tolerate a degree of informal influence in return for receiving a large share of formal power, because the participation of important states makes an international institution more valuable to all of the participants" (p. 14). Because the institutionally important states have greater informal power, they can afford to have less formal political power than what their underlying economic power would suggest. Hence, weaker states "must receive a share of formal political power that is out of proportion to their resources" (p. 18). Here, Stone argues that the options a state has outside of the institution increase with greater economic power. States with significant market size, for instance, can forum-shop (Drezner 2007). From this perspective, then, the leading states would be less likely to guard their formal political power jealously when they are at the top of their game than when they are in relative decline. Such was the United States' position at the end of World War II. Conversely, because the leading states likely experience loss of informal power during decline, they need to rely relatively more on formal power, which makes formal political power dearer. Hence, the declining states face pressures for "limited accommodation" and try to hold onto as much formal political power as possible.[14]

---

[14] Flipping this argument around would suggest that because the declining states continue to retain informal power, they are more willing to accommodate the rising states. While this is a possibility, it is less likely than the one I outlined here for a number of reasons. It is inconsistent with the most elaborate theory of informal influence we have – that of Stone's – where informal power correlates with structural power, which in turn relates to economic might. Further, as states enhance their economic power, it is more likely that they also enhance their informal power over a multilateral economic institution. Indeed, such has been the story within the IMF (e.g., Kaya 2012). In this scenario, even if the declining states retain their existing level of informal power, their relative informal power

From a different perspective, Ikenberry (2000) and Goldstein and Gowa (2002) reach the same conclusion. In examining the post-war multilateral order created under the leadership of the United States, Ikenberry argues that in order to ensure the legitimacy (broad acceptability) of the institutions, the United States pursued "restraint," which is critical in signaling to weaker states that the leading state will not "abandon" them. Restraint, broadly, suggests that the United States bound itself to a rules-based system – that is, the multilateral economic institutions.[15] In a narrow sense, Goldstein and Gowa argue restraint has translated into specific compromises within institutions based on other (weaker) states' demands. According to the "restraint" argument, weaker states have less to fear from abandonment during the decline of the leading state. In turn, the declining states could get away with showing less restraint in the face of lower fears of abandonment. The upshot for the discussions here is that institutionally leading states would and could be relatively more protective of their formal political power during decline, when "restraint" becomes less of an issue.

The interaction between the domestic and international levels may also tend declining states toward "limited accommodation." There is likely to be some domestic resistance to accommodation, assuming that accommodation translates into the declining states' loss of formal political power within the institutions. For instance, Congressional approval of US contributions to the IMF and the World Bank is necessary, which, in turn, suggests that Congress may be less likely to support further (and likely increased) contributions that come in the face of significantly lower influence in these institutions (see discussions in Chapters 1 and 5). A perusal of the Congressional Hearings related to the IMF and the World Bank reveals significant Congressional concern about the manner in which US taxpayers' money (in their words) gets used through the IMF (see, for instance, US House of Representatives 2013). Given that the US formal position in the institution insures and assures US influence over how the institution allocates funds, voting power in the institution matters for such Congressional concerns.[16] In this context, a crucial US Senate report on international financial institutions puts it bluntly: "U.S. voting

---

has declined, meaning their formal power becomes more important. Regardless, the possibility that the retention of informal power motivates accommodation does not affect the conclusions this book reaches (Chapter 8).

[15] For discussions that disagree, implicitly or explicitly, with Ikenberry's notion of restraint, see, e.g., Cox (1992); Foot et al. (2003); Lake (2010); Schweller (2001).

[16] As Lavelle (2011, p. 28) points out, the US Directors to the IMF approach Congress only when the institution's quota needs augmentation, whereas the concessional lending arm of the Bank, the IDA, requires annual appropriation. Chapters 4 and 5 discuss the funding of the institutions in greater detail.

shares and veto authority should be maintained" in adjustments of formal political power in the two Bretton Woods institutions (US Senate 2010, p. 4). Thus, while domestic audiences may concede (or even encourage) accommodation due to the rationale of burden sharing, they might also simultaneously prefer limited accommodation given the importance of formal political power as an instrument of influence and prestige.

To sum, *the leading states that are in decline face incentives to both increase formal political power of the rising states while limiting the extent of that accommodation.*

How institutional settings matter

The extent to which the tensions between accommodation and limited accommodation get resolved in favor of one or the other, specifically, and how the distribution of economic power manifests itself as states' formal political power in multilateral economic institutions, broadly, hinge upon key institutional features. As emphasized earlier, a point that gets side-lined in the current literature concerns the variation in the way in which inter-state power asymmetries make their way onto institutions. How then do institutional settings matter?

Functions and purposes of institutions   One of the key variables that the adjusted power approach pinpoints is the key states' conceptualization of the functions and purposes of institutions. For instance, as Chapter 3 will discuss, state actors did not resolve the core purpose of the World Bank until even after they constitutionalized the institution. Specifically, they debated the extent to which the World Bank should function as a guarantor of private funds into needy states versus the degree to which it should act as a lender of last resort to states for long-term development plans. Similarly, at the creation of the current multilateral trading system, the developing countries as well as a number of others, including the UK, emphasized the notion of a new trading institution as putting trade at the service of development, while the USA saw the new institution as primarily and almost exclusively as a medium for trade liberalization (Chapter 4). In this context, it becomes specifically important to "process trace" the dominant states' key officials' conceptualization of the purposes and functions of institutions. While this emphasis on institutions' "functions and purposes" is sympathetic to the notion of "deliberate design" advanced by RDT, the two approaches differ from each other in a number of fundamental ways. To begin with, the notion of "key states' conceptualization of functions and purposes of institutions" is prejudiced toward both state actors' subjectivity and power. Since I have above stressed how RDT leaves out power considerations by and large, it suffices here to say that the adjusted power approach inclines toward a design reflecting the dominant states' preferences relatively more.[17] The identification of dominant states requires institutional and temporal contextualization, which I provide in this book. This kind of argumentation does not leave out compromise – it would be unreasonable to suggest that the dominant states exclude the considerations of others. As the upcoming chapters show, for instance, and as we already know from the creation of the Bretton Woods system, the USA did make certain compromises (Eichengreen 1987). The approach here, however, suggests that each actor in the deliberate design of institutions cannot be weighted equally, and that functions and purposes of institutions cannot be understood as objective criteria that states negotiate.[18] Rather, they remain highly subjective and disputed. By the same token, power cannot be merely understood as helping identify *an* equilibrium (when institutions are seen by rational choice as equilibria),[19] it also plays a critical role in the shaping of *multiple equilibria* among which state actors end up choosing.

These discussions point to further fundamental differences with RDT. RDT does not factor in likely differences across states' preferences of the problems to be solved through institutions (either as a dependent or an independent variable or a necessary methodological tool). The history of the creation of the multilateral economic institutions, as well as their evolution, demonstrates that the role institutions should take on is a contested issue.[20] Again, while my approach does not reject deliberate design, it brings to the forefront the role of power in shaping the notion of deliberate design as well as the tensions among states as to what the institutions should do.

---

[17] Preferences denote "propensities to behave in determinate circumstances by people who discriminate among alternatives they judge either absolutely or relatively" (Weingast and Katznelson 2005, p. 7). In the context of international interaction, as Moravcsik (1997, p. 519) notes, preferences denote "an ordering among underlying substantive outcomes that may result from international political interaction."

[18] This point methodologically suggests that the process of inter-state negotiations, not just their outcome, should be the object of analyses on rational design. In contrast, architects of RDT emphasize: "Although the process of institutional design is usually contentious, we do not focus on bargaining among the participants but on the broad characteristics of the institutional outcomes they select" (Koremenos et al. 2001a, p. 21). This methodological lack of focus on bargaining, however, masks how power comes into play in shaping the outcomes.

[19] This is Krasner's (1991) response to the institutionalist literature's omission of power.

[20] A recently compiled volume on the Bretton Woods negotiations, for instance, reveals how difficult it was for the negotiators to agree on the primary function of the International Bank for Reconstruction and Development (see Schuler and Rosenberg 2012).

Since I have discussed above how RDT's "unique identifier" is the matching of specific collective action problems to design features (and not deliberate design), how my approach differs on this point also deserves an analysis. For one, my assumption of state actors as non-*homo economicus* suggests that state actors would not be disaggregating and differentiating between different collective action problems and matching each one of them to a specific design (this is the core of RDT as summarized above). While institutional crafters are likely to consider all of these pervasive problems in engendering institutions, it is unlikely they disaggregate these various problems. For instance, an analysis of 500 pages of Congressional testimonies by the US Treasury and State Department officials on the post-war economic order does not show any instance in which these designers justify or explain design features vis-à-vis distinct collective action problems (US Senate 1945). I do not claim that the designers fail to consider distinct impediments to cooperation, such as monitoring versus distributional issues. Rather, they likely approach these issues as undifferentiated goods in a basket of problems the institution should address. They plausibly bundle various collective action problems together, instead of matching each distinct barrier to an institutional feature.

This point questions the testable hypotheses of RDT. Consider, for instance, RDT's focus on the design feature of "control" within institutions, which includes member states' voting rights. RDT suggests: *a)* *"Individual control decreases as the number [of actors] increases"* *b)* *"Asymmetry of control increases with asymmetry among contributors [members of the institution]"; c) "Individual control (to block undesirable outcomes) increases with uncertainty about the state of the world"* [italics added] (Koremenos et al. 2001a, p. 791). These conjectures about voting rights relate to enforcement, distribution, uncertainty, and the number of actors. Leaving aside the already discussed issue of the vagueness of "asymmetry among contributors," if the designers disaggregate a, b, c, the implications for voting rights in the institution become ambiguous under certain conditions. For instance, if simultaneously an increasing number of actors encourage states to institute individual control but decreasing uncertainty about the world pushes them in the other direction, what happens to members' voting rights in an institution? The approach I present here does suggest that states' conceptualizations of the functions and purposes of institutions may embody self-conflicting elements, leading to tensions in the institutions, but RDT does not entertain that possibility.[21]

---

[21] Indeed, the empirical results support this point (see Chapter 8).

In short, although the rational choice approach's emphasis on actors' purposeful creation producing deliberate design is appealing, the adjusted power approach's contentions about the nature of that deliberation differ significantly from that of RDT's. Institutional designers are likely to be less precise in their design (aggregate the problems they face), and the leading states' preferences over the intended goods of the institution should matter relatively more for ascertaining design outcomes, all else equal. The import of these discussions for explaining the variation in the relationship between economic–political asymmetries across institutions *within the same time period*, is twofold. *One, the key state actors' conceptualization of core institutional functions and purposes affects the design of formal power asymmetries. Two, during decline, the leading states will permit greater "accommodation" if they see the rising states as crucial for (their interpretation of) the core functions and purposes of the institution.* How these factors unfold in practice depends, however, on the interaction of this variable with the following two factors.

Institution's financing   The understanding of key states' primary conceptualization of institutions' core functions and purposes illuminates other institutional features – particularly, the funding of an institution. If design, which is roughly rational, is at work, then the funding of the institution should relate to the institution's (actual or potential) core functions. Nonetheless, the manner in which states finance an institution deserves distinct attention, especially given its implications for institutional burden sharing, which is a concern from a number of distinct perspectives (e.g., Drezner 2008; Lake 1993). While financing is not the only concern in institutional burden sharing, it is likely to be a pressing concern. Further, there exists an explicit or implicit linkage between burden sharing and voice. Directly, financial burden sharing can be linked to formal political power. For instance, in the IMF and the World Bank, financial contributions determine members' voting power. Even in the absence of such a link, the more an actor contributes financially to an institution, the more they might demand voice within it. Taxation without representation, after all, is not a popular proposition.

The differences in the way in which members finance institutions, through their effects on burden-sharing arrangements, are likely to affect the declining states' tendency toward accommodation. For instance, scholars have rightly pointed out that member states contribute relatively little in actual disbursements to the World Bank because the International Bank on Reconstruction and Development (IBRD) can raise funds on international capital markets and thus relies mostly on "callable capital" (Kapur 2002; Woods 2006). Yet, studies have not explored the implications of this point for institutional discussions on political power.[22] How does this specific manner in which the World Bank is funded interfere with, if at all, states' thinking on the rising states' contributions to the funding of the World Bank? Reasonably, if member states make relatively little contribution to the IBRD, the pressure for immediate burden sharing there is relatively low.

At the same time, the financing issue likely interacts with the states' conceptualizations of the functions and purposes of institutions. In some cases, the two may reinforce one another. If, for instance, the declining states desire greater burden sharing with the rising states, which tends them toward accommodation, *and* they consider the rising states crucial for the functions and purposes of the institutions, the two variables complement each other to enhance the declining states' tendency for accommodation. In other cases, the two variables may work against one another. Regardless, a close examination of how the two factors interact is necessary for the analysis. Overall, *the greater the institution's need for immediate state financing, the greater will be the burden-sharing pressures, but how this burden-sharing impetus works in practice depends on its interaction with key states' preferences for the institution.*

Institutional rules and conventions

If institutions do indeed mediate the importance of inter-state asymmetries in economic power, then institutional rules and conventions that pertain to formal political power should matter in explaining the association between the inter-state distribution of economic power and the distribution of formal political power within multilateral economic institutions. Conventions, can sometimes work like habits, which denote "unreflectively utilized viewpoints," as Weber puts it, when they provide actors with "ready-made responses to the world" (Hopf 2010, p. 541; Powell and DiMaggio 1991, p. 26).[23] As habits, conventions point to behavior within organizations that connects to past actions with little or

---

[22] Kapur and Woods, like others, have drawn normative implications from this fact, suggesting for instance that the rich countries, which are the largest shareholders in the institution, are over-represented. But, to my knowledge, systematic analyses regarding how the precise manner in which the World Bank is funded affects inter-state discussions on formal political asymmetries have been missing. Moreover, a comparison to the IMF in this context with a focus on that institution's specific manner of funding has largely been absent.

[23] There is now a rich literature in International Relations, which has borrowed from sociology that focuses on the inner workings of organizations with a particular emphasis on organizational culture, including conventions and routines (e.g., Barnett and Finnemore 1999; Weaver 2008; Chwieroth 2010).

no institutional discussion. Conventions, however, can also be subjected to debate and nonetheless end up as the default option. In some cases, certain actors may reaffirm specific conventions because of the benefits they derive from them.[24] In other cases, conventions may endure simply because no better alternative seems available to institutional participants at the time. In either case, conventions limit the domain of available options for states, which suggests that states may pursue different avenues and hence reach different outcomes than they would in the absence of these existing institutional procedures.[25]

Institutional rules and conventions should, theoretically, create a tendency for the status quo. The content of those rules and conventions should illuminate power asymmetries at the creation of these institutions. Hence, political bargains struck at a specific time may not only work to reflect past asymmetries in power, but also explain *how* incremental change might be dominant in revising existing formal political asymmetries (Fioretos 2011). Orfeo Fioretos (2011, p. 373) explains: "Such changes [to rules] affect the extent to which people gain or lose access to the advantages (or disadvantages) they associate with past designs, including those that confer positions of privilege that translate into forms of enduring influence" (also Pierson 2004, p. 146). This rationale further justifies focusing on the institutionally dominant states' core preferences regarding formal political asymmetries.

Further, institutions exhibit in-built stickiness, to paraphrase Pierson (2004, p. 43). This innate stickiness stems from state actors' desire to reduce uncertainty and to have the institutions serve stability. In this regard, an institution's procedures, rules, and conventions tend to be relatively more status quo friendly by virtue of being difficult to overturn. With rules that can be changed at a whim, or conventions that could be renegotiated quickly, the institution's ability to contribute to predictability in inter-state relations would be reduced. In short, combined with the leading states' preference to maintain existing arrangements, to the greatest extent possible, the ingrained tendency of institutions for the status quo suggest that the existing rules and conventions will work toward maintaining, and not overturning, existing asymmetries in formal political power.

---

[24] Surely, individual actors – in their minds – may have reflected on a specific convention, but the issue here is whether there was collective, institutional consideration of certain procedures. The point that states may have reflected upon conventions and decided to pursue them nonetheless is reminiscent of Tetlock and McGuire (1986) quoted in Kahler (1998).

[25] While I take it seriously that conventions can often be habitual fallbacks for actors, because of the difficulties of differentiating between habitual and non-habitual fallback (when is an actor habitually acting? When are they conveniently ignoring a certain path?), I am primarily interested in actors' discussions surrounding conventions.

More broadly, *existing rules and conventions tend to create path dependence.* As Mahoney and Schensul (2006) note, scholars continue to disagree on the precise definition of path dependence. Here, path dependence points to the contribution of initial conditions to "narrow[ing] the range of possible future outcomes" (Mahoney and Schensul 2006, p. 460). As Pierson (2004) notes, one of the reasons as to why initial conditions limit the possible outcomes or processes has to do with those conditions removing certain factors from the agenda. Another way in which prior decisions narrow later decisions concerns "positive feedback" mechanisms in which "the *relative* benefits of the current activity compared with once-possible options increases over time" (Pierson 2004, p. 21). For instance, most fundamentally, creating new institutions is a highly costly process that arguably becomes more costly over time, as an institution matures. On a more micro-scale, departing from a certain rule or convention regarding the adjustment of formal political asymmetries, such as the World Bank's custom of tying its shareholding calculations to those in the IMF, may be difficult over time. Regardless, this study is less concerned in teasing out the reasons behind path dependence and more focused on the presence of existing rules and convention as a *mechanism* for path dependence regarding formal political asymmetries.[26]

The importance of institutional rules and conventions as a mechanism for path dependence offers two broad implications for this study. First is the significance of analyzing past design choices. If institutional rules and conventions do indeed matter, then the evolution of rules and procedures might relate closely to past design, and thus the detailed analysis of that past design matters significantly for unpacking institutional developments.[27] Even when departure from a path occurs, the effects of that supposedly departed path might live on.[28] Regardless, past design choices in an institution, specifically conventions and rules regarding the adjustment of members' formal political power, needs analysis.

As these discussions suggest, the existing rules and conventions concerning formal political asymmetries and their adjustment will tend

---

[26] This project's aim of identifying rules and conventions as a mechanism for path dependence is made more ambitious by the under-articulation in the existing literature of the mechanisms of path dependence.

[27] This point does not suggest that actors' preferences do not matter. As already noted, the observation that existing rules in t_1 reflect the power asymmetries of t_0 suggests that institutional evolution will lead to the preferences of actors that were dominant in t_0 to be preserved relatively more than the preferences of other actors.

[28] The period after the abolishment of slavery (a path that was abandoned) in the USA nonetheless saw discriminatory practices such as sharecropping contracts. In a more recent example, the "extractive institutions" of the Soviet era continued into the post-communist era (Acemoglu and Robinson 2013).

toward incremental change. The previous discussion makes clear one of the primary reasons for incremental change: institutionally dominant states will protect their position, to the greatest extent possible. Another reason for incremental change concerns the fact that the agenda of today will have been shaped by the agenda of yesterday. In other words, "today" does not offer a plethora of options, but rather those that are compatible with and branch out of the decisions taken "yesterday." Crucially, that big bang change might not have happened at a certain instance should not discourage from the close analysis of that instance. Understanding moments of incremental change might be the only way to be able to understand drastic change down the road, as historical institutionalists suggest (Pierson 2004; Thelen and Mahoney 2010).

Summary   The book focuses on three key explanatory factors in understanding the relationship between the distribution of economic power among states and formal political power within multilateral economic institutions (within a single period): (1) core states' conceptualization of the institution's key functions and purposes; (2) the financial burden sharing within the institution; (3) existing rules and conventions that pertain to the formal political asymmetries. As already noted, an interaction among these variables needs to supplement a distinct focus on each. At the same time, there is no expectation that each of these variables matters to the same degree across all the cases examined. For instance, in some cases the financial burden-sharing concerns may be muted. In that case, examining why such concerns are subdued serves the analysis as much as arguing that conflicts over burden sharing helped determine a specific outcome. Similarly, at the creation of an institution, the analysis will tilt relatively more toward explaining the origins of rules and conventions than accounting for their influence on the static or dynamic nature of formal political asymmetries. Despite these context-specific ways in which the variables demand analysis, they nonetheless provide the empirical studies in the ensuing chapters of the book with clear propositions as well as a systematic framework for analysis.

Conjunctural factors

This section discusses how the three key explanatory variables might interact with other factors that might plausibly explain the relationship between the inter-state distribution of economic power and the distribution of formal political power in multilateral economic institutions.

Differences across individual member states

While the previous discussion identifies three key factors in explaining the distribution of formal political power and how that distribution relates to the inter-state distribution of economic power, these factors do not pertain to the individual positions of members, but rather to broader factors, which stem both from actors' general preference-based behavior and institutional features. As an example, while core states' conceptualization of the institution's functions and purposes could explain the broad distribution of formal political power, this factor does not necessarily help identify how that core state affects a single member's formal political power. State 1's preference toward State 2 may be based on State 1's desire to get State 2 to contribute more to the financing of the institution. If State 1 thinks about States 3, 4, 5 as it does about State 2, State 1's interest in State 2 can be said to stem not from State 2's individualistic qualities, but its structural qualities that it shares with States 3, 4, 5 (e.g., its status as a rising state).

A different question to ask about State 1's relation to State 2 is whether there exist specific ties between these two states that could help explain State 1's preference regarding State 2's formal political power. In the context of this book, if State 1 denotes the institutionally dominant state, let us say the USA, then the question becomes: can State 2's formal political power have anything to do with its relation to State 1? This question is close to impossible to answer qualitatively: such a study might be not only be too lengthy (too many different states to analyze), but also indeterminate in terms of not being able to pinpoint *the kind of* inter-relationship that matters for understanding formal political power. A quantitative analysis, however, is more feasible.

Chapter 3 of the book, thus, undertakes a quantitative study that examines whether the USA exerts informal influence over members' quota adjustments in the IMF. While at the time of the creation of the institution, the leading states might have the opportunity to place key allies/friends/partners to advantageous positions of formal political power, once the rules and conventions have been set in motion, this kind of influence should be relatively out of the ordinary (Stone 2011). Existing work has shown that the USA, in particular, has conferred substantial influence over the decisions of multilateral economic institutions (e.g., Barro and Lee 2005; Copelovitch 2010; Fleck and Kilby 2006; Stone 2008 and 2011; Thacker 1999; Woods 2006). For instance, this literature has persuasively found that countries with political-economic ties to the USA receive greater and better credit (with fewer conditions) from the IMF and the World Bank, controlling for other relevant factors.

Extending this literature to the study at hand would suggest that within multilateral economic institutions, *political-economic proximity to the USA positively and significantly affects the individual member state's formal position, specifically the member's quota shifts in the IMF.*[29] Chapter 3 explores this proposition.

The upshot is while the meta-trends identified in the previous section may shape the parameters within which the determination of, or adjustments to, formal political power will occur, focusing on the individual (member state) positions offers an additional unit of analysis, thereby extending the scope of the study.

Distributional conflicts within groups

Another dimension that relates to individual positions concerns the within-group distribution of gains/losses. The previous analysis suggests that the institutionally leading states face pressures for "limited accommodation" during relative economic decline. A corollary to this point is: *distributional conflicts within the group of declining states likely intensify during the accommodation of rising states,* all else being equal.

The following logics back this proposition. While the declining states' accommodation of the rising states, and the rising states' corresponding position enhancement, does not constitute a zero-sum game, it is difficult to fathom a situation under which the rising states would enhance their position without any cost to the declining states at all. Although there does not have to be a one-to-one correspondence between the rising states' gains and the declining states' losses, position enhancement and accommodation are nonetheless likely to be inversely related particularly in institutions such as the IMF and the World Bank, where voting rights are distributed unequally. In those two institutions, not only is there likely to be not enough voting power to distribute within the developing world (away from the relatively poor to the rising states), but also a reform that leaves the voting power of the large advanced economies untouched is likely to be politically unfeasible.

In this context, the declining states, while conceding to accommodation, are likely to strive to minimize *individual* costs, having other members of the group suffer the losses that the group needs to experience as a whole. Such a strategy would ensure that a declining state would limit the costs to itself from accommodation. This cost

---

[29] To be sure, such proximity cannot be the only factor that affects adjustment in quotas, given the significance of the three key explanatory factors identified in the previous section.

shifting tactic would also overcome the tension between accommodation and limited accommodation. From an individualistic perspective, accommodation could be more easily achieved if one could shift costs. Cost shifting, thus, offers a relatively easy way for declining states to reconcile the motivations for accommodation with the tendency for limited accommodation. The expectation is thus for *members of the group of the declining states to engage in cost shifting,* in which each tries to have others in the group suffer more of the losses from the reduction in formal political power.

The flipside of these discussions concerns the distribution of gains within the group of rising states. The rising states face good reasons for wanting to increase their formal political power, given the importance of it for control within the institution (Chapter 1). In a similar vein, Grieco's (1995) "voice opportunities thesis" suggests that relatively weak states will care about asymmetric institutional arrangements and will try to use the opportunities to increase their voices. While Grieco advances this argument in the context of Europe, his study confirms this book's central position that states do care about asymmetries in institutions, and that "position enhancement" is a reasonable and likely strategy for the rising states, which are institutionally in a relatively weaker position.

Yet, there are a number of reasons for a rising state to avoid maximizing its position enhancement (increases in its formal political power), which in turn partially alleviates any potential within-group conflicts. Increasing its formal political power to some extent (whatever that extent might be) may give a rising state enough influence, and beyond this point, increases might have diminishing returns. For instance, these states might weigh the trade-off between increasing their formal power in the institution with increasing responsibilities, such as enhanced financial contributions, which come with that formal power. While not per se a responsibility, increasing formal political power in an institution also comes with greater scrutiny of that state's behavior within the institution or vis-à-vis the institution's policies. Furthermore, states might concede to shifts in the distribution of formal political power that do not fulfill all their preferences because they do not wish to hold up the reform process (namely, the adjustment of members' formal political power). Being designated as the reform-blocker might come with reputational costs or unwanted attention and affect future reforms.[30] In short, the rising states have a number of reasons for conceding to changes in formal political power that do not reflect all their preferences.

---

[30] Interviews confirmed this point.

The conjunctural factors outlined in this section go toward proposing details that are likely to matter in analyzing the relationship between (shifts in) the distribution of formal political power and (shifts in) the distribution of inter-state economic power.

Alternative factors?

In this section, I assess possible alternative explanations on the relationship between the inter-state distribution of economic power and states' formal political power in multilateral economic institutions.

Intentions of non-leading states?

Up to now, the analysis has treated the leading states as the most important actors regarding the design or the redesign of institutions. This assumption begs some questions: What about the extent to which other key states push for specific design options? The non-leading states could, for instance, be the leading state's key interlocutor at the creation of a specific multilateral institution (as in the case of the UK for the USA), or they could be the rising states in the case of altering existing formal political power. Kahler (2013), for instance, highlights the preferences and capacities of the emerging powers with respect to global governance as an important variable to examine in explaining the changes in contemporary multilateral institutions.

The book claims that non-leading states' *pursuit of* their preferences (regarding the distribution of formal political power) is likely to be endogenous to the leading state's pursuit of (differing degrees of) accommodation. The more the rising states serve the realization of the institution's functions and purposes in accordance with the aims of the leading states, for instance, the greater the room the rising states have for position enhancement. In this framework, the extent to which the leading states permit accommodation accounts for the bulk of the explanation about different levels of accommodation across institutions. This point does not dismiss the importance of the rising states' strategies, or their capacities (e.g., *International Affairs*, 2013 (89:3)). Rather, within the parameters of this study, it cautions against explaining the outcome of limited accommodation with a putative lack of interest on the part of the rising states. Rising states may not be pushing for greater degrees of position enhancement not because of their lack of enthusiasm in position enhancement, but because the leading states' willingness for accommodation might prejudice their pursuit of position enhancement. Regardless, I subject this assertion to empirical analysis.

States' concerns for the legitimacy of the institution?

Although legitimacy implicitly or explicitly features in the book's analysis, I do not use it as a central variable. The book recognizes the importance of legitimacy concerns. For instance, in outlining the background to the 2008–2010 shifts to members' formal political power in the IMF and the World Bank, the analysis draws particular attention to the declining legitimacy of these institutions in the eyes of both shareholders and stakeholders (see Chapters 4 and 5).[31] Moreover, the book discusses the ways in which the 2008–2010 changes in these institutions fall short of meeting some key actors' demands, thereby threatening the future legitimacy of the institution (Chapter 8).

Still, legitimacy is not a central concept and, pursuing it as such would subtract more than add. For one, even if "actors' legitimacy concerns" were a key explanatory variable, that variable would still have to focus on the kind of empirical issues on which this study focuses, such as the extent to which the distribution of formal political power meets actors' key preferences, or what kind of a burden-sharing arrangement the actors find preferable. Although the literature on legitimacy concurs that legitimacy has a normative quality, it also agrees that actors may have non-normative concerns when assessing the legitimacy of an institution.[32] For instance, Scharpf (1999) differentiates between input and output legitimacy. While input legitimacy denotes the acceptability of the process by which decisions are made, output legitimacy captures the acceptability of the substance of those decisions (see Hurd 2007, p. 7, for a similar distinction). Similarly, the causes of legitimacy failures are diverse. For instance, many authors recognize that lapses in actors' beliefs of an institution's legitimacy could stem from an institution's failure to deliver on its goals, namely from practical failures (e.g., Reus-Smit 2007; Steffek 2003). In this respect, understanding the legitimacy of an institution involves understanding actors' key positions (in this case, on the distribution of formal political power) – a task this book undertakes. At the same time, even when actors express an outcome/process as "illegitimate," we could not be sure what kind of an outcome would satisfy the actors' concerns for the legitimacy of the institution, unless the actors expressly indicate it. Most of the operationalization of legitimacy would involve focusing on actors' expressed preferences, which the book already does.

As for actors' normative preferences, which might also feature into their thinking on legitimacy, the analysis here contends that these normative

---

[31] Identifying legitimacy crises, as I discuss shortly, is a different task than capturing state actions based on concerns for the legitimacy of the institution.

[32] On this point see, Hurd (1999); Buchanan and Keohane (2006); Reus-Smit (2001).

concerns will not be absent, but will be tangential to understanding the relationship between the inter-state distribution of economic power and the distribution of formal political power in multilateral economic institutions. I expect the normative dimension to be relatively subdued when it comes to the distribution of formal political power because of the very sensitivity and the importance of members' formal political power. Formal political power permits the control of a state within an institution. Not only is the distribution of political power in multilateral economic institutions a domestically sensitive issue, it also relates to international prestige, which explains why states tend to guard their formal political power intensely (Chapter 1). Moreover, formal political asymmetries can easily confer upon member states tangible costs (such as financial contributions). In short, I suggest that the importance of formal political power will translate into states' prioritizing material concerns. Thus, although the empirical analysis pays attention to states' normative motivations, it does not expect these motivations to be a large factor in determining the outcomes.

Autonomy of institutions: the role of the staff and institutions

The discussions have so far centered on state actors. Existing work, however, shows the value of examining institutions as autonomous actors, where institutional bureaucracy and the staff, namely the non-state actors, generate most of that autonomy. While the rationalist literature regards this autonomy as relatively deliberate, resulting from the ideological or technocratic tendencies of the institutions' bureaucratic staff (e.g., contributions to Hawkins et al. 2006), the constructivist literature portrays it as an unintended by-product of existing institutional norms (e.g., Barnett and Finnemore 1999; Weaver 2008). Both strands assess the autonomy of multilateral institutions through the actions and influences of the staff (i.e., not member states) of institutions. How do those arguments on institutional autonomy mesh with the adjusted power approach?

In the case of the examination of formal political asymmetries, there is little room for the staff to exhibit autonomous action. True, the staff of these institutions possess expertise, and they can use this professionalism to push for their own preferences. At the same time, the staff play a key role in communicating and sustaining existing institutional conventions. Yet, the shift in formal political asymmetries provides little room for creative technical analysis. The state representatives tend to have a fundamental understanding of how different technical parameters impact upon their state's position within the institution, which permits their

interventions into staff's work. After all, not only do these state representatives tend to be highly trained in the relevant technical work, they are
also likely to be aware of the basic impact of different choices of variables.[33] More importantly, formal political power and discussions over
it are cases in which relatively little delegation to the staff occurs
(Chapters 1 and 3). Low delegation, in turn, translates into restricted
room for autonomy. Notably, most of the cases that are designated as sites
of autonomous organizational action are those that involve a significant
degree of delegation to the staff (see, Finnemore 1996; Weaver 2008;
Stone 2011). The bottom line is that while it is important to pay attention
to the effects of the staff on the design or redesign of formal political
asymmetries within multilateral economic institutions, their independent
impact is likely to be limited.

Conclusions and roadmap for the empirical analysis

While borrowing from both power-based and institutionalist approaches
on the relationship between the distribution of economic power and
political power within institutions, the adjusted power framework
differs from and improves upon these alternative frameworks. Table 2.1
summarizes these differences, and the ensuing discussion provides the
rationale for the points in the table.

The absence of a systematic treatment of power asymmetries in institutionalist works raises a number of questions. Particularly, the claim that
institutions tame power disparities suggests the realm of inter-state
cooperation functions with a certain degree of immunity from inter-
state asymmetries in economic power. In turn, how institutions would
react to shifts in inter-state power relations, such as the economic rise
of certain states, remains unclear. From a certain perspective, they
should not react at all given their immunity (by design and by definition).
At the same time, the institutionalist approaches do not problematize
adequately the variation in the taming influence of institutions – how do
different institutions alleviate the existing power asymmetries differently?
This variation seems critical in arguing for the effects of institutional
settings on inter-state power dynamics.

Perhaps it is less surprising that power-based approaches also overlook
the institutional variation in the interaction between economic-political
power, as these approaches not only privilege the importance of power,

---

[33] For example, representatives know whether their GDP is higher when GDP is measured
at market exchange rates or when it is measured using purchasing power parity (PPP) –
one of the key variables in measuring members' voting power in both the IMF and the
World Bank.

Table 2.1 *The adjusted power approach in a comparative lens*

	What is the primary relationship between the inter-state distribution of economic power and the distribution of formal political power in multilateral economic institutions?	How do shifts in the inter-state distribution of economic power relate to shifts in the distribution of formal political power among members states in a multilateral economic institution?	How do the relatively economically declining states (that are in an institutionally dominant position) handle the economically rising states within the institutional contexts?
Power-based approaches	Institutions *reflect* power relations among states.	As power asymmetries change, so should formal political power, but there will be a lag. How that lag gets overcome remains unclear.	Unclear, though if institutions reflect underlying power asymmetries, then change should happen in a way that reflects the rising states.
Institutionalist approaches	Institutions *tame* power relations among states; the importance of power relations is unclear. Also states may be important to an institution in ways that are not related to power differentials.	Unclear. In theory, changing inter-state asymmetries should not be a concern, as the institutions have tamed existing asymmetries in inter-state power.	Unclear due to the lack of emphasis on the variation in the degree to which different institutions tame power asymmetries.
Adjusted power approach	Institutions *adjust* power relations among states and three variables are of key importance in understanding that adjustment.	Institutions will exhibit variation in the manner in which they respond to shifts in the inter-state distribution of economic power.	The declining states' accommodation of the rising states (namely, increases in the formal political power of the rising states) should vary depending on the three features of institutions identified in this chapter.

but they also promote an understanding of state behavior that centers around the relatively myopic pursuit of interests. Moreover, although various realist accounts point to the fact that institutions mirror underlying power asymmetries with a delay, they still do not investigate the reasons for this "lag," the mechanisms that narrow it, or alternatively the manner in which the lag gets maintained. In short, institutionalist and power-based accounts both fall short in two primary ways: one, they do not explore institutional variation in the way in which inter-state economic asymmetries relate to political power disparities within institutions; two, they do not provide an understanding of how shifts in inter-state power dynamics affect institutional settings.

The adjusted power framework contributes to remedying these gaps. At its heart is the variation in the distribution of formal political power across different multilateral economic institutions (of the same period). Key to this variation, the approach explores why some institutions dial down the importance of the underlying distribution of inter-state economic power, while others are more sensitive to it.

By the same token, saying institutions matter to power relations is too indeterminate unless specific institutional features can be highlighted in examining how institutions significantly affect power differentials. The three institutional features the adjusted power approach highlights – core states' conceptualization of the functions and purposes of institutions, financial burden-sharing arrangements within the institution, and relevant institutional rules and conventions – aim to more specifically identify the manner in which institutions filter power. For instance, whether the institutionally dominant but economically declining states will tend toward relatively more "accommodation" hinges upon these factors and the inter action among them.

Further, the adjusted power approach contributes to understanding the lag between institutional settings and power dynamics, and how and why that lag may be easier to narrow under certain conditions than others. As an example, in certain cases, while institutionally dominant states' desire to burden share the financing of the institution may create a tendency for these states to reduce the supposed gap between institutions and power dynamics, existing institutional rules and conventions may nonetheless create inertia against such change. While all these factors may not be equally relevant across different cases – for instance, in newly founded institutions, conventions should matter relatively less than in mature institutions – taken together, they provide a systematic investigation of the intersection of power and institutions.

Finally, analyzing existing works (be they power-based or institutionalist-leaning) in a synthetic manner toward an integrative theory, while simultaneously expanding upon their discussions, yields propositions that differ from existing perspectives' core predictions (Table 2.1). This is perhaps not surprising, given power and institutions have been similar to two ships passing each other in the night. While prevalent works have focused on power or institutions, their intersection remains surprisingly under-explored. In the adjusted power approach, neither "institutions" nor "power" does the explanation – institutional settings cannot be analyzed as if they are immune from power differentials, nor can they be examined as if power seamlessly gets encapsulated in them.

3　The origins of states' formal equality in the global financial institutions

Why did the IMF and the World Bank end up with the same weighted voting structures that give their members' asymmetric formal political power?[1] What are the determinants of the shifts in members' formal political power over time? The study of these questions are not only central to the purposes of this book, they also address broader debates in international political economy, given the universal membership these two financial institutions have achieved and their centrality to the governance of contemporary multilateral economic relations. For example, the IMF's and the World Bank's policies on economic development from the 1980s until the early twenty-first century, known as the Washington Consensus, have been at the center stage of scholarly and public discussions.[2] Commentators have emphasized the Washington Consensus as intimately related to the USA's and a handful of other rich countries' asymmetric control over the IMF and the World Bank (Birdsall 2007; Wade 2002; Woods 2006). Scholars have, similarly, associated the developing countries' limited influence over the IMF with their lack of adequate formal voice. As Nancy Birdsall (2007, p. 12) puts it: "implicitly if not explicitly, better representation of developing countries on the boards of the [Bretton Woods] institutions would give the borrowing countries more influence in resisting pressure for constant liberalization of their markets and might create pressure to hire more professional staff with broader backgrounds." Birdsall's analysis draws a

[1] As noted earlier, voting in both institutions consists of two components – basic votes, which are distributed to member states equally, and quota (IMF) or subscription (World Bank) votes, which indicate members' shares in the organization. The shares, in turn, are calculated by the member's relative economic weight and other economic variables. The latter component is more important in determining a member state's total voting power.
[2] It is not possible to put an end date on the Washington Consensus; however, by the end of the first decade in the twenty-first century, many experts were considering the Consensus to have largely gone out of favor. Babb (2009) provides a detailed history of the Consensus, which basically prescribed privatization, deregulation, and liberalization in developing economies. For a critical assessment of the Consensus' success in engendering economic development, see Rodrik (2008), and for relatively favorable perspectives on the Consensus, see Dollar (2007) and Wolf (2005).

clear link between the disparities in formal political power within the two global financial institutions and the policies these institutions help facilitate (see also Chapter 1).

In exploring the origins and evolution of weighted voting in the IMF and the World Bank, this chapter pursues the following questions that are central to the book's core focus: (a) How did the US designers' conceptualization of the functions and purposes of these institutions affect their thinking on the institutional distribution of political power? What demands did other states make on the US actors' proposals? (b) What role did the financing of the institutions play in state actors' design of the institutions? (c) What rules and conventions have governed the maintenance and adjustment of formal political power over time? As the chapter shows, while there was very little dispute between the US actors and their key interlocutors over the desirability of weighted voting, the distribution of quotas in the IMF and hence the relative position of members within the institution proved contentious.

The chapter, thus, particularly focuses on IMF quotas and the changes in these quotas over time. Member quotas in the IMF constitute one of the most critical dimensions of the institution's governance and functioning. Quotas determine members' financial contributions and thus their relative voting power within the institution.[3] As Pauly (1997, p. 112) emphasizes, quotas indicate the "internal pecking order among Fund members." They also provide a benchmark, albeit rough and inconsistent, for the volume of loans the members can receive from the institution. Moreover, quotas have affected the members' shares in the World Bank for the majority of the Bank's history.[4]

Despite the centrality of quotas in both the IMF's governance and policy discussions, there is scant academic work that systematically analyzes them.[5] This point becomes even more unexpected when one considers that quotas also offer a window into the design of the IMF, a key interest within International Relations literatures (Koremenos et al. 2001a, 2001b). In addition to examining the rules and conventions surrounding IMF quota shifts, based on a panel dataset I compiled, the chapter probes whether the USA exerts informal influence over IMF quota adjustments. US informal influence over other aspects of the institution, particularly loan decisions,

---

[3] Basic votes currently account for only about 5.5 percent of the member's total voting power.

[4] As I explain in the Conclusion of this chapter, I could not construct a complete dataset for members' share adjustments in the Bank.

[5] Bird and Rowlands (2006) concur with this observation, and their study as well as Broz (2005); Broz and Hawes (2006); Blomberg and Broz (2006); Lister (1984); Pauly (1997) emphasize the importance of examining quotas, but do not analyze the determinants of quotas over time.

has been established, but the question of whether US actors can also similarly impact quota shifts has not been explored (Barro and Lee 2005; Copelovitch 2010; Fleck and Kilby 2006; Stone 2008; Thacker 1999). US interferences with quota adjustments could ensure the results, including member state rankings in formal political power, meet US expectations. And, since quotas are so important to member states, the USA can curry favors with other members by facilitating higher quota increases for them. Indeed, there is anecdotal evidence of the USA using quota increases as enticements (e.g., Lipscy 2003). There could also be economic rationale in US interference, since quotas affect access to IMF funds.

US informal influence over quota shifts should be relatively costly (compared to loan decisions in particular), but not so costly as to be unexpected. There are aspects of quota adjustments that fall under "formal governance" in the IMF (Stone 2011). Under formal governance, "legitimate procedures that embody a broad consensus of the membership" reign. In contrast, under informal governance "informal rules ... allow exceptional access for powerful states to set the agenda and control particular outcomes" (ibid., p. 13). Quota adjustments remain vested in the Board of Governors, and a set of well-defined rules and conventions determines how members will alter quotas, making quota adjustments relatively constitutionalized.[6] Importantly, these adjustments involve extensive member state scrutiny and debate over the quota shift each member will receive. Given quota adjustments are relatively more transparent, involve low levels of delegation (to the staff and the Executive Board), and receive a high level of member state oversight, the legitimacy costs of a US exercise of influence during quota adjustments should be relatively high (Stone 2011, p. 52).[7]

That the USA has a de facto veto power over quota adjustments does not alter this last point. The USA's veto power is of greater utility to the USA before and after the process of quota shifts. Beforehand, the members tend to negotiate a total quota increase to the IMF's quota. Here, if the largest shareholders of the institution are unwilling to increase the IMF's quota, it is unlikely this increase will happen.[8] After the quota adjustment, the USA can utilize its veto as a vote of disapproval on the outcome.[9] Yet, as just

---

[6] The IMF's Executive Board debates the quota shifts, but constitutionally the power to change them resides with the Board of Governors (high-level member state representatives), and this is one of the few areas where the Governors have specifically decided not to delegate their authority to the Board (Lister 1984).

[7] See Stone (2011) on why informal influence of this kind always incurs some legitimacy costs.

[8] See Broz and Hawes (2006) on total quota increases and the US Congress.

[9] Studies have found the veto power to generally confer only negative power on the USA, and any small majority can also utilize it, which explains why minorities within the institution have preferred its retention (Abdelal 2007; IMF 2010c; Leech 2002; Rapkin

noted, given the importance of quotas, the process of quota adjustments is highly politically sensitive and receives each and every member's detailed attention. In this context, the USA throwing its weight around would be more visible than in other issue areas, where there are relatively low levels of transparency and higher degrees of delegation to the Executive Board and the staff, such as in loan decisions (Stone 2011).

Still, there are also dimensions of quota adjustments that provide enough room for US informal influence. Particularly, members politically negotiate quota shifts, and these political negotiations provide opportunity for US interference. Indeed, the chapter demonstrates that political-economic proximity to the USA has positively and significantly affected the quota increases the members received at the IMF from 1965 to 2010. In addition to showing US informal influence where it is relatively more costly, this finding enriches the book's analysis by focusing on the determinants of individual formal political power. In the rest of the book a group of states constitute the unit of analysis, but here the unit of analysis is the member state.

The next section provides the history of weighted voting in the IMF/ World Bank, followed by a discussion of the contentiousness of IMF quotas, both at the institution's inception and now. That analysis leads to an examination of the aforementioned quota shifts in the IMF in 1965–2010. The conclusion draws the broad implications of these findings and outlines possibilities for future research.

The origins of weighted voting in the IMF and the World Bank

The US designers of these now global financial institutions as well as the USA's key interlocutors preferred asymmetric voting in the institutions, primarily because they reasoned that weighted voting would best serve the functions and purposes of the two institutions, particularly their mission of lending to their members.

The easy choice for weighted voting

As one of the main architects of the Bretton Woods institutions, Harry Dexter White, explained, together the IMF and the World Bank would "help [countries] not only to reestablish their economies but ... [they

---

and Strand 2005). In any case, the statistical specifications in this paper account for the US de facto veto over quota adjustments, which has existed throughout the institution's history.

would] help even more directly by promoting stability in exchange rates, by promoting the adjustment of exchange rates, by preventing economic warfare, thus enabling those countries to buy more" (US House of Representatives 1945, p. 101). According to the designers' original intentions for these institutions, the IMF would provide short-term assistance for members to maintain their currencies in the adjustable peg exchange rate system of the Bretton Woods order, while the Bank would provide relatively long-term loans for reconstruction and development. White emphasized that besides facilitating the goal of global financial and monetary cooperation, "the beneficial effect on our exporters [would be] a very important consequence of the adoption of these two institutions" (p. 101). In this respect, in creating the two institutions, the US negotiators' goal of boosting US exports meshed with their support for global economic stability and the reconstruction of war-torn countries. The next step in the analysis concerns the identification of how these institutional goals affected the design of voting in the IMF and the World Bank.

The US designers and other state representatives converged on the necessity for weighted voting in the IMF/World Bank given these institutions would require asymmetric financial capital subscriptions based on their intended functions as creditor institutions. For instance, White, in his plans for the Bretton Woods institutions (known as the White Plan), referred to the linkage between voting and financial contributions explicitly: "If each member of the board were to be given an equal vote, then a small country that invested one million dollars would have as much power in making decisions as a country that has subscribed a hundred or a thousand times that amount" (Gold 1972, p. 19). The Joint Statement, which the American and British officials co-penned, reemphasized this principle: "The distribution of voting power on the board [Board of Governors] and the executive committee shall be closely related to the quotas" (US Treasury 1944a). The discussions on the World Bank repeated the same principle: "subscriptions of member countries [shares in the Bank] will determine their relative share in the management of the Bank" (US Treasury 1944b, p. 1). In short, according to the designers, asymmetric capital contribution justified asymmetric representation.

Further, the notion that voting power should reflect capital contributions, specifically quotas, and hence be weighted, received widespread acceptance during the inter-state negotiations in Bretton Woods. Delegations from not just advanced economies, but also a group as diverse as Ecuador, China, Mexico, Greece, and Ethiopia expressed a preference for basing voting power on quotas. Here, the Mexican delegate's thoughts are representative: "It may appear inconsistent with

[Mexico's] normal position as a debtor country, but has it not always been true that creditors have more to say about lending money than borrowers? ... *we all thought it was a basic principle that, creditor nations should have proportionately more voting power than the debtor nations*" (Schuler and Rosenberg 2012, p. 481, emphasis added).[10] Along these lines, as the Chinese delegation explained, member states converged on the necessity for weighted voting for reasons White had outlined (pp. 475–7). In short, weighted voting in the two international financial institutions was not a controversial issue, and hence there was little discussion on the appropriateness of it during the negotiations (Gold 1981).

Differences across the IMF and the World Bank?

That the delegates found weighted voting as appropriate for both the IMF and the World Bank may, on the surface, seem unsurprising. Given the two institutions would serve complementary functions in the provision of financial and monetary stability *and* given both of them would provide loans, it may seem non-mysterious that the US designers and their interlocutors settled on the same voting system in both of the institutions.

Yet, there were (and are) a number of differences across the two institutions, and why these differences did not manifest themselves in different institutional designs deserves analysis. For instance, how the members would finance these institutions as well as the nature of the credit the institutions would extend to their members differed. Given that the book's analytical framework, the adjusted power approach, argues the key states' conceptualization of the functions and purposes matters for the distribution of formal political power within that institution, the question of why the differences across the two Bretton Woods institutions did not translate into differences in voting is a relevant question.

There were a number of differences in the way in which the member states would fund these institutions and the kind of credit the institutions would provide for the members. Particularly, in the IMF the quotas formed the primary basis of the short-term loans, or more precisely purchases of foreign exchange reserves, the institution would provide. The members had to pay the quotas in whole and within strict deadlines. In comparison, the US drafters initially envisioned the Bank as primarily guaranteeing the loans made by private banks in a foreign country, with

---

[10] Schuler and Rosenberg's book comprises the original transcripts of the Bretton Woods conference.

sovereigns as the clients of the Bank (e.g. Acheson 1945, p. 34; see also Morgenthau 1944; US Treasury 1944b). As one of the US drafters, Fred Vinson, put it: "The International Bank would help countries to secure the foreign capital they need for productive purposes" (US House of Representatives 1945, p. 160). Only as a side business would the Bank extend credit. As Acheson, the then US Secretary of State, explained, "[i]n addition to its guaranty of private loans, the international bank proposed may make direct loans within certain limits, when private capital is not available" (Acheson 1945, p. 34; parentheses in original removed). As far as the World Bank's own lending capacity was concerned, the discussions centered on the Bank participating in private loans, with a view to increasing the volume of those credits. In sum, originally the drafters considered the Bank's role as chiefly guaranteeing private credit, while the IMF would extend its own loans.

Correspondingly, the negotiators' thinking on how the Bank would be financed related to their central plan for the Bank as a guarantor of private investment. In this context, the Bank's callable capital would ensure that in the case of a default on a loan, the members would share the burden of paying for the default. The US designers, thus, referred to the creditor members as providing a "surety fund" (US Treasury 1944). Given the surety fund did not demand immediate contributions by members, most of the Bank's capital would be callable. Originally, the Articles of Agreement of the Bank required 20 percent of the capital to be paid-in and the remaining to be callable (see Chapter 6 for recent figures). Notably, the Bank's ability to issue bonds on international markets was not a central concern at the time of its creation (US Treasury 1944, p. 5). The negotiators considered this ability to raise debt as an additional resource for the Bank as opposed to a primary one, as it is the case today for the International Bank for Reconstruction and Development (IBRD).[11] In essence, a large portion of the members' contributions would be in the form of a liability to the Bank.

These discussions point to the following: the members' financial contributions to the Bank would be relatively less direct (the contributions would provide a "surety fund" primarily through callable capital) than their contributions to the IMF.[12] Relatedly, given only 20 percent of the capital would be "paid-in" in the Bank; whereas, the IMF quota would be provided in its entirety, the members' financial commitments to the IMF

[11] As noted earlier, the IBRD makes non-concessional loans and was the only institution that constituted the World Bank in 1944.

[12] Some of these details regarding the manner of the financing of the institutions have changed over time, a topic that the remaining chapters address, but the callable nature of most of the Bank's capital remains the same.

was relatively more upfront. Did these differences feature in the designers' thinking, and if so, why did they not spur different voting structures across the two institutions?

Two plausible answers come to mind here. First, it is possible that the designers recognized these differences, but they did not judge them as distinct enough to require substantially different voting structures. Second, it could be that the designers' prioritization of the IMF led to the World Bank ending with the IMF's voting structure by default. If the designers emphasized the slight differences in financing, but nonetheless deliberately decided on the same voting structure in the two institutions, then the first option would be vindicated. If the designers ignored the differences in the nature of state financing of the IMF versus the World Bank, then option two seems more likely.[13]

A careful examination of the transcripts of the Bretton Woods agreements, the available preparatory documents in the lead up to Bretton Woods, and testimonies of US drafters of the Bretton Woods agreements to US Congress provides evidence more for the first option than for the second possibility.

Designers' thinking on the IMF versus the World Bank   While the US designers intended the World Bank as complementary to the central role the IMF would play, this status of the Bank as a sidekick of the IMF does not explain why the differences in the two institutions' financing did not translate into differences in voting across the two institutions. The US drafters generally conceived the IMF as the central institution in the post-war financial and monetary order, as it would take on the primary responsibility of providing for collective economic security by managing a system of stable exchange rates, thereby preventing the beggar-thy-neighbor currency devaluations of the 1930s. But, the IMF was only allowed to make short-term loans; therefore, an institution with the ability to make long-term loans was necessary. The following explanation from Dean Acheson (1945, p. 42) illuminates these points:

the whole heart of the matter is contained in the fund agreement and in the operation of the fund, which provides for putting aside the instruments of economic warfare

It is one thing to make loans through a bank, under a system like that, and it is another to make loans through a bank, when you have no such system. The bank's loans will be infinitely safer, where you have a fund operating.[14]

---

[13] Again, the scope of these discussions pertains only to the creation of these two institutions and not to their evolution.

[14] For a similar conclusion about the centrality of the IMF, see Horsefield (1969, especially p. 5).

The US designers regarded the Bank as supporting the IMF's pursuit of sustainable balance of payment positions in member countries. The Bank's assistance (recall that it was originally seen as primarily guaranteeing private investment) would permit countries to import capital goods necessary for reconstruction and development without having to spend the country's exchange and gold reserves (US Treasury 1944b, p. 60). Further, only members of the IMF could, upon request, become members of the World Bank. More importantly perhaps, the majority of the Bretton Woods negotiations focused on the IMF (Schuler and Rosenberg 2012). Despite these points that support the prioritization of the IMF, there is no clear evidence that the designers without reflection imposed the IMF's voting system on the Bank.

Evidence suggests that the designers did not consider the differences in function and financing across the two institutions to justify different voting structures. The official documents and on-record testimonies demonstrate that the designers differentiated these institutions. Both Dean Acheson and Harry Dexter White, for instance, emphasized the callable nature of the capital in the Bank in their testimonies to Congress without being prompted on the matter (Acheson 1945; White 1945). Further, official documents also underscored the point that because the Bank's "direct lending activities [were] expected to be only of secondary importance," the members' paid-in capital to the Bank would be relatively small (US Treasury 1944b, p. 4). In this regard, the designers recognized that the financial commitments to the Bank would be relatively less upfront than those to the IMF.

It appears, however, that the US designers calculated the lower immediate financial involvement in the Bank would be balanced by the relatively risky nature of this commitment; whereas, the opposite held true for the IMF. The designers perceived the IMF's higher upfront financial involvement to be relatively less risky. Dexter White noted that the possibility of losing all the money put in the IMF was "sheer nonsense" made "impossible by the very nature of the make-up of the fund" (White 1945, p. 93). While not denying risk in the Fund, White went on to explain that the risk of a country refusing to pay its debt to the Fund was relatively less compared to the Bank because "governments are very, very hesitant to break their obligations on financial matters," as the USA had experienced in its preceding bilateral stabilization agreements (p. 93). In contrast, White noted that the USA, and others, could "lose substantial sums in the bank, because remember that the bank undertakes risky loans" (p. 93). Overall, the balance between the extent and the riskiness of the financial member contribution within each Bretton Woods institution was perceived comparable for the US designers.[15]

These discussions suggest the institutional designers appear to have considered the differences across the two institutions, but reasoned these differences would cancel each other out in a way that justified the same voting structure across the two institutions. More fundamentally, the to-be members agreed with the US design of weighted voting for both institutions.

IMF quotas and their adjustment over time

Even though the notion of weighted voting in the IMF/World Bank was not contentious, the same cannot be said about the distribution of quotas and thus relative voting power. The distribution of the quotas was in fact debated so extensively that the negotiators had to form the special Committee on Quotas during the Bretton Woods negotiations to discuss the matter in detail (see also Lister 1984). Even within this fifteen-member committee, however, five of the members dissented from the Committee (Schuler and Rosenberg 2012).

The initial quotas in the IMF, as would be the case in the rest of the institution's history, were determined in a highly political manner. Raymond Mikesell, the American economist who led the efforts to devise a formula for ascertaining the quotas, writes the following (1994, p. 22):

In mid-April 1943 ... [Harry Dexter] White called me to his office and asked that I prepare a formula ... He gave no instructions on the weights to be used, but I was to give the United States a quota of approximately $2.9 billion; the United Kingdom (including its colonies), about half the U.S. quota; the Soviet Union, an amount just under that of the United Kingdom; and China, somewhat less ... White's major concern was that our military allies ... should have the largest quotas, with a ranking on which the president and the secretary of state had agreed ... I went through dozens of trials, using different weights and combinations of trade data before reaching a formula that satisfied most of White's objectives.

While Mikesell's account would lead one to believe at least the US allies would be satisfied with the initial quotas, even France and China, which would be among the top five shareholders in the institution, regarded the quotas that the American team had generated not to reflect their self-assessed economic and political importance in the post-war world. China,

---

[15] To note, the discussions here only reflect the reasoning of the US designers that negotiated the Bretton Woods agreements. There were a group of bankers that regarded the loans of the IMF as relatively risky.

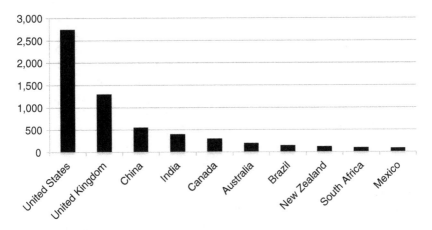

Figure 3.1 Initial quotas in 1945, top ten shareholders (in current millions USD).
Source: Author's own compilation from IMF documents.

for instance, noted the following: "The present quota, as stated by the Quota Committee, for China, when published, would be received with general disappointment by the people of China. The Chinese delegation is compelled to state that the quota is not acceptable and suggests that the Quota Committee reconsider the matter" (Schuler and Rosenberg 2012, p. 214).

France and China were not alone in their views. Iran, Greece, India, and New Zealand expressed similar concerns with their quotas. For most members the distribution of quotas was a sensitive issue because quotas determined ranking in the institution and voting power. One of the US designers of the IMF noted that "[m]ost requests for larger quotas were a reflection of the desire of the countries to maintain their prestige . . . There were only a few cases in which countries wanted larger quotas because they believed it would give them greater opportunity to use the resources of the fund" (US House of Representatives 1945, p. 168). This last point confirms the book's previous discussions about the importance of formal political power not just for practical reasons but also for prestige (especially Chapter 1). For the reader's reference, Figure 3.1 displays the initial quotas for the original ten largest shareholders of the IMF.

Cognizant of the sensitivity to the quotas, the US designers opted for combining weighted votes (based on quotas) with basic votes that were allocated equally to member states. Notably, the British proposal for the IMF was based only on weighted voting, but the US representatives preferred some basic votes. The inclusion of basic votes in the Bretton Woods institutions was to partially "[recognize] the doctrine of equality of states" (Gold 1972, p. 18). The US representatives also argued that basic votes would allow the smaller states to have large enough quotas to reflect "their true interests in [the] organization" (Schuler and Rosenberg 2012, p. 468). In other words, the US representatives thought the basic votes would be a way to get the small states vested in the institution. Basic votes would, however, only constitute 11.8 percent of the total votes, which small states in the negotiations found too little (ibid). While it may be tempting to see basic votes as the USA's concern with some sort of equality in the institution, the inclusion of basic votes resonates with the point that the rich, powerful states tend to let the small, poor states have formal institutional representation that is disproportionate to their economic power (Chapter 2; Ikenberry 2000; Stone 2011).

In sum, although the to-be members accepted the notion of weighted voting in the two international financial institutions without dissension, the distribution of these quotas, and hence voting power, stirred disagreements and tension between the negotiators. Further, although the US designers justified the original quotas based on technical calculations, these quotas were determined in a highly political manner, as Mikesell's account demonstrates.

IMF quota adjustments over time

Little has changed since the inception of the IMF – both in terms of member state sensitivity to quotas and of the political nature in which these quotas are determined. As one IMF document puts it, the rankings of members resulting from quota changes "represents a remarkable compromise among various economic and noneconomic considerations. This ranking can presumably not be reordered by reference to economic criteria" (SM/59/6 1959). Another document puts it even more bluntly: "quotas represent not only relative economic position but also, to some extent, relative political positions" in international affairs (EBD/69/165 1969). In this context, as one of the official historians of the IMF puts it, "[p]olitical battles over quota increases sometimes escalated to dimensions far out of proposition to the economic values at stake" (Boughton 2001, p. 857). Despite the political and economic significance of the quotas, scholarly work has not yet examined the determinants of IMF quota shifts, a gap the rest of this chapter begins to fill.

Table 3.1 *Increases to IMF's quotas*

	Date the Board of Governors adopted the resolution	Overall increase in IMF's total quota (%)
First Quinquennial Review	March 1951	0
Second Quinquennial Review	January 1956	0
1958/1959	February, April, 1959	60.7
Third Quinquennial Review	December 1960	0
Fourth Quinquennial Review	March 1965	30.7
Fifth General Review	February 1970	35.4
Sixth General Review	March 1976	33.6
Seventh General Review	December 1978	50.9
Eighth General Review	March 1983	47.5
Ninth General Review	June 1990	50
Tenth General Review	January 1995	0
Eleventh General Review	January 1998	45
Twelfth General Review	January 2003	0
Thirteenth General Review	January 2008	0
Fourteenth General Review	December 2010	100

Source: IMF documents.

What determines quota changes?   Table 3.1 summarizes the IMF quota reviews since the institution's inception until 2010, noting whether the reviews resulted in the institution receiving a total quota increase and thus a quota adjustment for the members. The institution's Articles of Agreement stipulates for quota reviews within a maximum of five-year gaps, though as the table indicates the members can decide not to increase the total quota following these reviews. In addition to the dates in the table, there was one other time that the institution adjusted a majority of the members' quotas. This exception occurred in 2008 when the members redistributed the existing quota in the absence of any increase to the IMF's total quota to give the developing countries greater representation in the institution.[16]

What determines the shifts in IMF quotas over time? On the surface, some kind of objective quota formula, which includes a number of core economic variables, is supposed to form a baseline for determining the members' initial quotas, as well as subsequent shifts. Although the calculation and combination of these variables in specific formulae have changed over time, the variables themselves have, more or less, stayed the same. These variables are: the member's GDP, its average imports and exports in a

[16] Exactly, only 14 members out of the 180 that are in my database did not experience a change in their quotas in 2008, while the rest of the members experienced either increases (54 members) or decreases to their quota (see also Chapter 5).

recent period, the variability of its exports, and the level of its reserves. Table 3.2 summarizes the range of datasets and formulae used at different times.

The quota formulae, however, cannot be seen as the only basis or the objective means for determining quotas and increases to them. It is not possible to ascertain which IMF quota formula has applied to which member state during the aforementioned quota changes Table 3.1 out-lines.[17] As Table 3.2 indicates, up to the 1990s, the institution was utilizing five different formulae and two different datasets (EBD/69/165 1969). Even though scholars and some IMF documents have generally noted that the formulae that gave greater weight to exports and variability were constructed to please the institution's developing country members (given these variables would indicate their potential demand for IMF resources), in reality, "no particular pair of quota formula [has applied] exclusively to any particular group or type of members" (SM/81 1981, p. 2; see IMF 2000b; Lister 1984 on the first point).

Complicating matters further, although different formulae applied to different members, one formula – the Bretton Woods Formula (BWF) – had an effect on all calculations (see Table 3.2 on BWF). Once the members were able to agree on a number for a total quota increase for the IMF, the distribution of this total to each member would need to be calculated. Because of the necessity of the sum of individual members' quota increases to equal the total negotiated increase, the formulae would have to be "normalized" (in IMF parlance). And the various formulae used for each individual quota increase were traditionally normalized using the BWF (SM/81/91 1981). The bottom line is that even when a specific formula could be identified for a specific country, that formula alone did not form the technical basis for that country's quota change. Because of these various layers of manipulation in the formulae, Jacques Polak (1981, p. 7), who served as the Director of Research at the IMF, once claimed that there is "one single formula hidden somewhere in the computer, which … produces the quota for each individual country."

Further, the quota formulae have in many instances provided *ex post* justifications for members' actual quotas in the institution. For instance, in discussing why the original BWF was revised in the early 1960s, an IMF document states: "the weights in the [BWF] were each reduced by 50 percent, thereby yielding a calculated set of quotas closer to the then existing size of quotas" (Table 3.2). In other words, the revisions to the

---

[17] Chapter 5 shows that the 2008 adjustment, just like any other adjustment, depended on political negotiations and tweaking of the formula, even though in 2008 officially only one formula was used.

Table 3.2 *IMF quota formulae*

Original Bretton Woods Formula (BWF)	$Q = (0.2Y + 0.5\,R + 0.1\,M + 0.1V)\,(1+X/Y)$ Q, calculated quota Y, national income R, gold and foreign exchange reserves M, Average annual imports (five-year average) X, Average annual exports (five-year average) V, Maximum fluctuation in exports defined as the highest and the lowest value of exports during a five-year period
Reduced BWF (early 1960s)	$Q_1 = (0.01Y + 0.025\,R + 0.05\,M + 0.2276V)(1+X/Y)$ $$V = \left| \frac{\sum_{t=3}^{11}(x_t - \bar{x}_t)}{9} \right|^{1/2}$$ x_t = value of current receipts in year t $\bar{x}_t$ = five-year moving average of exports, calculated over a thirteen-year period Q was also calculated with a second dataset where: M was replaced with C = average annual current payments (five-year average) X was replaced with Y = average annual current receipts (five-year average) VC = Variability of current receipts
Derivative BWF (early 1980s)	Formulae for Dataset 1, using imports and exports: $Q_2 = (0.0065Y + 0.078\,M + 0.5065V)(1+X/Y)$ $Q_3 = (0.0045Y + 0.070\,M + 0.9622V)\,(1+X/Y)$ $Q_4 = (0.005Y + 0.044\,M + 0.044X + 1.044V)$ $Q_5 = (0.0045Y + 0.039\,M + 0.039X + 1.304V)$ Formulae for Dataset 2, using current receipts and payments: $Q_2^\star = (0.0065Y + 0.078\,P + 0.5065VC)(1+C/Y)$ $Q_3^\star = (0.0045Y + 0.070P + 0.9622VC)\,(1+C/Y)$ $Q_4^\star = (0.005Y + 0.044P + 0.044C + 1.044VC)$ $Q_5^\star = (0.0045Y + 0.039P + 0.039C + 1.304VC)$
Changes to BWF (1990–1995)	Reduced BWF = $(0.01Y + 0.025\,R + 0.05P + 0.2276VC)$ $(1 + C/Y)$ Derivative BWF = $(0.0065Y + 0.0205125\,R + 0.078\,P + 0.5065VC)(1+C/Y)$
2008 Single Quota Formula	$CQS = (0.5Y + 0.3O + 0.15V + 0.05R)^k$ CQS = calculated quota share Y = a blend of GDP converted at market rates and PPP exchange rates averaged over a three-year period. O = the annual average of the sum of current payments and current receipts (goods, services, income, and transfers) for a five-year period V = variability of current receipts and net capital flows (measured as a standard deviation from the centered three-year trend over a thirteen-year period) R = twelve month average over a year of official reserves (foreign exchange, SDR holdings, reserve position in the Fund, and monetary gold) k = a compression factor of 0.95. The compression factor is applied to the uncompressed calculated quota shares, which are then rescaled to sum to 100.

Source: IMF documents.

formula aimed to match the technical calculations to the existing quotas rather than arrive at a new quota distribution (see also IMF 2000b, p. 12).

Another major reason as to why a simple link between the quota formula and changes in members' quotas remains elusive has to do with the fact that quota changes are subject to extensive political negotiations among IMF members (see also Bird and Rowlands 2006). And, the extent to which quota formulae formed the basis for quota shifts versus political negotiations has not only varied across different quota reviews, but also is unclear (SM/95/152 1995). Clearly, though, the formulae have, at no point, constituted the sole basis for quota changes; rather, negotiations among members have significantly affected the bottom line in quota shifts (EBD/69/165 1969).

The political negotiations over IMF quota shifts occur in multiple stages. Initially, IMF members undertake negotiations to obtain convergence on the overall quota increase (Table 3.1). Here, the largest shareholders tend to prefer modest increases, compared to the IMF staff, who have an inherent interest in expanding their role, and some developing countries, which see the quota increase as the basis for both greater voice within the institution as well as the ability to gain better access to institutional loans (see, e.g., Vaubel 1991; also EBM/89/154 1989; EBM/06/75–2 2006). Relatively larger quota increases happen when the ongoing or projected demand on the IMF's resources is significant.

Once the members agree on a total increase, they then extensively negotiate the manner in which it will be distributed among them. Crucially, members need to concur on a list of recipients for the "special increases." Quota increases tend to have uniform and non-uniform components. The uniform part of the increase constitutes an increase on the member's actual quotas, which have been traditionally a set percentage increase. The non-uniform part of the increase, prior to the 1980s, is referred to as a "special increase" and after the 1980s as a "selective" increase, namely an increase based on the member's calculated quota (using one of the formulae in Table 3.2). Table 3.3 lists these special increases.

Special or selective increases are politically contentious, as they benefit a small group of members and may disturb existing rankings. These special increases are justified with reference to statistics, which show the country is "under-represented" in the institution, though what constitutes under-representation remains open to negotiation. For instance, in 1959, the special increases were determined by a specific ratio of quotas and imports and exports (SM/59/6 1959). In 1978, many Executive Directors argued that only countries whose calculated quotas (based on one of the formulae) was four times more than their actual quotas should qualify for special increases, so that the number of special increases could be limited

Table 3.3 *Distribution of IMF quota increases*

	Date of adoption	Total quota increase (%)	Share of equi-proportional element (%)	Share of selective elements (%)
1958/1959	1959	60.7	82.4	17.6
Fourth GR	1965	30.7	81.4	18.6
Fifth GR	1970	35.4	70.6	29.4
Sixth GR	1976	33.6	0	0
Seventh GR	1978	50.9	98.2	1.8
Eighth GR	1983	47.5	40	60
Ninth GR	1990	50	60	40
Eleventh GR	1998	45	75	25
Fourteenth GR	2010	100	0	100*

Source: IMF documents.
* 100 = 60 percent selective (based on calculated quota shares) and 40 percent "ad hoc" based on specific criteria. GR = General Review

(SM/78/221 1978). Further, the members often decide on the economic criteria for determining selective increases in an *ex post* manner – after agreeing on the list of recipients for the special increases (e.g., EBS/58/59 1958).[18] Generally, the IMF staff provides the members with different calculations to show which countries could qualify for selective increases under different criteria, and the members negotiate for the most mutually palatable outcome (Boughton 2001, p. 875; EBM/90/79 1990).

Implications

These discussions suggest that while there should be opportunity for US informal influence, such influence should still incur relatively higher costs than in the case of US interference with loan decisions. The presence of extensive political negotiations over IMF quota shifts points to potential room for US interference with quota adjustments. Because of the importance of quotas for members, quota shifts are a crucial arena, where there could be some benefits to the USA exerting influence, including doling out favors to other states or ensuring that the quota shifts are to its liking. Hence the proposition: *Political-economic proximity to the USA positively and significantly affects members' quota shifts.*

Yet, the above discussions also suggest that the USA should face relatively high costs in influencing IMF quota adjustments (see footnote 7). As the contentiousness of quota adjustments itself suggests, the

[18] This does not suggest these increases are void of economic rationale.

members pay close attention to these shifts, jealously guard their own increases, and try to limit others' gains (such as imposing strict criteria on special increases). At same time, the presence of political negotiations should not distract from the point that a set of well-defined procedures govern quota shifts: members debate to converge on the most palatable set of calculations. In other words, IMF quota adjustments contain qualities of formal governance where playing by the established rules and procedures matters significantly more than in other circumstances in which transparency is lower and delegation (to staff and or the Executive Board) is higher (Stone 2011). For these reasons, while other members may need the USA's blessing for the total increase, given the USA is the largest shareholder and can veto quota adjustments, the USA intervening to ensure higher increases for certain states would be relatively less expected than in situations with higher delegation and lower transparency, such as with loan decisions.

Quantitative analysis of IMF quota shifts

To probe US influence over IMF quota adjustments, I have compiled a dataset of all quota shifts from 1965 to 2010 based primarily on IMF archives as well as more recent institutional documentation (see Tables 3.1 and 3.3).[19] The dataset consists of panel data (pooled cross-sectional data) and includes all IMF members for which consistent data on the dependent and the explanatory variables were available over time. The full sample contains over 160 countries, more than 85 percent of the IMF membership.

The dependent variable of interest, labeled as *quotashift*, is the rate of change in the member's quota from one quota review to the next. The following years are covered in *quotashift*: 1965, 1970, 1976, 1978, 1983, 1990, 1998, 2008, and 2010.[20] The dataset starts with the 1965 quota adjustment because the variables that one needs to control for in analyzing US influence over quota shifts, such as the economic factors in the IMF

---

[19] Boughton (2001) contains the data for Sixth to Eighth General Reviews. While the IMF's International Financial Statistics provides the members' quotas, this dataset was not suited to this study because it does not indicate the quota shifts the members decided on during general reviews (or any other time they adjusted the quotas). Further, the IMF dataset records the quota subscriptions over time as members place funds in the IMF (members can "subscribe" to the quotas they agree at general reviews at different paces within a set subscription period), which again made it not possible to use the IMF dataset to analyze the agreed quota increases. Also, the member's original quotas did not previously exist in a public dataset.

[20] *Quotashift* in 1998 is, for example, the member's quota in 1998 minus its quota in 1990 over the 1990 quota.

quota formulae, is available for most countries consistently only after 1960. If the member had joined the IMF in between the quota adjustments, then the member's starting quota is also taken into account in *quotashift*. Hypothetically, if the member joined in 1973, then the member's joining date falls between the 1970 and the 1976 quota shifts, the *quotashift* considers the change from 1973 to 1976. There is no centralized database that includes members' quotas at the time of joining the institution (original quotas), which I gathered through members' accession documentation. Given member states have joined the IMF at different times, not every *quotashift* contains all the countries in the sample, making the dataset unbalanced.

Quotashift captures the differential boosting of quotas across different members during quota adjustments that affect the entire membership because it includes both the uniform and the special increases the members receive. As discussed, since giving some members higher percentage increases on their quotas is politically contentious, it becomes particularly important to assess uneven increases across members. In International Relations terminology, *quotashift* allows the examination of US influence over some members' relative gains in quota adjustments.[21]

Following earlier studies on US informal influence on IMF/World Bank loans, I examine whether proximity to the USA significantly affects *quotashift*. Here, the two key explanatory variables of interest are: the logarithm of the volume of bilateral trade between the USA and the member state, and the logarithm of bilateral economic aid from the USA to the member. The volume of bilateral trade is a key indicator of political-economic proximity.[22] Higher levels of economic interaction between two sides can generate closer relations, and bilateral trade ties can help one explain the extent to which the two economies are vested in one another. Similarly, bilateral economic aid from the USA to the member could also indicate political-economic proximity to the USA. A rich literature extrapolates the political motivations in foreign aid, in general, and US foreign aid, in specific (see, e.g., Dreher et al. 2009; Lancaster 2007).[23] The trade and aid variables, plausibly, capture different kinds of proximity, with the latter one closer to approximating geopolitical closeness. In robustness tests, I include additional variables that could capture proximity to the

---

[21] The analysis answers a different question when the level of the member's quota is taken as the dependent variable. Nonetheless, political-economic proximity to the USA (specifically, the volume of bilateral trade with the USA) was still a significant explanatory factor for the level of the member's quota.

[22] See, e.g., see Barro and Lee (2005); Morrow et al. (1998); Kastner (2007); Kilby (2013); Mansfield and Pevehouse (2000).

[23] Throughout, I ran the regressions substituting bilateral economic aid with bilateral military aid, but the military aid variable was insignificant.

USA, such as voting affinity with the USA at the UNGA, which can better capture geopolitical/strategic ties.[24]

The specifications control for the economic criteria contained in the IMF quota formulae (Table 3.2). The aim here is not to replicate the IMF formula; rather, the goal is to assess whether, even after controlling for some key economic indicators the IMF considers, political-economic proximity to the USA significantly affects *quotashift*. Because the IMF indicates relying on nominal values in the quota formulae, including nominal GDP and reserves, the economic variables are in nominal form. And, because *quotashift* is a growth variable, following standard practice, I also include all economic variables in the equation as growth variables. Specifically, for GDP, imports, exports, and reserves, I include the three-year average of the annual growth rates. For the variability variable in the IMF formulae, I include the standard deviation of the member's trade balance over the ten-year period preceding *quotashift*.[25]

The estimations also have to control "ad hoc" increases.[26] IMF designates shifts in members' quotas that happen outside of a general quota review as ad hoc. Similar to special increases, members frown upon these ad hoc increases given the selective benefits such increases deliver. For instance, in 2006 only China, Mexico, South Korea, and Turkey received increases to their quotas based on the justification that they were the only members under-represented (the difference between their actual and calculated quotas based on formulae) by more than 60 percent, and they were also under-represented by all the variables the formulae included. Convention dictates these increases to be rare. After 1965, for instance, there are only six instances of ad hoc increases. Based on IMF documentation, the panel dataset includes a dummy variable, which is coded as 1 if the member received an ad hoc increase prior to *quotashift*.[27] Appendix 3.A includes a full list of the variables as well as their descriptions and sources.

[24] Relevant studies that use this variable include Barro and Lee (2005); Kilby (2013); Thacker (1999).

[25] These three years begin with the year prior to the quota shift and exclude the year when the quota shift occurs. Qualitatively and quantitatively very similar results are obtained when five-year averages are utilized.

[26] Although the IMF labeled the 2008 shift in members' quotas "ad hoc" because it occurred outside of a general review, the dataset here measures the 2008 shifts as any other quota adjustment because unlike other ad hoc increases, the 2008 quota changes extended to almost the entire membership, with 166 countries out of the 180 on which I collected data receiving a quota change. Crucially, during 2008 all members were subject to a quota shift, which suggests that even those whose quotas remained the same could have hypothetically seen changes. In the case of ad hoc increases, however, there is no institutional logic or expectation that all the members are eligible for shifts.

[27] While in the future, it might be good to examine the determinants of these ad hoc increases, my aim is to simply control for their influence.

Estimation model

The estimation model is based on a fixed effects model, which includes fixed effects for both year and country and is specified as:[28]

$$y_{it} = x_{it}\beta + c_i + d_t + u_{it} \qquad t = 1, 2, 3 \dots .T$$

Here, y denotes *quotashift*; x_{it} is the vector of the aforementioned explanatory variables; "t" stands for the time periods; "i" stands for country (i.e. member state); c_i designates the unobserved time invariant country effects; d_t captures the common time effects; and u_{it} stands for "idiosyncratic errors," namely unobserved country effects that vary across time (Woolridge 2002).[29]

The results

Table 3.4 Column (1) displays a baseline model that explores the impact of the control variables on the dependent variable, *quotashift*. Column 1 shows that growth in *reserves*, the *variability* in the trade balance, and *ad hoc increases* significantly and positively relate to *quotashift*. The higher the average growth in the member state's reserves over the three years preceding the increase in its quota, the greater the member's *quotashift*. Similarly, receiving an ad hoc quota increase prior to the member state experiencing a quota adjustment significantly and positively relates to *quotashift*.

Table 3.4 Column (2) demonstrates that the member's volume of bilateral trade with the USA positively and significantly affects *quotashift*. In other words, as the member's volume of bilateral trade with the USA increases, the quota increase the member receives also goes up. Quantitatively, if bilateral trade between the USA and a member country increases by 1 percent, the country's quota shift would increase by 5.2 percentage points. Given the average *quotashift* is 50 percent, this impact of the volume of bilateral trade on *quotashift* is quantitatively and qualitatively important.

Table 3.4 Column (3) shows the logarithm of the volume of US bilateral economic aid to the member does not significantly relate to *quotashift*.[30] Column (4) includes the full model results, which

---

[28] In the fixed effects framework, it is assumed that time invariant unobserved heterogeneity, c_i, is correlated with one or more of x_{it}. The fixed effects estimator controls for this correlation. Hence, scholars prefer the fixed effects model for cross-country analysis (e.g., Woolridge 2002). I confirmed the usage of fixed effects through a Hausman test.

[29] d_t accounts for the US de facto veto power which all members face and have faced since the institution's inception.

[30] When the bilateral trade variable is excluded and only the aid variable is added to the baseline model, this aid variable still does not significantly affect *quotashift*.

Table 3.4 *Effects of political-economic proximity to the United States*
Dependent variable: *quotashift*

Variables	(1) Economic variables	(2) US bilateral trade	(3) US bilateral trade and US bilateral aid	(4) Full model
Average GDP	0.652	0.523	0.038	0.031
growth	(0.552)	(0.578)	(0.235)	(0.237)
Average growth in	0.118*	0.132*	0.088	0.078
reserves	(0.071)	(0.073)	(0.086)	(0.084)
Average growth	−0.282	−0.216	0.203	0.189
in imports	(0.431)	(0.444)	(0.169)	(0.165)
Average growth	0.367	0.289	0.070	0.085
in exports	(0.225)	(0.236)	(0.187)	(0.182)
Variability in the	0.0003***	0.0003	0.0005***	0.0005***
trade balance	(0.0002)	(0.0002)	(0.0002)	(0.0002)
Ad hoc increases	0.429***	0.403***	0.365***	0.378***
	(0.100)	(0.102)	(0.092)	(0.092)
Bilateral trade		0.052**	0.061**	0.062**
with the		(0.024)	(0.025)	(0.025)
USA (ln)				
Economic aid			0.014	0.006
from the			(0.008)	(0.009)
USA (ln)				
Population (ln)				0.310**
				(0.143)
Observations	930	893	707	707
R-squared	0.152	0.152	0.564	0.569
Number of	162	160	157	157
countries				

Notes: Robust standard errors in parentheses.
*** $p<0.01$,
** $p<0.05$,
* $p<0.1$. All estimations presented include country and year fixed effects (see text).

additionally includes the logarithm of the member's population. The member's population significantly and positively impacts *quotashift*, suggesting the larger countries tend to be relatively more at the forefront of negotiations on quota changes.[31] The significance of the trade variable withstands the inclusion of the population variable.

---

[31] The trade and aid variables are included in logarithmic form because the intent is to capture how the level of trade or aid ties with the USA affects *quotashift*. Put differently, of interest is how the level of political-economic proximity to the USA affects *quotashift*.

Table 3.5 *Sub-sample analysis*
Dependent variable: *quotashift*

Variables	(4) Full model	(5) Advanced economies	(6) Non-advanced economies
Average GDP growth	0.031	0.289	0.063
	(0.237)	(1.116)	(0.243)
Average growth in reserves	0.078	0.510	0.020
	(0.084)	(0.553)	(0.057)
Average growth in imports	0.189	−0.388	0.146
	(0.165)	(2.435)	(0.168)
Average growth in exports	0.085	−2.203	0.193
	(0.182)	(1.790)	(0.167)
Variability in the trade	0.0003***	0.01	0.0005***
balance	(0.0002)	(0.006)	(0.0002)
Ad hoc increases	0.378***	0.187	0.466***
	(0.092)	(0.143)	(0.105)
Bilateral trade with the	0.062**	0.178	0.058**
USA (ln)	(0.025)	(0.193)	(0.027)
Economic aid from the	0.006	−0.009	0.010
USA (ln)	(0.009)	(0.039)	(0.009)
Population (ln)	0.310**	−0.452	0.348**
	(0.143)	(0.415)	(0.153)
Observations	707	79	628
R-squared	0.569	0.635	0.583
Number of countries	157	27	130

Notes: See Notes for Table 3.4. The specification in Columns (4)–(6) is the "full model" in Table 3.4, Column (4).

Overall, the specifications reported in Table 3.4 demonstrate that political-economic proximity to the USA, measured as the member's volume of bilateral trade with the USA, enhances the increases a member receives to its quota. This finding provides a significant step toward demonstrating the US effect on quota adjustments.

Robustness and extensions   This section tests the robustness of the full model in Table 3.4 Column (4).

Table 3.5 splits the sample into two sub-samples that distinguish the members' level of economic development based on the institution's own classifications: advanced economies and non-advanced economies,

Likewise, the intention is to capture the effects of the size of population on the dependent variable. Similar results are obtained when the log variables were lagged by one year.

which includes all developing countries.[32] Most institutional discussions on quota changes revolve around changes to the position of "developing countries."

Table 3.5 demonstrates that the fundamental findings of the full model presented above largely hold. The coefficient on the bilateral trade variable is statistically significant for the sub-sample of the non-advanced economies, with a coefficient similar to that of the full sample (Table 3.5, Column (6)). Likely, given the small sample size for the advanced economies, the coefficient for the advanced country sub-sample is not precisely estimated. The non-advanced economies constitute the largest group of countries within the institution, and contemporary as well as past discussions have revolved around the formal representation of these members (see Chapter 5). In this context, the finding that these countries are more likely to see increases to their quota with increasing bilateral trade ties with the USA stands as a significant finding.[33] Further, variability in the trade balance positively affects *quotashift* for the non-advanced sub-sample, which is in line with potential economic need from the institution. The non-advanced economies need to rely relatively more on quotas to access funding from the institution, since loan amounts tend to be calculated as a multiplier of quotas. In this regard, their needs would suggest that the greater the variability in their trade balance, the greater their need for quota increases. In fact, as previous discussions in this chapter noted, commentators have explained the original inclusion of variability in the IMF formula as indicating the need for countries to rely on IMF funds. The member's population also significantly affects its *quotashift* for the non-advanced economies (Table 3.5, Column (6)).

To further test the robustness of the results, Table 3.6 excludes the 2010 quota changes from the calculations. The quota adjustments in 2010 occurred during highly unusual circumstances, namely following the greatest economic downturn since the Great Depression.[34] Here, the question is whether the unusual increase the member states provided to the IMF could be affecting the results. Table 3.6 shows that the results from the previous table generally carry over. Particularly, the volume of bilateral trade with the USA significantly affects *quotashift* for non-advanced

---

[32] Any member which the IMF does not deem advanced is included in the sub-sample of non-advanced economies.

[33] This finding withstood the addition of other control variables, particularly the member's trade relations with the rest of the world included in logarithmic form. It also withstood the addition of the member's GDP as another control variable.

[34] According to NBER, which is the official business cycle dating agency, the 2008 recession ended in June 2009, though different scholars date the Great Recession differently.

Table 3.6 *Pre-2010 quota shifts*
Dependent variable: *quotashift*

Variables	(7) Pre-2010	(8) Advanced/ pre-2010	(9) Non-advanced/ pre-2010
Average GDP growth	0.119	0.010	0.090
	(0.212)	(1.022)	(0.217)
Average growth in reserves	0.088	1.412	0.030
	(0.079)	(0.865)	(0.049)
Average growth in imports	0.022	0.958	0.013
	(0.163)	(2.134)	(0.168)
Average growth in exports	0.011	−3.574*	0.107
	(0.170)	(1.899)	(0.159)
Variability in the trade	0.0006***	0.0056	0.0006***
balance	(0.0001)	(0.0101)	(0.0001)
Ad hoc increases	2.078***		2.100***
	(0.061)		(0.055)
Bilateral trade with the	0.056**	0.368	0.056**
USA (ln)	(0.023)	(0.238)	(0.024)
Economic aid from the	0.001	−0.037	0.007
USA (ln)	(0.008)	(0.046)	(0.008)
Population (ln)	0.058	−1.198	0.090
	(0.139)	(0.924)	(0.152)
Observations	560	53	507
R-squared	0.412	0.655	0.428
Number of countries	149	23	126

Notes: See Notes for Table 3.4. The specification in Columns (7)–(9) is the "full model" in Table 3.4, Column (4).

economies.[35] A difference between Table 3.5 (Column 6) and the pre-2010 years concerns the effects of population. With the exclusion of 2010, population loses its significant impact on *quotashift*. This point is suggestive: non-advanced countries may have benefitted from their population size during the 2010 negotiations only. In turn, focusing on the qualitative differences between 2010 changes and previous ones becomes important, which Chapter 5 will analyze.

To expand upon the core findings and test their robustness, Table 3.7 changes all the variables in the full model to real values. Because the IMF indicates relying on nominal values in the quota formulae, including nominal GDP and reserves, the previous specifications have also used the

---

[35] Again, this finding withstood the addition of another control variable, the member's trade relations with the rest of the world included in logarithmic form.

Table 3.7 *Robustness using real values*
Dependent variable: *quotashift*

Variables	(10) Real	(11) Advanced/real	(12) Non-advanced/ real
Average real GDP growth	−0.678	0.879	−0.751
	(0.457)	(2.780)	(0.477)
Average growth in real	0.074	0.519	0.012
reserves	(0.081)	(0.562)	(0.053)
Average growth in real	0.089	0.347	0.045
imports	(0.156)	(1.985)	(0.163)
Average growth in	0.089	−2.305	0.209
real exports	(0.160)	(1.599)	(0.140)
Variability in the real trade	0.0002***	0.006	0.0002***
balance	(0.00006)	(0.008)	(0.0096)
Ad hoc increases	0.321***	0.201	0.409***
	(0.097)	(0.144)	(0.114)
Real bilateral trade with the	0.068**	0.166	0.063**
USA (ln)	(0.026)	(0.176)	(0.027)
Real economic aid from the	0.006	−0.005	0.009
USA (ln)	(0.009)	(0.035)	(0.009)
Population (ln)	0.213	−0.489	0.233
	(0.144)	(0.386)	(0.153)
Observations	684	78	606
R-squared	0.592	0.618	0.613
Number of countries	156	27	129

Notes: See Notes for Table 3.4. The specification in Columns (10)–(12) is the "full model" in Table 3.4, Column (4).

variables in nominal form (see Table 3.2). Here, nominal values may be misleading because they do not distinguish between growth due to inflation and that due to a genuine increase in economic activity. Table 3.7 demonstrates that real bilateral trade with the USA significantly affects *quotashift* again for the full sample and the sub-sample of non-advanced economies (Table 3.7 Columns (10), (12)). Here, population is insignificant in the non-advanced country sub-sample, but variability in the trade balance and ad hoc increases are significant.

Finally, Table 3.8 includes the estimation results when a number of other variables that can potentially affect *quotashift* are included. Column (13) in Table 3.8 incorporates a dummy variable that records whether or not the member belongs to a club of lenders to the IMF (*nab* and *gab*). In addition to quotas, member states can provide funds to the IMF through credit lines, which function effectively as loans when the

Table 3.8 *Additional variables*
Dependent variable: *quotashift*

Variables	(13) NAB, GAB	(14) UN voting	(15) UNSC	(16) DAC	(17) Polity2
Average GDP growth	0.026	0.098	−0.003	0.134	0.030
	(0.238)	(0.237)	(0.235)	(0.248)	(0.247)
Average growth in reserves	0.079	0.093	0.099	-0.007	0.088
	(0.084)	(0.084)	(0.085)	(0.056)	(0.086)
Average growth in imports	0.190	0.142	0.213	0.148	0.108
	(0.166)	(0.165)	(0.167)	(0.178)	(0.172)
Average growth in exports	0.084	0.046	0.093	0.140	0.097
	(0.182)	(0.182)	(0.182)	(0.161)	(0.189)
Variability in the trade balance	0.0006***	0.0005***	0.0004***	0.0006***	0.0005***
	(0.0002)	(0.0002)	(0.00008)	(0.0002)	(0.0002)
Ad hoc increases	0.381***	0.312***	0.368***	0.522***	0.362***
	(0.102)	(0.075)	(0.098)	(0.131)	(0.098)
Bilateral trade with the USA (ln)	0.062**	0.076***	0.058**	0.051**	0.063**
	(0.025)	(0.025)	(0.025)	(0.026)	(0.026)
Economic aid from the USA (ln)	0.006	0.004	0.002	0.012	0.006
	(0.009)	(0.008)	(0.008)	(0.012)	(0.009)
Population (ln)	0.307**	0.294**	0.339**	0.340*	0.324**
	(0.142)	(0.147)	(0.144)	(0.177)	(0.156)
NAB	−0.011				
	(0.068)				
GAB	0.120				
	(0.117)				
Aid from DAC (ln)				−0.010	
				(0.025)	
Voting similarity at the UNGA		0.000			
		(0.230)			
Membership on UNSC			0.010		
			(0.079)		
Polity2					−0.002
					(0.005)
Observations	707	695	686	611	661
R-squared	0.570	0.585	0.565	0.580	0.567
Number of countries	157	154	151	132	139

Source: See Notes for Table 3.4. The specification in Columns (13)–(17) is the "full model" in Table 3.4, Column (4). See Appendix 3.A for variable descriptions.

IMF draws from them. Both scholars and current affairs resources have paid particular attention to these credit lines during the 2008 financial crisis, as the IMF bolstered its arrangements (Kaya 2012; Truman 2013; Woods 2011).

The General and New Arrangements to Borrow provide two separate mechanisms through which the IMF can borrow from its members. The General Arrangements to Borrow (GAB) was established in 1964 with funds from the ten main industrial countries. GAB was extended and enhanced in 1983 and has been renewed regularly since then. Since 1998, with the establishment of New Arrangements to Borrow (NAB), NAB has become the main borrowing resource for the IMF.[36] Its members extended the NAB in 2009 to include emerging economies, such as Brazil, China, India, and Russia as new members.

Anecdotal evidence suggests lending to the IMF might confer advantages during quota shifts, but this issue has not been subjected to systematic analysis. As an example, Saudi Arabia, which joined the Fund in 1957 with an "exceptionally small quota," enhanced its position (through increases to its quota) in the Fund after the 1970s oil shock by becoming a major lender to the institution especially through the Oil Facilities (Boughton 2001, p. 890). Interestingly, the G10 did not invite Saudi Arabia to join the GAB because some G10 states were "reluctant to expand their club" (Boughton 2001, p. 898). In sum, it seems plausible that the member states who lend to the institution position themselves well in the political bargaining for the quotas. Yet, Table 3.8 Column (13) does not show a significant effect for NAB and GAB membership on the dependent variable, *quotashift*. Future studies could more fully explore why this is the case, though plausibly other variables in the equation pick up the potential effects of NAB and GAB. More importantly, the bilateral trade volume with the USA remains significant with the inclusion of "nab" and "gab."[37]

Table 3.8 also examines the impact of a number of other political variables. One of these is voting similarity with the USA in the UN General Assembly (Column (14)).[38] As previous discussions emphasized, scholars have relied on voting similarity with the USA in certain contexts to approximate political proximity to the USA. This kind of proximity, however, does not appear to have a significant effect on *quotashift*. Column (15) incorporates another UN-related variable to the full

---

[36] In addition to GAB and NAB, the IMF has relied on credit lines from member states in increasing access limits for its lending operations, such as the Oil Facilities in the 1970s and the Supplementary Financing Facility (1979–1984).

[37] Using the loan amounts the states made available to the IMF, as opposed to NAB and GAB membership, does not produce different results.

[38] I used Strezhnev and Voeten's (2013) dataset and followed their categorization of the incidence of voting similarity with the USA, where votes are divided into yes, no, or abstain. Agreement with the USA is coded as 1, disagreement with the USA is coded as 0, and abstaining votes are coded as 0.5. I tried the binary categorization for the voting similarity variable (1 or 0), but there was no difference.

model – temporary membership on the UN Security Council (UNSC). Kuziemko and Werker (2006) show that US aid to a temporary member on the UNSC increases, and Dreher et al. (2009a) show a positive relationship between temporary membership on the UNSC and being part of an IMF program (i.e. receiving financial assistance from the IMF).[39] Temporary membership on the UNSC, however, does not significantly relate to *quotashift*. Further, Column (16) examines the impact of foreign aid the members of the OECD's Development Assistance Committee (DAC) provide to the IMF member as an explanatory variable. Again, this variable was not significantly related to *quotashift*. Finally, the member's level of democracy, based on Polity IV categorizations, did not affect *quotashift* (Column (17)).[40] In all of these cases, the volume of bilateral trade with the USA significantly and positively affects the member's shift in quota.[41]

Conclusions

This chapter enriches the understanding of the relationship between the inter-state distribution of economic power and the distribution of formal political power within multilateral economic institutions in a number of ways. First, it discusses the institutional means and methods for how the formal asymmetries initially emerged in the IMF and the World Bank and how they have evolved over time.

Those discussions affirm the adjusted power approach developed in the previous chapter (Chapter 2). The way in which the US designers conceptualized the design of the Bank and the IMF was closely related to the functions and purposes they foresaw for the institution. Specifically, the designers closely linked the formal asymmetries within the two institutions to the nature of the financing of the two institutions. The manner in which member states would fund the two institutions was in turn a by-product of the institutions' intended primary functions. Moreover, the US designers did not fuss over the differences across the two institutions. The designers were not unreflective: they did not impose the IMF's structure on the Bank without any contemplation, as they emphasized the differences in function across the two

[39] The UNSC membership dataset comes from Dreher et al. (2009b).
[40] Here, this finding again withstood the addition of one other control variable, the member's trade relations with the rest of the world included in logarithmic form.
[41] US foreign claims in the member country (i.e. US banking exposure in the country) based on the Bank for International Settlements' (BIS) consolidated international bank claims (quarterly data were averaged into yearly data) did not relate significantly to *quotashift*. Similarly, US direct investment in the country based on the US Bureau of Economic Analysis data did not significantly affect *quotashift*.

institutions. Neither were they meticulously rational in design, how-ever. Had they functioned as textbook rational designers, they would have likely dissected each collective action problem (distributional issues versus uncertainty versus enforcement problems) and matched it to a design feature, which would have in all likelihood resulted in the Bank having a different structure of decision-making than the IMF (Chapter 2). Yet, their financial commitment versus risk calculus in the Bank and the IMF was done in more of a "back of the envelope" manner than scrupulous engineering of institutional design. Additionally, as evidenced by the inclusion of basic votes in the two international financial institutions, while the US designers harbored some normative concerns about sovereign equality and perhaps the fairness of representation in the institution, these normative concerns were marginal to their thinking.

Second, the chapter details how IMF quotas, which constitute the basis for members' voting power within that institution, are adjusted based on both technical calculations and political negotiation among members. The technical calculations rest on formulae, which have been at least partially politically determined throughout the IMF's history (see also Chapter 5). While the formulae embody economic logic, such technical logic cannot be understood in a sterile manner that excludes politics.

Third, following on from these points, this chapter provides a quantitative analysis of IMF quota changes in 1965–2010 based on an original dataset. This analysis contributes to the understanding of the determinants of IMF quota changes. It also demonstrates that political-economic proximity to the USA positively and significantly impacts a member's changes in quota. Given that IMF quota adjustments do not fully provide the conditions that are conducive to informal influence – specifically, relatively low transparency and high delegation by the states – this finding is, reasonably, more unanticipated than US meddling with loan decisions. I do not suggest that this finding should be wholly surprising and unexpected, but rather that even when the conditions are relatively less opportune for it, the USA appears to exercise informal influence.

Future research

The chapter leaves some issues under-explored. A quantitative analysis of the kind undertaken here for the IMF could be extended to shifts in shareholding at the World Bank. The discussions on the IMF quota shifts are relevant to changes in Bank shareholding. The Bank has followed

IMF quota adjustments in numerous instances, including in 1965, 1970, 1976, and 1984. The institutional jargon for this convention is "parallel share adjustments" (e.g., World Bank 1995). Moreover, many times in determining whether a member is "under-represented" in the institution, the Bank has relied on IMF quota calculations (e.g., World Bank 1998). In short, the examination of shifts in IMF quotas also roughly illuminates about shifts in shareholding within the World Bank. Yet, because the Bank's convention of paralleling the IMF quota changes has not been consistent and one-to-one, it would be worthwhile to extend the kind of quantitative analysis this chapter provides to the World Bank. Unfortunately, while I have been in the process of collecting the data for some time, this process requires much more time for worthwhile meaningful analysis. Still, the book delves further into the issue of path dependence between the IMF and the World Bank in later chapters (Chapter 6).

Also, this chapter touched upon the role of the IMF staff in guiding quota changes, but there is greater room for exposition on that subject. Questions remain, for instance, regarding the extent to which the staff can steer the direction of quota reviews. Given the quota reviews are centered on member states and formally controlled by them, the staff's independent maneuvering is expected to be minor. Nonetheless, it is worth analyzing this question with greater detail, a point to which the book returns in Chapter 5.

Another issue that deserves further analysis concerns the motivations for US influence over IMF quota adjustments. Two plausible motivations are: the pursuit of domestic interest group preferences and currying favor with IMF members. Interest group pressure over quota shifts is unlikely in reality. Quota changes remain highly member state-centered, and they are an issue area for which interest groups tend not to be activated (e.g., Lavelle 2011). It is unclear why interest groups would choose the issue of quotas to pressure US action because quota changes do not constitute an easy target for interest groups vested in another country's economy. Yet, the US actors could, nonetheless, be looking out for the interests of specific domestic groups. Plausibly, US influences quota adjustments because US actors are doling out favors. And, through such favoring the USA utilizes multilateral opportunities in a self-beneficial manner. Given the importance of quotas for ranking and prestige in the institution, it is apparent why the recipients would welcome relatively higher quota increases.

Future analyses can also explore *quotashift* as an independent variable, exploring whether others return the US favor provision in different institutional contexts. Finally, future studies can explore whether there is US exceptionalism, or whether other dominant shareholders also influence quota shifts. Although not reported for space reasons, I explored the impact of the member's bilateral trade with G4 countries (UK, France, Germany, and Japan) and aid from G4 countries on quota adjustments, and found such G4 influence insignificant on *quotashift* (with or without the inclusion of US trade, which retained its significance in those specifications). Nonetheless, a thorough examination of other great power influence, including the range of proximity variables this study considers, over quota adjustments would be interesting.

A question that this chapter leaves unaddressed is the story of how the linkage between the distribution of economic power and formal political power unfolded in the third multilateral economic institution of the post-war era, the International Trade Organization (ITO). The next chapter turns to this question.

Appendix 3.A *Summary statistics and variable descriptions*

Variable	Observations	Mean	Standard deviation	Min	Max	Source
Quotashift	756	0.5103	0.4576	−0.0384	3.4990	Author's own dataset compiled from IMF documentation
Bilateral trade volume with the USA, logarithm (n)	756	20.0301	2.5559	12.93284	27.12014	UN Comtrade
Average growth in GDP (n)	756	0.1036941	0.0859708	−0.348896	0.5810254	WDI
Average growth in imports (n)	756	0.1121196	0.1088324	0.1088324	0.6301066	WDI
Average growth in exports (n)	756	0.1022514	0.1141585	−0.4177418	0.6544806	WDI
Average growth in reserves (n)	710	0.1162925	0.2509309	−0.9440106	1.811604	IMF
Variability in trade balance (n)	751	4136.02	46670.18	0.85	1260980	Calculated based as the standard deviation of the previous 10-year trade balance, which was obtained from WDI
Bilateral economic aid from the USA, logarithm (n)	756	16.15122	2.723717	3.713572	22.21428	US Overseas Loans and Grants (Greenbook)

Appendix 3.A *(cont.)*

Variable	Observations	Mean	Standard deviation	Min	Max	Source
Population, logarithm	756	15.82715	1.735768	9.826822	21.01422	WDI
Bilateral trade volume with the USA (r)	756	16.48368	2.452094	3.609331	22.11003	UN Comtrade
Average growth in GDP (r)	734	0.0429101	0.0401494	−0.099418	0.3736305	WDI
Average growth in imports (r)	734	0.0517048	0.0919366	−0.4209073	0.6301066	Calculated using the deflator for the country for the year, obtained as nominal gdp/real gdp
Average growth in exports (r)	756	0.1022514	0.1141585	−0.4177418	0.6544806	Calculated using the deflator for the country for the year, obtained as nominal gdp/real gdp
Average growth in reserves (r)	693	0.054162	0.2415861	−0.9871421	1.733232	Calculated using the deflator for the country for the year, obtained as nominal gdp/real gdp
Bilateral economic aid from the USA, logarithm (r)	756	16.48368	2.719566	3.609331	22.11003	Calculated using the deflator for the country for the year, obtained as nominal gdp/real gdp

Variable	Obs	Mean	St. dev.	Min	Max	Source
Variability in trade balance (r)(10-year st.dev)	723	5725.529	86248.22	5.745831	2313790	Calculated using the deflator for the country for the year, obtained as nominal gdp/ real gdp
Ad hoc increases	756	0.0648148	0.2463618	0	1	Author's own database
NAB	756	0.0515873	0.2213388	0	1	Author's own database
GAB	756	0.0039683	0.0629106	0	1	Author's own database
Similarity of voting with the USA in UNGA	742	0.3638119	0.1600333	0	0.9	"agree3un" variable from Strezhnev and Voeten (2013)
Temporary membership on the UNSC	735	0.0639456	0.2448226	0	1	Dreher et al. (2009b)
Aid from Development Assistance Committee (DAC) donors, logarithm	660	18.57569	1.540683	13.08154	22.47623	OECD's DAC database
Polity2	701	1.114123	7.11747	−10	10	"polity2" variable from the The Polity IV project, www.systemicpeace.org/polity/polity4.htm
Advanced economies	756	0.1044974	0.3061072	0	1	IMF
Non-advanced economies	756	0.4312169	0.499053	0	1	IMF

4   The origins of states' voting equality
     in the post-war multilateral trading system

The multilateral trading institution that governs contemporary trade relations among states, the World Trade Organization, emerged in 1995 out of
the 1947 General Agreement on Tariffs and Trade – an evolution that
scholarly literatures have extensively analyzed. The GATT itself was signed
as a "temporary agreement" during and as a part of the negotiations on the
International Trade Organization (ITO) (Jackson 2000). The ITO was
planned as the third institution, alongside the IMF and the World Bank,
of the post-war multilateral economic system. Although fifty-four states
signed the ITO Charter in Havana in March 1948, the US Congress never
ratified the Charter, with the Truman Administration eventually abandoning
the quest for its approval in 1950. The loss of its primary architect spelled the
demise of the ITO. Because the ITO is a failed organization, the scholarly
literature has paid much less attention to it, and when it has done so, it has
been with the intention of explaining that very failure (Bidwell and Diebold
1949; Diebold 1952; Goldstein 1993).

   The importance of understanding why history relegated the ITO to its
dustbin withstanding, there is much to be gained from analyzing the ITO
itself. After all, the GATT inadvertently emerged as the progenitor of the
current multilateral trading institution, and the ITO, had history worked
differently, would have been the central multilateral trade organization.
In this respect, the provisions of the ITO capture the intentions of the
US designers of the institution, the compromises they struck, and the
negotiations they underwent with key domestic audiences, such as the US
Congress.

   One of the most crucial, but yet under-analyzed, dimensions of the
ITO concerns the nature of member state representation in the institution, particularly members' voting power.[1] Interestingly, the ITO would

---

[1] McIntyre (1954) devotes some space to the discussion of states' voting rights at the ITO
   and provides useful insights for this study, but the core of her largely descriptive article is
   not the ITO. The following also mention voting at the ITO, but voting issues are not their
   central focus: Wilkinson and Scott (2008); Goldstein and Gowa (2002); and Irwin et al.
   (2008).

have endorsed voting equality (one-member-one-vote), while the IMF and the World Bank had already endorsed weighted voting (Chapter 3).[2]

Why did the prominence of US economic power at the time translate into different institutional designs (regarding member state representation) across the three inter-related multilateral economic institutions?[3] While voting equality does not necessarily mean the US designers thought every member of the institution would be on equal footing, the question of why the US designers enshrined voting equality in the ITO Charter remains an important question to answer not only for the sake of understanding the relationship between states' economic power and their formal political power in multilateral economic institutions, but also toward explaining the design of multilateral institutions, as states' formal political power constitutes a critical dimension of institutional design (see Chapter 1; Koremenos et al. 2001a, 2001b).

Based on extensive analysis of archival material on inter-state negotiations on the ITO, internal Department of State documentation, as well as Congressional testimonies in addition to scholarly material, the chapter finds that the US designers of the multilateral trading regime preferred voting equality because they considered it to suit the intended objectives and functions of the ITO better than weighted voting, which they, along with other critical actors, found appropriate for the IMF and the World Bank. However, when faced with negotiations that undermined their goal to provide a link between the trade institution and the IMF on the issue of balance of payments, the designers advanced a proposal for weighted voting. This proposal suggested the mirroring of the IMF weighted voting within the ITO on balance of payments discussions. In the end, when the ultimate draft of the ITO established the desired ITO-IMF linkage, the US drafters reverted back to their original equal voting proposal. In this respect, as their ability to pursue US preferences on balance of payments (BOP) oscillated, the designers adapted their proposal on voting.

The chapter supports the adjusted power approach advanced in Chapter 2, while also offering implications for additional theoretical frameworks. It shows that the manifestation of economic power asymmetries within the multilateral regime was mediated by the functions and purposes the designers intended for the institution. The ITO was

---

[2] Voting in in the IMF and the World Bank consists of two components – basic votes, which are distributed to member states equally, and quota (IMF) or subscription (World Bank) votes, which are based on the member's shares in the organization. The latter component is more important in determining a member's total voting power (Chapter 3). The notion of voting equality here denotes merely one-member-one-vote and does not suggest anything about fairness or other normative concerns.

[3] On the US economic preeminence at the end of the war, see Ikenberry (2000); Kennedy (1989); Mearsheimer (2001).

designed primarily as a platform for inter-state negotiation on trade issues, which motivated the designers' inclination toward voting equality. At the same time, the designers thought the differences in the funding of the ITO versus the IMF and the World Bank removed any institutional rationale for the former embodying asymmetric voting. This said, taking funding differences across the three institutions as *the* explanation for voting equality is inadequate because, as just mentioned, the US delegates at the ITO negotiations tabled a proposal for weighted voting without any change in the nature of the funding of the institution. In this respect, how the funding factor intersected with the US designers' conceptualization of the planned functions and purposes of the ITO becomes critical to analyze (Chapter 2). Methodologically, the chapter demonstrates the importance of tracing negotiators' thinking and intentions through the available paper trail and not attempting to define intentions from observed outcomes (Elster, 2000; Wendt, 2001).

In making its core arguments, the chapter rules out a number of competing explanations. It tests rational design theory (RDT)'s predictions relevant to the distribution of voting power in multilateral institutions, finding limited support for them. For instance, unlike what RDT predicts, the number of actors does not seem to have been a significant factor on the decision for voting equality. Again contrary to RDT, the US designers do not appear to have disaggregated distinct collective action problems, but rather have approached institutional design with broader brushes. More importantly, the paper shows that the ITO's drafters pursued both design that intends to solve collection action problems, let me call this "macro-purpose," and design that serves the narrow interests of their state, which is "micro-purpose." This point is substantial because if design reflects micro-purpose, then multilateral institutions could be understood as instruments of specific states to advance exclusive goals. If design instead reflects macro-purpose, then institutions can be understood to further a collective good, as RDT contends. The findings suggest that a framework that explores both the possibilities for micro- and macro-purposes offers more promise to explain outcomes.

From another institutionalist perspective, the voting equality at the ITO could be interpreted as the US actors showing "restraint" in creating the post-war multilateral order, binding the USA to rules-based frameworks embodied in the institutions (Goldstein and Gowa 2002; Ikenberry 2000). While evidence suggests that other states preferred voting equality, they were also not against some weighted voting. More importantly, the US designers' preferences on voting in the ITO came prior to other states expressing their preferences on the matter.

The chapter also does not find enough support for power-based arguments. For instance, potential conjectured differences in informal power across the three multilateral economic institutions do not explain well the differences in voting across them. The US actors did not doubt they would be able to informally dominate the IMF and the World Bank, given the US credit would bankroll these institutions in their early years (Gold 1981). Yet, the US designers opted for weighted voting in these institutions, placing the USA at the top of a formal hierarchy in voting. There is also no evidence for the possibility that US designers thought they would have more informal power in the trade institution compared to the two international financial institutions. In fact, the US designers were unsure of their informal influence in the ITO. In any case, the US designers faced a number of options for enshrining equal voting in the ITO – they did not have to make voting completely equal among members. Instead they could have chosen to combine weighted votes with some equal votes, as in the World Bank and the IMF (see Chapter 3).

Another power-based explanation – the onset of the Cold War – also does not offer much explanation. When the GATT was created in 1947, the Cold War was beginning, whereas, the Bretton Woods institutions were created toward the end of the world war in 1944. In this context, one might argue that the American negotiators' pursuit of voting equality in the ITO intended to sweeten the deal for other states in attracting them to the US sphere of influence at the onset of the Cold War. A dominantly realist perspective on the ITO would, thus, point the analysis to changing inter-state power dynamics affecting voting design in the ITO. However, for a number of reasons, the evidence does not support the supposed correlation between intensifying tensions between the USA and the Soviet Union and voting equality at the ITO.

Finally, the chapter shows the US negotiators' attitude to be not tightly linked to the demands of key domestic audiences. Specifically, while members of the US Congress and critical business groups expressed discomfort with voting equality, the US negotiators pursued it nonetheless. This point does not undermine two-level games (Putnam 1988), but it does raise a question about whether a linkage between domestic and international levels can always be assumed.

The rest of the chapter is organized as follows. The next section provides an overview of the inter-state negotiations during the ITO, followed by a section that is devoted to explaining the US attitude throughout those inter-state negotiations. The concluding section stresses the significance of the chapter for analyzing the relationship between the distribution of economic power and the distribution of formal political power within multilateral economic institutions.

Inter-state negotiations on states' voting equality

As noted at the onset, the ITO Charter was signed in Havana, Cuba, in March 1948, following two years of negotiations among more than fifty states.[4] While the origins of the ITO date back to discussions between the US officials and their British counterparts in the early 1940s, the skeleton of the institution emerged with the US Proposals for the Expansion of World Trade and Employment at the end of 1945 (herein, 'the Proposals'; US Department of State 1945). The Proposals then evolved into the 'Suggested Charter for an International Trade Organization' (US Dept. of State, 1946a). This Suggested Charter formed the basis of inter-state negotiations on the ITO starting in London in 1946 and ending in Havana in 1948. In Havana, the signatories for the USA were two State Department officials – William Clayton, the Under Secretary for Economic Affairs, and Clair Wilcox, who headed the US delegation at the Charter negotiations. An inter-Departmental/agency committee, known as the Executive Committee on Economic Foreign Policy (ECEFP) formulated the Charter, with the State officials playing a central role.

The US designers hoped the trade institution would engender economic cooperation and freer trade among states, which would in turn facilitate peace (Truman 1949). Also, given that the US negotiators feared the significant upsurge of US exports during World War II was an aberration, they envisioned the ITO would continue to facilitate the openness of foreign markets to US exports (Wilcox 1949a).

States' voting power and representation in the ITO were subject to debate in various key inter-state negotiations. The first of these was in November 1946 in London, which was followed by a meeting in Lake Success, New York, in January–February 1947, and then a meeting in Geneva in May–June 1947. It was following these meetings that twenty-three states signed the GATT in October 1947.[5] The GATT was signed as a component of the ITO, specifically as Chapter IV of the ITO Charter (Jackson 2000).[6] As one expert notes, "[m]uch of the GATT was taken verbatim from the draft of the ITO Charter as it stood at the end of the Geneva Conference deliberations on ITO" (Jackson 2000, p. 22). Moreover, the "government officials who drafted the GATT were, with few exceptions, the very same men who were drafting the text of the ITO Charter" (Hudec 1998, p. 21). The question of member state representation and voting power in the ITO was, however, not resolved in Geneva and was subjected to further discussion at the last set of meetings in Havana (see, e.g., Bronz 1949; Irwin et al. 2008; Wilcox 1949a).

---

[4] More than half of these countries were developing countries.
[5] For a list of original GATT signatories, see Irwin et al. (2008, p. 106).
[6] The GATT evolved into the World Trade Organization (WTO) in 1995.

Three key developments transpired during these various negotiations on member state representation and voting at the ITO. First, at the first meeting in London, the USA and the UK tabled different plans for states' voting rights and representation in the new trading institution. The US drafters proposed voting equality (one-member-one-vote) at the ITO in the "Suggested Charter for an International Trade Organization," which formed the basis of their position in London (US Department of State 1946a). Internal documents preceding inter-state discussions show that the US officials preferred voting equality in the Conference with special majorities on issues of particular concern to the USA (e.g., ECEFP D-72/45 1945; ECEFP D-63/44 1945). In the Suggested Charter, the US officials proposed one-member-one-vote both at the ITO's would-be fifteen-member Executive Board (EB) and the Conference, where all members would be represented (Articles 52, 53). The Suggested Charter also stated that the Conference would choose the members of the EB, though it did not specify how this selection would occur (Article 55.2). Despite this vagueness, the US drafters did not include a clause for permanent membership on the EB. The decisions at both the Conference and the EB, the Suggested Charter stated, would be taken by a majority of the votes, except in special circumstances. One of those special circumstances that required a special majority (two-thirds) was the Conference's waiving of members' obligations under the Charter (Article 55).

The UK tabled a contrasting plan for voting in London. According to the UK plan, both the Conference and the EB would have weighted voting (E/PC/T/C.V/14 1946). Votes, the UK delegation explained, could be weighted by the following factors: external trade, national income, and population (E/PC/T/C.6/W.3 1947). The selection of countries to the Board, under this proposal, would also be based on weighted voting. The UK proposal, generally, underlined the importance of reflecting countries' asymmetric economic importance in the institution. This differential importance, the proposal noted, could be achieved by giving "a number of the more important trading countries ... permanent seats on the proposed Executive Board of the Organization" (E/PC/T/C.V/14 1946).

The second primary development on the voting issue surfaced during the New York meetings in Spring 1947, where the US delegates presented a plan for limited weighted voting. The US drafters proposed weighted voting in the ITO on two different issues: (a) where the ITO and the IMF had a "common interest," namely discussions on countries' balance of payments; and (b) when the ITO Conference, composed of all member states, selected the members to the ITO's EB. Weighted voting in the ITO on these two issues would mirror the weighted voting in the IMF (E/PC/T/C.6/W.6/Add.1 1947; E/PC/T/C.6/62 1947). Under this scenario, the USA, the

UK, the USSR, China, France, and India would, in that order, have the highest number of votes and therefore would be Board members. Other states would have to build coalitions to be elected to the Board. Other issues, the US plan went, would be governed by one-member-one-vote.

The third major development regarding voting happened during the negotiations in Havana, when the US negotiators abandoned their afore-mentioned plan for weighted voting in December 1947 (Porter 1947). The Havana negotiations resulted in the ITO consisting of, as the US drafters had all along planned, a Conference and an EB. The Conference would guide the agenda of the Organization and steer its work, including the selection of the Board and the delegation of certain tasks to it. In this regard, the Conference held the "final authority." The Board would consist of eighteen member states, eight of which would be countries of chief economic importance, and the Conference would select the rest of the Board with due attention to regional representation. The ITO Charter indicated the members would consider "shares in international trade" in assessing countries' economic importance (E/CONF.2/7 1948).

What explains the evolution and the outcome of states' negotiations on members' voting rights at the ITO? Specifically, why did the US designers prefer voting equality initially, but later table a proposal for weighted voting, only to revert back to voting equality eventually?

Explanations

This section rules out some plausible explanations before demonstrating that the US designers' original preference for voting equality at the ITO related to the purposes and functions they intended for this institution.

Informal power

An easily accessible and plausible answer as to why the ITO enshrined voting equality goes along the following lines: "because the US designers knew the USA would always dominate informally, they did not worry about formal voting equality." This answer is tempting partially because scholarly work on the WTO has shown the informal dominance of the economic heavyweights, such as the USA and the EU (see particularly Steinberg 2002). However, in evaluating whether this answer holds one has to try to ascertain the original US designers' thinking and not what is known in hindsight.

The US negotiators did count on some level of informal power in the institution, but it is difficult to suggest that this foreseen informal power explains why the ITO would have had voting equality. As one US negotiator put it:

I think it is fair to anticipate on the basis of experience in other international organizations, that even if the formula is one country or one member, one vote, there is no such thing as equality among votes; and the announcement that the United States, for example, intends to vote a certain way on a motion is far more important than the announcement that some small country intends to vote that way. (US Senate 1947, p. 548)

Here the US negotiator makes the reasonable point that voting equality does not mean equality of states in practice. Yet, not much more can be read into this quote for a number of reasons. First, the quote comes from State Department assurances to Congress that voting equality in the institution would not be detrimental to the pursuit of the USA's interests. The reasons behind the ITO's voting equality remains unclear just based on this point. Second, it is not clear that the US negotiators were confident of the high level of US informal power well into the post-war era, assuming reasonably that they saw informal power as being underwritten by relative economic importance. For instance, William Clayton reasoned the USA would face decreasing relative economic importance as the post-war era matured: "While perhaps we have the large proportion of international trade today, that may not continue, of course. As other countries get into production, our percentage will, of course, go down" (US Senate 1947, p. 37). Without the wisdom hindsight affords, the US designers were modest about how much informal power the USA would exactly have because they did not count on the USA dominating world trade indefinitely. Third, negotiators' confidence in informal power cannot explain the choice of institutional design, since that confidence would be consonant both with an institution that included weighted voting (as in the IMF and the World Bank) and one that did not (as in the ITO). Originally only US dollars were used in IMF loans, and as was expected, US credit and the backing of the US financial markets bankrolled the IFIs in their initial years (Gold 1981). Given the US dominance in the post-war financial system (let alone other factors, such as these institutions' location), the US negotiators would have been assured of US informal influence in the two multilateral financial institutions. Hence the reasons for why confidence in the USA's informal power was coupled with different designs on formal voting across the multilateral economic institutions needs to be explained with factors other than informal power itself.

Predictions of rational design theory

The "rational design" theory (RDT) of institutions, which argues that states create institutions to handle collective action problems, also offers potential answers to the core question (see e.g. Abbott and Snidal 2000;

Koremenos 2005; Koremenos et al. 2001a, 2001b; Rosendorff and Milner 2001; Thompson 2010). Koremenos et al. (2001a, p. 791) draw the following conjectures about control, which includes member states' voting rights: a) *"Individual control decreases as the number [of actors] increases"*; b) *"Asymmetry of control increases with asymmetry among contributors [members of the institution]"*; c) *"Individual control (to block undesirable outcomes) increases with uncertainty about the state of the world"* [emphasis added].[7]

Conjecture a concerns the number of actors, and there is no evidence to suggest that the number of actors affected the US negotiators' original tendency for voting equality, or their subsequent proposal for limited weighted voting. It is true that the number of signatories to the ITO (54) exceeded the number of signatories to the Bretton Woods agreements (44). Yet, none of the writings of US designers of the ITO, nor any of their Congressional testimonies or inter-state negotiations on the ITO provide any suggestion that the number of actors was a concern that motivated voting equality. And the GATT, which also enshrined voting equality, had fewer signatories than the ITO Charter (23), again calling into question voting equality significantly relating to the number of actors.

In any case, given it is unlikely that there is an automatic relationship between number of actors and the design on voting, other states' demands on the US negotiators regarding voting rights requires analysis. Presumably, as the number of actors increase, each of them demands a bit of control, which explains the putatively inverse relationship between these two factors. As already indicated the USA's main partner, the UK, preferred weighted voting, but what about the role of other states? This question is also pertinent in assessing whether the USA was signaling "restraint" and meeting others' demands in choosing voting equality.

Although some other states expressed a preference for voting equality, this point does not explain well the US behavior on voting. Upon the UK's tabling of its proposal for weighted voting in London, other states raised objections to it. The Benelux countries emphasized "it is desirable to find a solution which will give satisfaction to all countries represented, for the success of the ITO depends largely on the extent to which various member states will feel that their opinions have been taken into consideration and their interests safeguarded" (E/PC/T/C.V/21 1946). Thus, the delegation for the trio backed one-member-one-vote in the

---

[7] The architects of RDT mention not being able to offer explanations on "control" in institutions, which includes voting power: "The findings on control . . . are sparse, so we do not claim too much for them" (Koremenos et al. 2001b, p. 1060).

Conference. Similarly, the Chinese delegation noted: "The general application of weighted voting to all provisions of the Charter would ... not only be unfair to Members in the early stages of industrialization but would also be unrealistic" (E/PC/T/W/221 1947). Some of those against weighted voting argued the "successful functioning of the Conference would depend in large measure upon a feeling of equality" (E/PC/T/33 1946). Others reasoned that the contribution of weighted voting to inter-state negotiations on the reduction of trade barriers remained unclear.

Still, there is thin evidence to suggest these objections formed the basis of the US tendency for voting equality. Particularly, other states' protests of weighted voting followed the UK's proposal for extensive weighted voting during the first meeting in London, and the USA had already expressed a preference for voting equality *prior* to that meeting. Further, following the timeline above, the US negotiators proposed weighted voting *after* having heard objections to the UK proposal. The chain of events suggests that other (non-British) states' opinion did not affect US behavior significantly. Moreover, other states' objections did not categorically rule out weighted voting. The aforementioned representative quotations from the Benelux and Chinese representatives objected to the wholesale application of weighted voting throughout the institution (in the spirit of what the UK had proposed). But, as the London draft on the negotiations remarked, "several [who supported voting equality] expressed willingness to consider alternatives" (E/PC/T/33 1946).[8] The US delegates could have, thus, plausibly pushed for a combination of basic votes (equal votes) and some weighted voting, had they considered weighted voting important for the institution. Overall, while other states' objections against weighted voting could have *reinforced* the US designers' tendency for voting equality, they do not explain well the origins of that inclination.[9]

Regarding *conjecture b*, the rational design theory argues: "an actor's control over an institution relates to that actor's importance to that institution" (Koremenos et al. 2001a, p. 792). While this point is compelling, the notion of "importance to that institution" remains unclear. I discussed why this indeterminacy is problematic in Chapter 2. An example the authors provide to asymmetric importance is asymmetric financial contributions, but this is only one among many different kinds of uneven input actors could make to an institution (Duffield 2003; see Chapter 2). It is conceivable that asymmetric contribution in this case

---

[8] London Draft, Section E2.
[9] In any case, showing others also wanted voting equality would not suffice to support *conjecture a*.

carried a different meaning, such as the USA's importance to world trade. This point, however, does not contribute much to understanding why the ITO would have enshrined voting equality. More importantly, these two factors – financial contributions and the USA's importance to world trade and to the institution – could plausibly affect voting equality in different directions. As I discuss shortly, the financing of the institution did play a role in the US designers' thinking, but it cannot, on its own, explain their inclination for voting equality, given without a change in the institution's financing, the designers presented a proposal for weighted voting.

Conjecture c above suggests that as the uncertainty in the world increases, a dominant player like the USA should want to increase its individual control to be able to fend off undesired outcomes. There is a rich literature on uncertainty and its interpretation (e.g., see discussions in Koremenos 2005; Thompson 2010). In the case of the post-war world, there is perhaps no doubt that the world was fraught with uncertainty of different kinds – how economic reconstruction would have occurred, whether stability in monetary and trade relations could have been obtained, and whether the Soviets would join the new international trade organization were among the pressing issues. But, such uncertainties do not appear to have encouraged the US push for veto power, nor weighted voting (namely, increased individual control).

Nonetheless, one might argue the safeguards within the ITO (would have) permitted "individual control." One such safeguard was the escape clause that would provide the USA with the ability to suspend commitments on liberalization. The escape clause could hypothetically mean that had voting equality produced undesirable outcomes from the US perspective, the USA had an option to protect itself, thereby lessening the potentially adverse consequences of voting equality. Another safeguard more generally allowed for a member to suspend its commitments to the organization contingent upon a two-thirds majority. Each of these points deserves attention.

Safeguards in the ITO   The escape clause in the ITO, which has survived to this date through the GATT and the WTO, permitted a member to suspend its obligations (namely, the lowering of trade barriers) if a surge of imports caused domestic injury (Article 40 of the ITO Charter). With this safeguard, it is foreseeable that, if other states took action that harmed US domestic interests, the USA could opt out of its commitments under the ITO. Is it possible the presence of the escape clause affected the US designers' as well as domestic audiences' thinking on voting in a way that benefitted the plan for voting equality within the institution?

There is no evidence that the escape clause positively inclined the US designers toward voting equality, while there is good evidence to suggest that Congressional members worried about the escape clause in achieving the very opposite of protecting US interests. As the Congressional members rightly recognized, the escape clause was not a privilege unique to the USA and other states could exercise it. As one member put it, "it is a two-way road." Another Representative chimed in along the same lines: "It is alright to talk about an escape clause, but now you know, the other countries can do this" (US Senate 1947, p. 12 and p. 404). Importantly, the US designers of the institution agreed with this diagnosis. Further, the Congressional members appeared to have worried, in my words, about the moral hazards the escape clause could create. The presence of the escape clause would compel the US negotiators to agree to reductions in barriers that they would not have otherwise agreed. As one Senator put it, "without the existence of the preagreement [the escape clause] protection that we may be inclined to take chances in making the agreements that we would otherwise not take" (US Senate 1947, p. 28). This moral hazard argument again suggests the difficulty of seeing the escape clause as insurance against voting equality. Moreover, the escape clause remained subject to the approval of the ITO Conference by a two-thirds vote, where each state had a single vote. In this context, Congressional members worried about every member state in the ITO having a single vote on (dis)approvals on the escape clause (US Senate 1947). In short, there is good evidence to suggest that the escape clause contained in the ITO cannot be seen as a facilitator of voting equality at the ITO.

The presence of the escape clause also fails to contribute to understanding the voting design of the ITO in comparison to the IMF and the World Bank. Although the escape clause in the GATT has received great scholarly attention, the IMF agreement also originally contained a safeguard. While the IMF agreement fixed members' exchange rates, members had nonetheless the discretion to adjust these rates without consultation within the institution as long as the adjustment remained within a 10 percent band. Indeed, the US Congressional members and the US designers of the Bretton Woods institutions identified this allowance within the IMF as an escape clause. As one Representative put it, "You have several escape clauses in your Monetary Fund provisions," to which a State Department official answered affirmatively: "On parities, it is a 10 percent change without permission" (US Senate 1947, p. 281). In this context, even if we downplay other relevant evidence and take merely the presence of the escape clause to be a significant explanatory variable in the outcome of voting equality, one would still need to explain why the escape clause in the case of the ITO was paired with voting equality, while in the context of the IMF it was combined with weighted voting. Overall, the escape clause offers limited explanatory value.

Two-thirds majority   The ITO Charter also foresaw:

the Conference may waive an obligation imposed upon a Member by the Charter; Provided that any such decision shall be approved by a two-thirds majority of the votes cast and that such majority shall comprise more than half of the Members. The Conference may also by such a vote define certain categories of exceptional circumstances to which other voting requirements shall apply for the waiver of obligations. (Article 77.3 of the ITO Charter)

One the one hand, this clause suggests that on important issues, a special majority would be required, which in turn implies the enhancement of "individual control," as special majorities would have increased each member's individual say. The US designers did actually plan for the special majority rule for issues of particular concern to US interests. As one of the State Department officials emphasized, "where the interests of the United States are directly at stake, in actions of the Organization, we might ask for special majorities" (US Senate 1947, p. 533). On the other hand, it is difficult to argue that this potential for higher individual control justified voting equality, though it can be taken to provide enough protection in the midst of voting equality (United States Delegation 1947, p. 9). Such special majorities in the Bretton Woods were paired with weighted voting. In short, the presence of special majorities itself does not illuminate the origins of voting equality in the ITO.

Power-based explanations

Possibly, during the onset of the Cold War in 1946–1948, when the ITO was being negotiated, the US negotiators faced increasing costs in a potentially failed ITO deal, so their choice of voting equality was to sweeten the deal for others (see, e.g., Zeiler 1999). This argument runs into problems.

If voting equality was offered due to the Cold War, it remains a mystery as to why the US negotiators tabled a proposal for weighted voting when the potentiality of the Cold War was becoming more real. As noted previously, the US negotiators tabled their original plan for the ITO (equal voting), and a proposal for weighted voting in 1947. By 1947, the Soviet intentions – at least regarding the trading system – were much clearer than they were a year earlier, before any negotiation on the ITO had commenced. The Soviets had not attended any of the meetings and had expressed no interest in the organization by that point (Zeiler 1999). In this respect, the international environment was more pressing when the US designers tabled their weighted voting proposal than when they expressed a preference for voting equality in 1946. Moreover, voting equality was not attractive to the UK, and elite opinion within the UK turned from positive to skeptical toward the ITO, as the negotiations on the ITO advanced (Gardner 1980). Thus, voting equality might have potentially increased the costs of a non-deal, when the USA's main partner was concerned. In this respect, if voting equality were there only to lure other states to the ITO, it would have been a costly move on the US negotiators' part, given the growing British discontent with it. Finally, the onset of the Cold War would have been more consequential for other features of the ITO, such as the inclusion of non-capitalist economies, than voting (Zeiler 1999).

Normative concerns?

Could normative concerns for sovereign equality explain the US negotiators' choice for voting equality? In the IMF and the World Bank, weighted votes were combined with basic votes, which were distributed to member states equally. Two primary rationales existed for basic votes: to enshrine the sovereign equality of member states, and to entice the small states' interest in the organization, which they might not have had with the negligible votes they would be given under a purely weighted voting system (see Chapter 3). Could it be that similar concerns carried the day at the ITO?

Again, why such putative normative impetus for sovereign equality in the ITO would have been paired with formal equality, while it was combined with weighted voting in the other two institutions, remains to be answered. It is doubtful that the only way to highlight sovereign equality in the ITO would have been through voting equality. Given the USA was the architect of the Bretton Woods model of voting, that model or a version of it could have plausibly served as an alternative for the trade institution, if the concern was to reflect sovereign equality. Further, there is no documentary evidence to suggest that normative considerations shaped the US negotiators' thinking. For instance, when the US negotiators were comparing the design and functions of the ITO to other international organizations, they made explicit references to the two multilateral financial institutions and not to the United Nations, as they regarded the ITO as the indispensable third institution in the multilateral economic system. Given that the UN General Assembly symbolized the sovereign equality of states, some comparison to the UN could have conceivably been interpreted as indicating normative concerns.[10] If normative considerations occupied center stage, their absence from a diverse set of sources, ranging from the US designers' documents and memoirs to Congressional hearings to inter-state negotiations on the ITO, is confounding.

US designers' thinking of the functions and purposes of the ITO

The US designers preferred formal voting equality at the ITO because they thought such formal equality would best serve the intended functions and purposes of the institution. The US drafters conceptualized the ITO as primarily a platform for inter-state bargaining on members' trade policies, given the institution would be a "centralized agency for the coordination of the work of Members regarding the reduction of trade barriers" (US Department of State 1946a, Article 1). Toward this end, the US negotiators reasoned that the institution would engender "consultation and collaboration among Members" (US Department of State 1946a). Further, the ITO was envisioned to act as the centralized information agency on members' trade policies (Article 5).

This conceptualization of the institution as a bargaining and consultation platform, in turn, necessitated wide participation by members, which militated against weighted voting. Particularly, given the nature of the ITO as a forum for "continuous consultation," each member would be expected to reveal information about its trade policies and would have to be engaged in an open discussion with others regarding those policies (Wilcox 1949a, 1949b). And, had a member state's willing acceptance of a specific trade policy been lacking during the inter-state negotiations, then that state's enforcement of the policy could not be trusted. As a US negotiator explained:

since most of the acts of the Conference [of the ITO], and for that matter, the executive board, are in the nature of recommendations to governments for action, which has to be implemented by governments, the importance of the recommendation is not merely determined by the weights of the votes that you can collect on an issue, but on the number of countries that are willing to accept the obligations (US Senate 1947, p. 533).[11]

US drafters expressed this opinion during internal discussions also, noting that in an "essentially recommendary body" like the ITO there would

---

[10] This is not to suggest that the design of the UN was completely disregarded – the way in which the EB of the ITO would have paid attention to regional representation would have been reminiscent of the rotating membership of the UN Security Council based on regions. Still, the IFIs were the main point of reference.

[11] Also quoted in McIntyre (1954, p. 490).

not be much to "gain by allowing the more heavily weighted Members to vote down the smaller Members" (ECEFP M-20/46 1946, p. 4). It was better to grant the members the voice to be heard during the negotiations, so that their inclinations toward compliance with the outcome of the negotiations could be ascertained.[12] The key rules of international trade embodied in the institution also emphasized the importance of inter-state bargaining. Consider, for instance, the most-favored-nation (MFN) rule, which has survived to date. While MFN generally precluded a member from treating different members of the ITO unequally, the substance of this rule would gain meaning only through inter-state negotiations.

On this point, the ITO's aim was to create a *multilateral* mechanism for reducing trade barriers. The multilateral nature of the institution would work toward assuaging states' hesitations about lowering trade barriers, since State A's reservations about reducing barriers to imports from State B could, theoretically, be offset by the gains that State A's exporters would make in other members' (States C, D, etc.) economies (Hoekman and Kostecki 2001). US drafters of the ITO emphasized this point: "If each country could be attracted by the chance of securing new opportunity from *all* the rest, it might be bolder and more assured in granting opportunity to others" (Feis 1948). Without each state's participation, the multilateral nature of negotiations on reductions to trade barriers would be undermined. Here again, the ITO would need to rely on as widespread member participation in the reductions to trade barriers as possible (US Senate 1947, 543).[13]

Additionally, the US negotiators reasoned that in the ITO there would be fluid coalitions and shifting interests, which insured against stable coalitions in opposition to the USA. In Wilcox's words, in the ITO, "[t]here [would be] no sharp division of interest that [would] appear in every case. The line-up of votes [would] be constantly shifting, from issue to issue and from time to time" (Wilcox 1949a, p. 147). Such fluidity stemmed directly from the ITO's standing as a bargaining platform. For instance, negotiations of tariff reductions on hundreds of different commodities would compel the emergence of a diversity of interests. Such diversity of interests promised changing coalitions. In turn, shifting coalitions meant that the effects of one-member-one-vote on the USA would be mitigated because there would likely be no permanent coalitions against US interests. In contrast, divisions between creditor and debtor countries were expected to mark the IFIs, with the USA as a creditor

---

[12] At the same time, the powerful states have used this "information" generated during the discussions to their advantage; see Steinberg (2002).

[13] Note that this conclusion does not suggest that each participant's voice mattered equally.

(Gold 1972, 1981). And, on certain issues, where the USA predicted stable groupings against its views, particularly on the issue of "restrictive business practices," the USA thought weighted voting would be to the detriment of the US interests because others would be able to obtain "a large number of votes ... and be in a better position to outvote the U.S." and so in these situations, equal voting would be preferable too (Office Memorandum 1947, p. 9; also United States Delegation 1947a).

Among the primary by-products of the ITO's intended core functions and purposes were the ITO's relatively limited bureaucratic capacities and its relatively limited need for financing. The first point is self-explanatory: the ITO's conceptualization as an inter-state bargaining platform suggested a weaker bureaucracy compared to the IMF and the World Bank. The Secretariat of the ITO, for instance, was planned as relatively small (US Department of State 1946a, Section F).

On the second point, the US contribution to the ITO would not constitute shareholding as in the IMF and the World Bank (Article 77.6 of the ITO Charter). The US financial commitment to the ITO would have been higher than those of other members as contributions would be based on a pre-negotiated ability to pay. Still, the nature of member financing differed significantly across the three economic institutions. The US financial contributions in the Bretton Woods institutions, along with other states' contributions, have formed the primary basis of the credit the institutions have extended to borrowers.[14] As one of the leading State Department officials emphasized, the USA was not placing "any capital" in the organization, which in turn undermined a rationale for weighted voting. The official explained, "in [the IMF] we have a weighted voting position because we put in capital there" (US Senate 1947, p. 37). Simply, the ITO's reliance on member finances for its operations would have been much lower than the Bretton Woods' institutions.

It also seems that the US contributors were concerned that if there were to be weighted voting at the ITO, an institutional logic was needed for it. For instance, William Clayton remarked:

As other countries get into production, our percentage [of international trade] will, of course, go down. It is a thing that would not be static like, for example, our contributions to the International Bank and Fund. They are fixed there where we have a right to demand, and we did demand and we got a weighted voting provision. (US Senate 1947, p. 37)

[14] There are substantive differences across the IMF and the World Bank as to how member states finance these institutions (see Chapter 3).

These remarks may seem strange, since a contemporary view of the USA's contributions to the Bretton Woods institutions as "static" does not make sense. Yet, at the time of the creation of the institutions, many were concerned about increasing original levels of commitment, preferring to see them as more or less fixed (US House of Representatives 1945). Clayton's points primarily emphasize that the US financial contributions to the Bretton Woods institutions justified, at least partially, weighted voting. Clayton suggests the capital contributions in the financial institutions created an institutional logic for weighted voting, and this logic, not the underlying power differentials, constituted the reason for asymmetric voting, but such logic would have been lacking in the ITO. Interestingly, other state representatives echoed this very rationale. For instance, the Brazilian delegate to the ITO negotiations put it simply: "The [s]ystem of weighted voting of the Fund cannot apply to the [ITO] as there is no analogy. Weighted voting in the Fund is justified by capital contributions for operation" (E/PC/T/C.6/25 1947). The ITO would, as the drafters emphasized, "have no money to lend and no equipment to provide" (Wilcox 1949a, p. 190). Accordingly, members' contributions to the organization would have covered operational expenses only. Undoubtedly, the relatively rich states would have provided more toward these operational expenses, but their so-called asymmetric contributions appear to be a non-issue in the US designers' thinking.

These discussions offer some general points regarding the relationship between members' financial contributions and voting design. The presence of asymmetric financial contributions alone does not substantiate one voting design over another. After all, in all three multilateral economic institutions some members were slotted to make greater contributions than others. Rather, the meaning of those contributions within specific institutional contexts contributes to understanding the choice for voting. While in the two international financial institutions, unequal contributions not only meant different levels of shareholding but also creditor-debtor relations, in the ITO, there was no such institutional logic for weighted voting. Even in this context, however, the outcome of voting equality cannot be understood with only a reference to the nature of the funding of the institution, as the latter was a by-product of the planned functions and purposes of the institution, which in the first place justified voting equality. Crucially, without any change in the institution's financing structure, the US negotiators tabled a proposal for weighted voting. In this respect, while a lack of financial logic for weighted voting seems to have reinforced the US designers' tendency for voting equality, it cannot be taken to explain that inclination.

Why the switch to weighted voting   Although the US negotiators'
conceptualization of the core functions of the ITO, and the by-
products of these functions, such as the financing of the ITO, played
a key role in disposing the US negotiators toward voting equality
in the ITO, none of these aforementioned explanations account for
why the US negotiators tabled a proposal for weighted voting during
the course of the negotiations. To understand their weighted voting
proposal, we must turn to the evolution of the inter-state negotiations
on the institution.

The London negotiations (1946) on the ITO led to a number of
changes to the USA's original draft of the ITO Charter, which altered
the US negotiators' thinking on the balance of payments (BOP) question,
which in turn motivated their weighted voting proposal (Irwin et al. 2008;
see also Odell and Eichengreen 1998). From the start, the US negotiators
regarded exchange rate restrictions, which were under the IMF's authority, and quantitative restrictions on trade, which would have been under
the purview of the ITO, as two sides of the same coin in countries' efforts
to deal with BOP problems (e.g. E/PC/T/C.6/62 1947). Through the
ITO the US designers wanted to circumscribe others' ability to use
quantitative restrictions, while having the members also observe
exchange rate rules set by the IMF. The drafters, thus, foresaw that all
members of the ITO would be members of the IMF, and failing that
would sign "special exchange agreements with the organization" (US
Senate 1947). Interestingly, however, the original US draft on the ITO,
the Suggested Charter, did not clearly delineate the relationship between
the IMF and the ITO. For instance, it did not devote a section to the two
organizations' inter-relationship. That said, Article 22 of the Suggested
Charter on quantitative restrictions emphasized that these restrictions
would conform to Article VII of the Articles of Agreement of the IMF,
which outlined exchange rate restrictions that could arise if a certain
currency was deemed scarce.

The US compromises during the London draft, directly or indirectly,
affected the BOP question. For instance, the US negotiators conceded to
the inclusion of provisions for full employment, and thereby the imposition of trade restrictions that were aligned with the domestic provision of
full employment (Wilcox 1949a, p. 536). Moreover, yielding to requests
from developing countries, the London negotiations produced a draft
with a section on economic development (Wilcox 1949a). As William
Clayton noted, this chapter "was added because a number of under-
developed countries felt that provisions for dealing explicitly with this
subject are a necessary and proper part of an International Trade
Charter" (US Senate 1947, p. 7). These changes permitted the

possibility of trade restrictions beyond the US intentions. Further, the London Draft explicitly foresaw "greater flexibility in the exceptions permitted" on the question of the discriminatory application of quantitative restrictions (Wilcox 1947, p. 534). The London draft specified the period for countries to transition out of quantitative restrictions as 1951, whereas in the Suggested Charter it was 1949 (Wilcox 1947; US Department of State 1946a, Article 20).

In this context, as the US designers' thinking on how the ITO would function shifted through the course of the negotiations, they seem to have regarded the weighted voting proposal as insurance against the ITO not reflecting their preference on balance of payments questions (e.g., ECEFP M-20/47 1947, pp. 5–6). For instance, Wilcox specifically emphasized that the ITO-IMF linkage was the proper counterweight to the London Draft's relaxation on quantitative restrictions because the London draft contained "more adequate safeguards and more effective supervision through the collaboration of the [IMF] and the ITO" (Wilcox 1947; US Department of State 1946a, Article 20). He also noted in his internal notes on the ITO that the question of voting could not be finalized until the substantive elements were completed (US Department of State 1946b). Given the compromises they made in London, the US negotiators' weighted voting proposal during the subsequent New York meeting ensured a relatively stronger link between the ITO and the IMF.

By the same token, the shift back to voting equality at Havana can be explained by the fact that the Havana Charter drew a robust link between the ITO and the IMF *and* gave the upper hand to the IMF on BOP issues (e.g., ECEFP D-62/47 1947). The Havana Draft, unlike the Suggested Charter, included an entire section on the two organizations' inter-relationship (Article 24). This section stated clearly that the IMF, where the USA formally dominated through weighted voting, would have the ultimate say on BOP matters:

In all cases in which the [ITO] is called upon to consider or deal with problems concerning monetary reserves, balance of payments or foreign exchange arrangements, the Organization shall consult fully with the Fund. In such consultation, the Organization *shall accept all findings of statistical and other facts presented by the Fund* relating to foreign exchange, monetary reserves and balance of payments, and *shall accept the determination of the Fund* whether action by a Member with respect to exchange matters is in accordance with the Articles of Agreement of the [IMF]. (E/CONF.2/7 1948, Article 2 Paragraph 4. Emphasis added)

In short, the weighted voting proposal can be understood as the USA's insurance policy during the ITO negotiations. In their original thinking, the US drafters thought the institution could achieve its desired ends, including the pursuit of US interests, without weighted voting, but the subsequent negotiations shook US confidence in the ITO Charter attaining those interests. Thus, the weighted voting suggestion during the negotiations served as an insurance policy had the penultimate draft steered uncomfortably away from the US preferences. But, the Havana draft ended up drawing a close link between the ITO and the IMF, capturing the original intention of the US negotiators on the BOP issue without resorting to weighted voting.

The influence of the UK?   Bolstering the point that the US drafters pursued their weighted voting proposal as an insurance policy against the negotiations undermining their pursuit of key interests, the evidence suggests that the UK proposal did not affect the drafters' calculations. As late as November 1946 (almost a year after the US Proposals), the US officials "had not seen an concrete British proposals for weighted voting" and could not conceive of weighted voting being applied wholesale (Office Memorandum Letters 1946). In addition to this lack of conversation between the two parties on voting, internal US documents indicate that the US drafters specifically disliked the British proposal because they saw it as designed to give disproportionate influence to the British Empire through extensive basic (equal) votes because a number of countries would have individually contributed to the Empire's views (ECEFP M-20/47 1947; Paper on Organizational Chapters 1947).

Domestic factors?   Interestingly, although key domestic audiences expressed a clear preference against voting equality, this domestic preference does not contribute to the understanding of the US negotiators' weighted voting proposal. The timing of the US weighted voting proposal precedes the Congressional scrutiny of ITO documents. During the 1947 Senate Committee on Finance Hearings on the ITO Charter, the voting equality enshrined in the Charter came under critical scrutiny (US Senate 1947). Further, the US drafters defended voting equality at the Congressional Hearings. For instance, the Chairman of the Finance Committee, Republican Senator Millikin of Colorado, indicated that there was a "substantial field of power" in the ITO Charter in which the Organization, and not individual member states, had a say and thus "the question of one member one vote [became] very important" (US Senate 1947, p. 533). But, Clayton defended voting equality to Millikin. The following exchange is illustrative:

THE CHAIRMAN   May we assume, Mr. Secretary, that it is a fact that the United
  [MILLIKIN]:   States, so far, has been for one vote in the Executive
                  Committee [Board] and in the Conference?
MR. CLAYTON: Yes, sir; that is right.
MR. CHAIRMAN: May we assume, for purposes of this inquiry, that that will continue
             to be a fact?
MR. CLAYTON: Yes, sir, Senator. I think we ought to do it that way (US Senate
             1947, p. 44).[15]

Millikin was not alone, and other Senators also showed their concern with voting equality.[16] For instance, Senator Hawkes from New Jersey indicated that:

you are putting the future welfare of billions of dollars worth of industry into this picture, and certainly you and I [Millikin], as individuals, would not make a deal with some fellow who had one-thousandth of part of what we had, to have an equal vote as to what was going to happen in an organization that we would belong to (US Senate 1947, p. 37).[17]

Still, despite this Congressional skepticism to voting equality, the US negotiators were hesitant to discuss their weighted voting proposal with the Committee, even though it had already been tabled by the time of these hearings (US Senate 1947, p. 44). For instance, upon Clair Wilcox's mentioning of the "possibility" of weighted voting under questioning from the Committee, Senator Millikin enquired more about it, only to receive vague answers from Wilcox. To Millikin's question of "Has the formula [for weighted voting] been evolved?" Wilcox replied "It has been explored, but there is no final position." The Senator, then, pressed – "Is it on paper?" only to get a an evasive reply from Wilcox – "We do have something on paper" (US Senate 1947, p. 44). If the weighted voting proposal intended to please Congress, the negotiators would have been less coy about discussing it during the hearings.[18] Also, on this evidence, US negotiators' commitment to weighted voting was questionable, even under pressure from Congress.[19]

[15] Given Clayton's remarks, this exchange also bolsters the previous point about the US designers' tendency for voting equality.

[16] This concern with weighted voting in ITO was in line with general Congressional attitudes toward the whole post-war multilateral economic system (see Gardner 1980, p. 129).

[17] The Committee on Finance contained a number of influential Republicans, such as Taft and Millikin. Still, the partisan divide within the Committee is not as relevant to this study as it is to understanding the failure of the ITO.

[18] Instead of Congressional ratification, the GATT was approved, as Jackson (2000) explains, through a mixture of existing law on trade and Executive authority.

[19] I explored the potential of discord among the US negotiators regarding the rules for voting in the institution, but found no evidence for it in the documents, including the State Department cables (1945–1952). Regardless, the presence of such disagreements would explain neither the content nor the timing of US proposals on weighted voting.

In addition to Congressional members, key US domestic businesses were also concerned about voting equality, which also suggests that the US negotiators' switch back to voting equality at the end of the ITO negotiations came at the displeasure of yet another key domestic group. Ultimately, the failure of the ITO Charter was closely related to the lack of domestic support from key interest groups that represented export-oriented businesses (Bidwell and Diebold 1949, p. 231; Diebold 1952). These groups, such as the International Chamber of Commerce (ICC) and the National Foreign Trade Council (NFTC), were originally and in principle supportive of the ITO. Their support was critical in counteracting the protectionist business groups, which opposed the institution, and in lobbying protectionist Republicans and Democrats in favor of it. Yet, these business groups judged that the ITO Charter ended up tipping the balance between multilateral openness, on one hand, and domestic interventionism to provide for national publics, on the other, too much in favor of the latter (e.g. Diebold 1952, pp. 14–20; Ruggie 1982).

The voting rules influenced the way in which these groups interpreted the ITO Charter, especially in the context of other US compromises (see also Diebold 1952). For instance, the ICC argued that:

In view of the inconsistencies, ambiguities, and differences in philosophies the voting procedure proposed for the ITO would be of utmost importance, for it is within the organization itself that differences in interpretation are to be compromised or resolved. And here is one of the great weaknesses of the [Havana] charter, for it is based on the one-nation-one-vote principle (US Senate 1947, p. 568).[20]

Voting in the ITO was also problematic according to the NFTC. The group was particularly concerned about the rule that a two-thirds majority of the members could "waive an obligation imposed upon a member by the Charter" (Loree 1950, p. 57). The NFTC reasoned that the waiver could be relatively easily attained, and it would opt states out of "unwise policies" that would harm the USA. For instance, ("unwise") inflationary policies by governments could facilitate balance of payments problems, for which states could seek a waiver. According to the NFTC, given voting equality, the successful pursuit of US business interests could be jeopardized.

In sum, the voting equality enshrined in the ITO magnified the business community's worries about having a Charter in which the

---

[20] See also similar statement by the National Association of Manufacturers in US Senate (1947).

USA had compromised, from their perspective, too much. Had the voting distribution been different, it is plausible that the business community could have interpreted all the "opt-outs" or compromises from free trade in the Charter with less skepticism.

The failure of the domestic level to make an impact on the negotiators' international position defies expectations from the two-level games because the US negotiators pursued voting equality contrary to the opinions of Congressional and business members, namely domestic agents of ratification.[21] As is well known, according to the two-level analysis, negotiators bargain with each other on the international platform (Level I) for an agreement that will be acceptable on the domestic level (Level II). The "win-set" denotes the agreements acceptable on Level II, and the intersection of states' win-sets is necessary for an international agreement. This framework offers a straightforward, but important implication to the discussions at hand: designers of institutions will have to balance their own design preferences with the preferences of those that will domestically ratify the agreement. Presumably, if designers fail to construct institutional features that receive the approval of key domestic audiences, then the designers will have failed in their ultimate objective of getting the multilateral institution accepted, regardless of the institution's design. The findings here do not necessarily weaken the two-level approach, as voting equality in the ITO contributed to the domestic skepticism about the institution. The findings suggest, however, caution against taking it for granted that international negotiators integrate the concerns of key domestic audiences.

Conclusions

This chapter has shown that the US designers' conceptualization of the unique specifics of the institutional setting of the ITO adjusted the importance of the underlying inter-state distribution of economic power. Although the USA was the preeminent economic power when the ITO was being created in 1946–1948, just as it was in 1944, when the IMF and the World Bank came into being, US economic dominance carried differing significance across the three institutional settings. Unlike its Bretton Woods predecessors, the ITO enshrined voting equality because the US designers judged formal equality to best suit the intended purposes and functions of the ITO as primarily an inter-state forum for bargaining. Specifically, the negotiators not only aimed to create a collective mechanism for addressing trade barriers, but they also

---

[21] See, for instance Milner (1997); Putnam (1988).

wanted to ensure that the USA, as a surplus country, would not be disadvantaged by other countries' restrictive trade and exchange rate policies in the post-war period. The designers aimed to tie the ITO to the IMF. When that institutional linkage seemed to loosen during the initial negotiations, the US designers tabled a proposal for weighted voting, which would primarily apply to discussions on balance of payments. The UK's own weighted voting proposal and domestic-level factors fail to explain the US negotiators' actions.

This conclusion partially agrees with other works that argue for the rationality of state actors in creating institutions. After all, the US negotiators followed the planned functionality of the institution in engendering its voting design.

Still, the conclusions of this chapter differ significantly from those of existing theories. Unlike the expectations of rational design theory (RDT), voting equality did not stem from the numbers of states negotiating the ITO charter and each of their demands for control over the institution. Further, even if one takes RDT's indeterminate conjecture about "asymmetric importance" to be about financial contributions to the institution, that point still does not illuminate US behavior during the inter-state negotiations. More importantly, while RDT conceptualizes institutional design choices as intended solutions to collective action problems (distribution, enforcement, and uncertainty), in the case of the ITO, this macro-purpose co-existed with the US designers' micro-purpose of having the institution deal with BOP problems in a way that served the USA's anticipated post-war position as a surplus country. While surely BOP issues can breed a collective problem, the US designers were viewing the BOP question from the narrower lens of the anticipated US position in the post-war era. This point is reminiscent of the US negotiators for the Bretton Woods institutions rejecting John M. Keynes' proposal for a mutual adjustment process at the IMF that placed the burden equally on surplus and deficit countries (and not merely the latter, as has been the case).

In any case, institutionalist theories do not tell us much about how power asymmetries get reflected onto institutions, even though as this chapter has shown key actors' conceptualization of the specifics of institutional settings adjusts the significance of those asymmetries. One might argue that the very notion of collective bargaining for the pursuit of mutually beneficial goals tames those asymmetries, but as this chapter has demonstrated there is variation in the degree of taming. While at the institutional setting of the ITO, the US designers chose voting equality, hence formally taming the US economic preeminence in the institution, in the case of the IMF and the World Bank, the institutional settings contributed more to the reflection of those asymmetries than their taming. Further, collective bargaining on voting does not seem to have swayed the US designers' thinking on voting *toward* meeting others' demands. The US designers tabled their proposal for voting equality prior to hearing others' preferences and despite the fact that their key interlocutor, the British, pressed for weighted voting.

Do these points not suggest that power-centered explanations do a good job of telling why the ITO ended up with voting equality? The answer "US negotiators preferred voting equality" appears to be a nod to those theories that base their explanations on the preferences of the mighty. As Stephen Krasner (1991) wrote, there are different possibilities on the Pareto-frontier.[22] In other words, a number of different designs on voting could have been acceptable through strategic bargaining among different states, and the bargain chosen (the spot on that Pareto frontier) has to do with the interests of the dominant states. Some of the chapter's assertions including the US negotiators' concerns with others' balance of payment positions appear in line with this kind of thinking. Both implicitly and explicitly, however, these power-based theories assume that the dominant states will choose the spot that leverages their power the most (see also Chapters 1 and 2). In other words, it is puzzling from these perspectives as to why the US actors did not push for a combination of weighted votes and equal votes in the ITO when the evidence suggests they could have. On their own, power-based analyses do not tell us why the dominant state chooses one out of the numerous acceptable design outcomes. Also puzzling from this perspective, the evidence does not match the assertion that the onset to the Cold War affected the institutional design on voting. Crucially, a power-oriented approach does not lend itself to the suggestion that different institutional settings adjust the importance of the inter-state distribution of power differently. It merely lends itself to the assertion that power asymmetries get reflected onto the institutions. In the end, when institutional design features are concerned, the analysis of the intersection of power and institutions offers significantly different conclusions than the independent examination of those realms.

---

[22] Pareto efficient outcomes are those where no actor can be made better off without someone being made worse off. Put differently, there are different equilibria that would be consistent with the outcomes from strategic bargaining.

5 Shifts in political power in the IMF in 2008–2010

Prologue: contemporary cases

Rising and declining states

In the last decades of the twentieth century and into the twenty-first century, economic strength has been shifting from advanced economies to fast-growing developing countries, known as emerging markets. This trend is apparent when states' economic sizes are examined. For instance, in 1990 the G7's share of world economic output was about 51 percent, while in 2008 this number had dropped to, roughly, 42 percent (Canuto and Lin 2010). Additionally, the G20 emerging economies accounted for approximately one-fifth of the world's economic output in 1990, while they accounted for almost one-third of the world's economic output in 2008 (World Development Indicators 2010).[1]

Critically, the large emerging markets have been growing faster, on average, than the large advanced economies in the last two decades.[2] In the period 1990–1994, the G7 countries accounted for about 50 percent of world GDP growth, while the emerging market members of the G20 accounted for only 24 percent of the world's GDP growth. A decade later, in 2000–2004, the G7 countries' share of world growth had declined to 28 percent, while the G20 emerging economies had increased their share of it to 39 percent. In 2005–2008, the declining states' share of world growth had declined further to 19 percent, while the rising states increased their share to 49 percent.[3]

The large emerging markets' enhanced importance for trade flows also indicate these economically rising states' growing importance for the

---

[1] GDP measured in constant 2005 PPP international US dollars. GDP measures, despite their imprecision, are good proxies for the size of a country's economy, given that GDP is the best available indicator of the aggregate level of economic activity.

[2] Even though it was only in 2010 that China surpassed Japan in economic size, the stagnation in the Japanese economy since the early 1990s had long subdued discussions of Japan as a great economic power.

[3] These numbers were calculated from Canuto and Lin (2010).

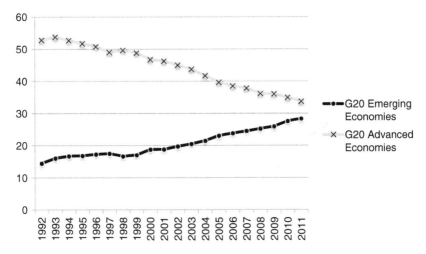

Figure 5.1 Share of world exports (%), G20 emerging and advanced economies. *Source:* Author's own calculations from WDI.

global economy, including the financial transactions within it. In 1995, the rising states' (the emerging economies of the G20) value of exports constituted just under 17 percent of the value of the world's total exports; whereas, the same number for the economically declining states (the advanced economies of the G20) was over 51 percent. A decade later, the rising states' share of world exports had climbed to over 23 percent, and the declining states' share of world exports had fallen to under 40 percent. In 2010, the same numbers had, respectively, changed to approximately 27 and 35 percent. Figure 5.1 displays the convergence in the two groups of states' shares of world exports, and Figure 5.2 compares the exports of the BRICs and the USA as a share of world exports.[4]

The rising states' increasing attractiveness for foreign direct investment (FDI) has followed a similarly upward trend. For instance, in 1990, the largest seven emerging markets (EM7) accounted for about 5 percent of the world's net inflows of FDI, while the G7 accounted for 54 percent of the same inflows. In 2005, EM7's share of the world's total inflows of FDI had increased to approximately 16 percent, while the G7's share of it had decreased to about 39 percent. By 2008, the same numbers for EM7 and G7 were, respectively, 20 percent and 29 percent.[5]

[4] These statistics were calculated from the IMF's International Financial Statistics database, using the value of exports in US dollars.
[5] These numbers were compiled from World Development Indicators.

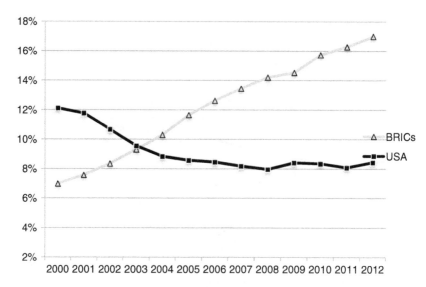

Figure 5.2 Exports from BRICs and the United States (as a share of world exports). *Source:* Author's own calculations from WDI.

At the same time, the increased foreign exchange reserves of large emerging markets point to their enhanced liquidity position (Cohen 2006; Helleiner and Pagliari 2011). According to one count, the reserves held by emerging economies increased from $1.5 trillion to $7 trillion between 1999 and 2008 (Wolf 2009).[6] These reserves not only provided the large emerging markets with a cushion in the latest global crisis, but they also emphasize the increasing importance of these rising states as investors in international capital markets. For instance, the EU asked China to invest in European sovereign debt instruments in their efforts to mend the broken economies of Union members, particularly Greece, during the Great Recession.[7] The Europeans' asking for Chinese investment also symbolizes a qualitative shift in multilateral economic relations. While before the crisis the preoccupation of multilateral institutions, particularly the IMF, was with the prevention of the financial crisis in the developing world, the 2008 crisis has shown the lopsidedness of this perspective (see also Chapter 8).[8]

[6] I discuss the rationale behind the build-up of these reserves in Chapter 5.
[7] See, e.g., "China Signals Reluctance to Rescue E.U.," *The New York Times,* December 4, 2011.
[8] While economic strength could be about perception (should we continue to invest in the dollar? Is China really a safe place to engage in foreign direct investment?), the aforementioned basic economic indicators embody those perceptions as much as inform them.

Table 5.1 *Real GDP growth (%) in key economies*

	2009	2010	2011	2012	2013	2014	2015
World	−2.3	4.1	2.8	2.3	2.2	3.0	3.3
Euro Area	−4.2	1.7	1.5	−0.5	−0.6	0.9	1.5
Japan	−5.5	4.5	−0.5	2.0	1.4	1.4	1.3
United States	−3.5	3.0	1.8	2.2	2.0	2.8	3.0
China	9.2	10.4	9.3	7.8	7.7	8.0	7.9
Indonesia	4.6	6.1	6.5	6.2	6.2	6.5	6.2
Russia	−7.8	4.0	4.3	3.4	2.3	3.5	3.9
Turkey	−4.8	9.0	8.8	2.2	3.6	4.5	4.7
Brazil	−0.2	7.5	2.7	0.9	2.9	4.0	3.8
Mexico	−6.1	5.5	3.9	3.9	3.3	3.9	3.8
Argentina	0.9	9.2	8.9	1.9	3.1	3.0	3.0
India	9.1	8.7	6.2	5.0	5.7	6.5	6.7
South Africa	−1.8	2.8	3.1	2.5	2.5	3.2	3.3

Source: Compiled from World Bank Global Economic Prospects 2013. Projections start in 2014; 2013 is estimated. Real GDP calculated using constant 2005 US$.

Indeed, for many commentators, the effects of the Great Recession appear to underscore the long-term trend of the rise of the large emerging markets and the relative decline of the large advanced economies (e.g., Hurrell 2008; Kahler 2013; Layne 2012; MacDonald and Parent 2011; Schweller and Pu 2011). The rising economies, such as China, Brazil, and India, have proven relatively more resilient to this severe global economic crisis in comparison to the declining economies. Table 5.1 provides real GDP growth figures for 2009–2012 (the table also includes projections). As this table shows, even though the crisis hit some emerging economies relatively more severely, by 2010 almost all of the emerging economies had recovered economic growth more impressively than the advanced economies and were growing faster than the average world growth. In short, Table 5.1 shows the continuation of the divergence in the growth of the emerging and advanced economies.

Overall, the above statistics suggest that there has been a long-term trend in which the large emerging markets are of *rising* importance in the global economy; whereas, the larger advanced economies are of *declining* importance. Hence, the rest of this book refers to the large emerging economies as the *rising states*, and to the large advanced economies as the *declining states*. This shorthand does not, however, suggest that the economically declining states are also in a declining position within the multilateral economic institutions. Rather, the upcoming chapters examine the shifts in the formal positions of the institutionally dominant but economically declining states versus the rising states, which putatively seek greater formal political power within the same institutions. Of key interest is the extent to which the declining states "accommodate" increases to the rising states' formal political power ("position enhancement").

Operationalizing accommodation

Accommodation and position enhancement can be conceptualized as continuous variables, with higher and lower degrees of them. The next question becomes how to differentiate between these differing degrees. The issue of position enhancement within a single institutional setting is not straightforward, but nonetheless discernible. For instance, hypothetically, how big of a shift is a 3 percent shift in voting power away from the declining states to the rising states? In order to answer this question adequately, one would have to have a prior conceptualization of how much of a shift, measured by specific criteria, would be desirable and for what end. While this is a worthy approach and one that numerous studies undertake (e.g., Virmani 2011), I do not adopt this method here because different commentators are bound to disagree on the normative appeal of different outcomes. This lack of agreement, in turn, makes the analysis a shifting target. Moreover, this book does not aim to advance a normative framework for assessing the (in)adequacies in formal political power.[9]

For these reasons, in assessing the extent to which shifts in the distribution of formal political power within an institution reflect position enhancement and accommodation, the case studies to come, first, examine different reform proposals/discussions that took place on adjustments to formal political power. This focus on various reform proposals permits the assessment of different states' (expressed) preferences as well as how they would have fared under different outcomes. For instance, to what extent did the change in formal political asymmetries (outcome) fulfill the rising states' expressed preferences during that process of change? The case studies, second, provide an understanding of the degrees of accommodation in a comparative sense, across institutions. For instance, was there greater position enhancement in the World Bank versus the IMF? In sum, this chapter and the next one will assess accommodation both within and across institutions.

---

[9] Yet, the book offers findings that could be used in normative evaluations, such as the implications of reforms for low-income countries (LICs) (Chapter 8 especially).

Why focus on groups of states?

In analyzing the contemporary shifts in members' formal political power in 2008–2010, the book focuses on three groups of states – the large advanced economies, the large emerging markets, and the poorest countries.[10]

Besides following shifting patterns in the inter-state distribution of economic power, another key advantage of examining groups of states, as opposed to a focus on a select few, has to do the multilateral economic institutions' own custom of analyzing and treating states in different categories, based on their levels of economic development. Particularly, almost always, the IMF and the World Bank documents discuss shifts in formal political power in terms of advanced economies versus developing countries.

Yet, I also pay attention to disparities within these groups, suggesting that the category of "developing" countries in the case of the 2008–2010 changes is too broad for useful analysis. Particularly, the increase in the significance of the large emerging markets for the global economy has also meant greater diversity within the group of countries known as developing countries. The relatively poor members of the developing world, referred to in the book as low-income countries or the poorest states, are lagging substantially behind the rising states (some of them are still failing to develop). For instance, the poorest states' economic output constituted less than 1 percent of the world's total economic output in 2000–2009.[11] Crucially, the rising states can access international private capital much more easily than the low-income countries. As an example, although the Great Recession overturned the inflow of capital into both emerging and low-income economies, by 2010, key emerging economies were facing the problem of regulating capital inflows to moderate volatility, while the low-income countries had the opposite problem (Griffith-Jones and Ocampo 2011).

Also, although both the emerging economies and low-income countries continue to wrestle with extreme poverty, the rising states have made substantial progress in that realm. In 2005, in the least developed countries over half of the population continued to live in extreme poverty, on

---

[10] Throughout, the G20 states are the reference point for the large advanced economies and the large emerging markets. The low-income countries comprise the following categories: (1) the Sub-Saharan African states (minus South Africa), (2) the UN classification of Least Developed Countries (LDCs), (3) the World Bank's classification of low-income countries. The ensuing discussions elucidate the institutional relevance of these classifications.

[11] This statement is true for the GDPs of "low-income" and "least developed" countries as categorized by the World Development Indicators; GDP in constant 2000 US$.

less than \$1.25 a day (2005 PPP).[12] In contrast, in China while 60 percent of the population lived in extreme poverty in 1990, in 2005 the same number was only 15 percent, which is an astounding reduction in just fifteen years. Similarly, Brazil reduced the portion of its population living in extreme poverty from 15 percent in 1990 to 8 percent in 2005. While much of India continues to live in extreme poverty, the country's extreme poverty declined from 54 to 42 percent in 1990–2005.[13] More importantly, the large emerging markets' increasing economic prowess indicates their relatively higher capacity (compared to low-income countries) to tackle poverty.[14]

Taking these points as background, the rest of this chapter begins with the analysis of the 2008–2010 shifts in members' formal political power at the IMF.

Introduction to changes in the IMF, 2008–2010

The IMF's crisis of credibility in the early twenty-first century facilitated reforms to member states' representation in the institution in 2008, and, urged on by the Great Recession, the members supplemented these reforms in 2010.[15] These 2008–2010 changes constitute, arguably, the most extensive set of reforms to members' voting power in the institution as well as the nature of state representation in the IMF's Executive Board (EB) since the institution's inception in 1944. For instance, for the first time in the IMF's history, in 2008 the members agreed to calculate their quotas in the institution based on a single formula.[16] Additionally, the 2008 changes tripled the basic votes in the institution and fixed their percentage at about 5 percent of the total votes, another first for the

---

[12] http://mdgs.un.org/unsd/mdg/Host.aspx?Content=Data/Trends.htm (Last accessed: November 20, 2011).

[13] These numbers are calculated from: http://ddp-ext.worldbank.org/ext/ddpreports/ViewSharedReport?REPORT_ID=1336&REQUEST_TYPE=VIEWADVANCED (Last accessed: November 20, 2011).

[14] The argument here is not that throwing money at development problems can simply solve them. Rather, the argument is simpler and a lot less controversial – large emerging markets have higher capacity than low-income countries to tackle development challenges, and this has been borne out by the numbers cited above.

[15] The 2008 global economic crisis that commenced as a panic in US financial markets is now widely dubbed as the Great Recession.

[16] There are two components of a member state's voting power in the IMF: basic votes, which member states hold in equal amount, and quota votes, which are determined by the member's quota. Quotas are based on the member's relative economic importance, measured by GDP and a number of other variables, in the global economy. The quota-determined voting share is more important than basic votes. In short, voting is weighted in the IMF. On the significance of quotas, see Chapter 3.

institution.[17] In 2010, the members converged on the most aggressive increase in the IMF's quota, its doubling, since the institution's inception (Chapter 3). This increase has, on average, enhanced the members' quotas more than any other previous change, with the greatest beneficiaries being the large emerging economies, such as China.[18] At the same time, in 2010, the members decided to make the Executive Board an all-elected body, ending the rule that the top five shareholders can appoint their own Directors.[19] Further reforming the EB, the Europeans agreed to give up two seats on the Board in order to increase the number of Directors from "developing countries."[20]

Such seemingly substantive shifts in member states' formal political power raise a number of critical questions. What explains these 2008–2010 changes to the distribution of formal political power in the IMF?[21] What accounts for the extent of the quota and thus voting power adjustment in favor of the large emerging economies, namely the rising states?[22] These questions, in turn, demand an analysis of the 2008–2010 shifts to members' formal political power. Not just the evolution of inter-state negotiations on the issue, but also how different groups have fared in the process needs to be sorted. While most analyses have attempted to explore this last question on the gains and losses of different groups based on normative yardsticks (e.g. Virmani 2011), this chapter focuses on how the reform outcomes compared with the reform discussions in the institution going as far back as 1999. Because the intent here is to examine how institutional mechanisms, including institutional rules and conventions, interacted with changes in the world economy and the inter-state

---

[17] These reforms came into effect on March 3, 2011.

[18] This point was calculated based on data introduced and discussed in Chapter 3.

[19] The IMF is governed by both a Board of Governors (BG), to which all members are entitled to appoint a governor, and an EB. Voting at both the BG and the EB is weighted. The Governors have delegated (and can delegate) almost of all of the tasks to the EB. Tasks that the BG cannot delegate include decisions that will affect the institutional structure of the IMF, including quota adjustments, distribution of the Fund's income, relations with other international organizations, acceptance of new members, changes in the value of currencies, and the number of EBs (Lister 1984, p. 103). The EB, with its directors resident in the IMF headquarters, carries out day-to-day work of the IMF. For discussions on the functioning of the IMF's EB, see Gold (1972, 1974), Lister (1984), Woods and Lombardi (2006).

[20] In the IMF jargon, the group of countries that will benefit from a reduction in the European chairs are "dynamic emerging market and developing countries" (EMDCs). The EB approved the 2010 reforms on November 5, 2010.

[21] To recall, formal political power is defined as a state's right to voice in the institution, as outlined by the rules and procedures of that institution. Formal political power has two dimensions – states' voting rights in the institution and state's representation in the constituent organs of the institution, such as the EB (Chapters 1 and 2).

[22] Given the book's focus, references to IMF reform only pertain to changes in members' formal political power.

distribution of economic power to facilitate the 2008–2010 shifts, the normative approach is not preferable (Chapters 1 and 2).

To preview some of the key discussions, the chapter finds that the 2008–2010 changes redistributed relatively more voting power to the rising states, the large emerging economies, than the prior reform discussions had anticipated. And, three meta-factors help one understand this outcome. First, the dominant states within the institution, which this book has identified as the economically declining states, reasoned that the rising states' position enhancement was essential to steer the IMF in a direction they desired. Specifically, the declining states consider increases in the rising states' formal political power as critical for more effective surveillance of these countries' economies as well as their greater involvement in burden-sharing the financing of the institution.

Second, the manner in which the member states fund the IMF affected the content as well as the timing of the 2008–2010 changes. The institution relies heavily on state financing, whether through quotas or loans, with little ability to raise capital on its own. This state of affairs not only enhances the importance of burden sharing, but it also makes the institution sensitive to shifts in the distribution of economic power, in this case the rise of large emerging economies. Notably, however, this financial dimension should be analyzed in conjunction with the institutionally dominant states' conceptualization of how the rising states contribute to institutional priorities (Chapter 2). In this case, the manner of the IMF's financing reinforced the declining states' willingness to boost the rising states' formal political power.

Third, the 2008–2010 changes cannot be understood outside the context of the IMF's existing rules and conventions on how to alter quotas (and thus voting power). For one, as emphasized in Chapter 3, quota shifts remain politically sensitive and thus remain subject to lengthy interstate negotiations. Such bargaining creates inertia against change. Moreover, the IMF has traditionally relied on adjustments to members' formal political power only when the institution's overall quota is boosted (Chapter 3). In this regard, that the 2008 changes to members' formal political power occurred without any changes to the institution's overall quota indicates the significance of the 2008 quota adjustment. Nonetheless, because the 2010 changes provided a boost to the institution's overall quota, the shifts in formal political power in 2010 were more extensive than in 2008. Generally, institutionally set ways affected the nature of the 2008–2010 changes.

While these three factors are by no means the only ones relevant to understanding the shifts in formal political asymmetries in the IMF in the period examined, they explain the majority of the outcomes of the

2008–2010 shifts in members' formal political power. In terms of the importance of other factors, the chapter details the role the IMF staff played. The staff provided the members with technical calculations and guided the process along. By reminding the IMF member states how previous quota calculations and adjustments occurred, the staff sustained existing institutional conventions. Nonetheless, there is little evidence that in the case of the shifts in formal political asymmetries, which remain controlled by states and subjected to formal votes, the staff have had much room for maneuver. In others words, the fact that quota adjustments involve little delegation to the staff limited the staff's ability to independently affect the shifts in formal political power (see also Chapter 3).

Similarly, the chapter finds that while the reforms, and the documentation surrounding them, paid lip service to the position of the poorest states in the institution, the 2008–2010 changes brought little gains to these states in terms of a boost to their formal political power in the institution. Although the tripling of the basic votes benefitted these states, this boost in the basic votes was part of a package deal that greased the wheels of negotiation, and the other beneficiaries of the deal fared much better compared to the poorest states at the end of the changes. Further, subsequent shifts undermined the gains the poorest states made through changes in voting power. Normative concerns, understood in this case as a concern for the position of the weakest members of the institution, did not play a significant role in the 2008–2010 changes.

What about the role of the Great Recession, the deepest worldwide economic recession since the Great Depression? The chapter argues that the timing of the 2010 reforms owes a great deal to the economic crisis that began in 2008, but the crisis does not explain well the content of the changes. The chapter also shows that the crisis did not overturn existing institutional routines within the institution, which contributes to the understanding of institutional continuity and the difficulty of radical institutional change.

The rest of the chapter is organized as follows. Section 2 provides the background on the IMF's crisis of legitimacy leading up to the 2008–2010 reforms. Section 3 discusses these changes with a view to showing how they enhanced the position of large emerging markets relatively more than preceding institutional discussions. Section 4 explains this outcome with reference to the three primary aforementioned factors, while considering why alternative explanations fall short. Section 5 concludes with a view to highlighting the long-term effects of the shifts in member states' formal political power.

Background to the 2008–2010 shifts

While the IMF's legitimacy crisis had long been in the making, by 2007, there were a number of visible symptoms of the institution's declining credibility and relevance. For instance, in 2007, its outstanding loans to member states had dipped to roughly 10 percent of its level in 2003. This reduction in the demand for IMF loans was due to a number of factors, including primarily its emerging market clients' rush to pay down their debt to reduce the need for IMF funds that came with conditionality.[23] In this context, Mervyn King (2006), a former Governor of the Bank of England, remarked that: "Certainly, the Fund's remit is unclear. Its lending activities have waned, and its role in the international monetary system is obscure." Given the dip in the demand for its loans, the institution had to cut about 15 percent of its staff soon after its former Managing Director Dominique Strauss-Kahn took office in 2007 (*The Economist* 2009). Strauss-Kahn (2007) remarked at the time: "What might be at stake today is the very existence of the IMF as the major institution providing financial stability to the world."

The IMF's crisis of relevance was intrinsically related to its declining legitimacy (acceptability) in the eyes of member states, which was, in turn, related to the institution's perceived lack of even-handedness. The institution's lack of even-handedness was widely regarded as a by-product of the asymmetries in member state representation and influence in the institution.[24] Here, the IMF's treatment of its emerging market clients during the 1997 Asian financial crisis is emblematic. When the Asian emerging markets, such as South Korea and Indonesia, turned to the IMF for assistance during the 1997 crisis, the IMF loans imposed extensive conditionality on these countries, such as increasing interest rates to unprecedentedly high levels and imposing painful cuts in public spending. Critics considered these conditions as prioritizing the bailing out of Western creditors as opposed to aiding the recovery of these economies (Stiglitz 2002; Woods 2006).[25]

Regardless of the intentions of the conditionality, the lesson of the crisis for the Asian countries was to reduce their future need on the IMF, given the emergency funds came with curbs on their economic autonomy.

---

[23] Author's calculations from www.imf.org/external/np/fin/tad/extcred1.aspx. In 2007, the only emerging market member of the G20 that had an outstanding loan from the IMF was Turkey.

[24] For discussions on the IMF's legitimacy crisis, see Best (2007) and Seabrooke (2007). The reforms' wholesale implications for the institution's legitimacy falls outside the scope of this book (see Chapter 2 and Chapter 8).

[25] For an overview of the 1997 crisis, see Radelet and Sachs (1998); for a perspective that defends the IMF's actions, see Rogoff (2003).

Thus, in the aftermath of the crisis, emerging economies in the region, and others affected by the crisis, such as Brazil and Russia, started building up their foreign exchange reserves as self-insurance mechanisms in future financial crises (Eichengreen 2007). In short, the IMF's handling of the crisis economies in Asia damaged its reputation and, along with it, its prospects as a creditor.

The IMF's behavior during the Asian crisis, its critics reasoned, was intrinsically related to the control the USA, and a handful of other G7 countries, have had over the institution.[26] In contrast, not only were the Asian economies in the weak position of demanding IMF funds, but they also had little meaningful say over the IMF's policies because of their limited voting power in the institution. Thus, as two experts put it in a typical statement prior to the onset of reform at the institution, "[a] realignment of voting shares is central to preserving the support of the Fund by all its members and thereby to the Fund's relevance and legitimacy in promoting global growth and economic and financial stability" (Cooper and Truman 2007, p. 1).

Because the institution's lack of even-handedness was seen as being closely related to political asymmetries in states' representation at the institution, the IMF began its efforts to reform member state representation in 1999.[27] As this chapter discusses, these efforts culminated in years of reform discussions at the institution. By 2006, as the "Singapore Resolution" captured, the members had converged on the point that reform to the distribution of formal political power in the institution was to achieve two ends: one, to increase the voting power of countries that had experienced sustained levels of high economic growth; two, to focus on the voice of low-income countries (LICs). The members finally agreed to the first set of reforms in 2008 and then further supplemented these reforms in 2010. The next section describes these shifts in members' formal political power.

Shifts in members' formal political power: descriptive analysis

The 2008 formula reform

In 2008, IMF members revised the formula for determining a member state's underlying economic importance in the global economy, and hence that state's quota in the IMF ("the quota formula"). Chapter 3

---

[26] For works that show the influence of core shareholders on the IMF's loans (see, e.g., Copelovitch (2010); Momani (2004); Thacker (1999); Stone (2008); Vreeland (2007)).

[27] 1999 is the key year because the IMF's member states commissioned an external group of experts to carry out quota reform in the institution in that year.

has already provided the history of changes in the IMF's quota formulae. As that history has shown, not only has the formulae's role as determinants of the shifts in members' quotas been obscure, but also the member states have always subjected quota changes to intense political negotiation. The 2008 alterations to the quota formula were motivated, partially, by the formulae's lack of transparency given the presence of a number of distinct formulae that guided different members' quota contributions and the lack of knowledge about which formula applied to which member state (Chapter 3; also Bird and Rowlands 2006). The other primary motivation for the 2008 change stemmed from the membership's general discontent about the results the formulae yielded, which were considered as "unrepresentative of actual conditions in the world economy" (IMF 2000b, p. 4). This lack of representativeness, many argued, arose from the widely held conviction that the formulae did not adequately reflect the large emerging markets' economic rise.

A brief background on pre-2008 attempts to reform the quota formula is necessary to appreciate the contentious and prolonged nature of the issue. Toward tackling quota formula reform, in 1999, the IMF commissioned a group of experts known as the Quota Formula Review Group (QFRG). The QFRG, led by Richard Cooper of Harvard University, presented a report to the IMF in 2000. In this report, the QFRG proposed a single formula with only two variables – GDP, which was calculated at market exchange rates, and variability in current receipts and net long-term capital flows. The GDP variable would be weighted twice as much as the variability factor.

The IMF membership, however, generally found this proposed formula politically unacceptable because it would have led to an increase in the quota of advanced economies, when one of the main existing problems related to the IMF's legitimacy was identified as the asymmetric influence of these states over the Fund at the expense of developing states, both emerging and low-income. Nearly a decade-long debate ensued from the ruling out of the QFRG's suggestion. Ultimately, these institutional discussions culminated in the 2008 revision of the quota formula.

The 2008 formula includes the same four variables the institution has all along relied on, but alters their weights and, in the case of the GDP variable, the manner of its calculation: the GDP variable, which is a blend of GDP converted at market exchange rates (60 percent) and at Purchasing Power Parity (PPP) (40 percent), an openness variable, a variability factor, and a reserves variable.[28] The openness variable

---

[28] See Chapter 3 for a detailed discussion of the quota formulae. PPP exchange rate is the rate at which the same bundle of goods and services can be purchased in different countries.

comprises the annual average of the sum of current payments and receipts for a five-year period, and the variability factor consists of variability of current receipts and net capital flows. The GDP blend measure has a weight of 50 percent; the openness variable has a weight of 30 percent; and the variability and reserves components have, respectively, 15 and 5 percent weights.[29] The formula was compressed by a factor of 0.95.[30]

The 2008 voting adjustment

In 2008, the members partially (and putatively) relied on this new formula to adjust members' formal political power in the institution, boosting the quota and hence the voting power of some members, while decreasing or retaining the quotas of others. From one perspective, this 2008 shift in formal political asymmetries was out of the norm for the IMF because it was done outside of an increase to the institution's overall quota. As Chapter 3 explained, because increases outside of a general boost benefit only a select group of members, they remain politically contentious and thus unpopular with the membership. For instance, in 2006, the members converged with difficulty on giving four of the fastest growing emerging economies – China, Mexico, South Korea, and Turkey – "ad hoc" increases, namely special increases outside of a general boost to the institution's quota. The only way the rest of the membership agreed to enhancing the quota of only these four states was to regard this selective boost as the first step of a two-step process, with the 2008 changes constituting the second step (EBM/06/75–1 2006). Because fifty-four members, largely from the developing world, received increases to their quotas in 2008, this so-called second step (following the 2006 shift) was relatively more politically appealing. Yet, with the third of the members experiencing a positive shift in their quota, the 2008 changes differed from similar adjustments in the past, where only a handful of members would be able to enhance their quotas outside of a general increase.[31]

Not all institutional conventions were forsaken in 2008, however, because as usual the quota adjustment was only roughly based on the quota formula with additional measures taken to ensure the acceptability of the outcome to the large emerging markets (Chapter 3). For instance, given that the calculations alone did not achieve what the membership generally regarded as a desirable redistribution of voting power away from the large advanced economies to the large emerging markets, the G7 countries that were

---

[29] For an economic analysis of the formula, see Bryant (2008).
[30] The formula was raised to the power of 0.95.
[31] The author's own calculations based on data presented in Chapter 3.

Table 5.2 *Changes in states' voting power (%) after the 2008 reforms*

Group/state	Pre-2006	Post-2008	Rate of change
G20 Advanced	46.62	44.35	−4.88
USA	*17.02*	*16.73*	−1.74
G20 European	19.07	17.53	−8.07
Japan	*6.11*	*6.23*	1.92
G20 Emerging	17.41	18.97	8.97
China	*2.93*	*3.81*	29.99
Sub-Saharan Africa	4.08	4.48	9.65
LDCs	3.03	3.58	18.30
LICs	2.44	2.78	14

Source: Author's own calculations from IMF sources. Sub-Saharan Africa excludes South Africa, which is included in the G20 Emerging Economies. LDC is a UN classification, and LIC is the World Bank classification. Numbers were rounded.

eligible for increases (based on the new formula) agreed to forgo some of these increases. For instance, the USA retained its post-2006 quota share and did not pick up any increases that were available to it. Furthermore, again to attain a desirable redistribution in voting, some countries' GDPs were calculated merely with reference to PPP (and not the aforementioned blend in the formula). Those developing countries whose pre-2006 quotas were lower than their quota-shares based on this GDP PPP criterion by more than 75 percent were eligible for a nominal quota increase of 40 percent from their pre-2006 levels. As these complicated tweaks suggest, the formula provided only a vague guideline in the 2008 quota and voting redistribution and the members employed other methods to make the results politically acceptable to the rising states. In this regard, the established custom of using the formula as a vague guidepost persevered even in the 2008 reforms, which broke with the past in other important ways.

Table 5.2 provides the redistribution in voting power that resulted due to these changes with reference to the large advanced economies' and the large emerging economies' pre-2006 and post-2008 voting power.[32] The table also shows the changes to the voting power of the poorest states, referred to as low-income countries (LICs) by the institution, in three different categories: Sub-Saharan African countries (excluding South Africa), the least developed countries (LDCs), and the World Bank's classification of LICs.[33] The table demonstrates that G20 emerging economies as well the poorest states, judged by the rate of change, were

[32] As noted earlier, China, South Korea, Mexico, and Turkey received increases in 2006.
[33] LICs refer to the poorest members of the IMF.

the greatest beneficiaries from these shifts; whereas the G20 European countries as a whole were the greatest losers (among the group of countries observed).[34]

The 2010 reforms

The 2010 shifts to members' quotas and voting power were relatively more in keeping with the traditional method of engendering quota increases as they followed a boost to the IMF's overall quota (Chapter 3). The members doubled the IMF's quota (from SDR 238.4 billion to about SDR 476.8 billion) and distributed this quota increase unevenly among themselves. Also, the 2010 quota changes, like their predecessors, relied on complex economic calculations that primarily reflected the political rationale of boosting the rising states' position in the institution. 60 percent of this quota increase was "selective," which was distributed in proportion to a member's quota share calculated based on the 2008 formula. The remaining 40 percent of the quota increase was referred to as ad hoc. The ad hoc increases relied on a distinction between two sets of calculations: one set of calculations relying on the whole of the 2008 formula and another relying only on the GDP component of the formula (to recall, this GDP variable was a blend of market exchange rates and PPP) (IMF 2010a).

Table 5.3 expands upon the previous table to summarize the effects of the 2010 changes on the voting power of different groups of states. The rate of change reported in the table pertains to the comparison between pre-2006 and post-2010 numbers and shows that, among the key countries examined, the greatest beneficiaries from the quota adjustments were the G20 emerging economies, especially China, while the greatest losers were once again the G20 European economies. Not shown, the G20 emerging economies, including China, made greater gains from 2008 to 2010 than from pre-2006 to post-2008, while the opposite holds true for the poorest states (measured across all three categories).[35]

It was not just in voting power that the 2010 reforms altered the asymmetries in formal political power within the IMF, but also in terms of state representation on the IMF's Executive Board (EB). First, these changes placed China as the third top shareholder in the institution, after the USA and Japan. Prior to the 2010 change, the largest quota holders were the USA, Germany, Japan, France, and the UK. After 2010, the UK

---

[34] The rate of change is the difference between the post-reform voting power and the pre-reform voting power divided by the latter and multiplied by 100.

[35] As noted earlier, while domestic authorities are still implementing some of these reforms, this point does not change the conclusions reached in the book, though it may require a re-visitation of how the "two-level games" are exactly structured (see Chapter 8).

Table 5.3 *States' voting power (%) before and after the reforms*

Group/state	Pre-2006	Post-2008	Post-2010	Rate of change
G20 Advanced	46.62	44.35	42.54	−8.76
USA	*17.02*	*16.73*	*16.48*	−3.20
G20 European	19.07	17.53	16.37	−14.14
Japan	*6.11*	*6.23*	*6.14*	0.49
G20 Emerging	17.41	18.97	22.24	27.74
China	*2.93*	*3.81*	*6.07*	107.34
Sub-Saharan Africa	4.08	4.48	4.25	4.14
LDCs	3.03	3.58	3.63	20.04
LICs	2.44	2.78	2.79	14.45

Source: Author's own calculations from IMF sources. See notes for Table 5.2.

theoretically lost its place as the top fifth shareholder, but in practice France and the UK requested their quota shares to be equalized and co-retained the fifth spot. The 2010 reforms also moved India (8), Russia (9), and Brazil (10) to be among the top ten shareholders (rank indicated in parentheses). Second, prior to the 2010 change, members with the five largest quotas in the IMF were entitled to appoint their own EDs to the Board, and the rest of the membership elected the remaining EDs. The 2010 reform changed this rule, making the IMF's EB an all-elected board. The actual repercussions of this change remain to be seen at the time of writing. For instance, how this reform will affect the dual position of EDs as both officials of their states and as international bureaucrats of the IMF is unclear.[36] A sudden shift in the EDs' interpretation of their role is unlikely. However, the shift to an all-elected EB has equalized the formal standing of different members of the Board.[37]

Identifying the outcome: the relatively higher level of accommodation

In comparison to institutional discussions prior to 2008, the 2008–2010 shifts displayed a relatively higher degree of accommodation in a number of ways.

---

[36] The following quote from Lister (1984, p. 114) captures the position of the EDs well: "The intermediary position of the directors—certainly not full-fledged international officials, but something more than national officials representing governments—may be regarded as somewhat unique."

[37] As Truman (2013) notes, it will also likely lead to shifts in the European representation on the Board.

Table 5.4 *GDP of G20 emerging economies*

Country	GDP (2007–2009 average) at ME	GDP (2007–2009 average) at PPP
Argentina	300.19	560.25
Brazil	1544.71	1951.92
China	4334.91	8205.99
India	1223.01	3377.39
Indonesia	493.97	904.53
South Korea	938.24	1333.33
Mexico	1002.79	1503.81
Russia	1394.18	2170.86
Saudi Arabia	413.11	575.03
South Africa	281.79	498.24
Turkey	664.62	893.68

Source: Author's own calculations from WDI.

The revised quota formula, contrary to what previous reform discussions indicated, reflected some of the key preferences of the rising states. The inclusion of GDP PPP (and not just GDP calculated at market exchange rates) in the formula was a more extensive change in favor of the rising states than what previous discussions had envisioned. Relying on calculations of GDP at market exchange rates, as opposed to at PPP, boosts the importance of the large advanced economies for the world economy, while having the opposite effect for large emerging markets. According to one calculation (Bryant 2008), the G7 countries hold 63 percent of the world's GDP calculated at market exchange rates, while they hold about 42–46 percent of the world's GDP calculated at PPP. For illustrative purposes, Table 5.4 shows the difference between large emerging markets' share of world GDP at GDP PPP versus GDP converted at market exchange rates. As the table demonstrates, relying on GDP PPP yields to greater economic importance for the large emerging markets.

The large emerging markets had long argued for the inclusion of GDP PPP in the quota formula. For instance, at a key meeting in 2003, six of the Executive Directors from the developing world indicated their desire for GDP to be measured solely by PPP. Director Le Fort, representing Southern Cone countries, reasoned that GDP PPP was relatively more suited to determining "long-term economic prospects and to make cross-country comparisons" (EBM/03/76 2003, p. 7). The Brazilian representatives made a similar point in emphasizing market exchange rates did not "capture the significant variations in the price of similar non-tradable goods" (p. 25). The Indian representative put it more bluntly that the GDP PPP provided a better measure of the "relative position of a country in the world economy" (p. 27). Developing countries also articulated their preference for GDP PPP at the level of the institution's Board of Governors. For example, the Chinese central bank's Deputy Governor noted, "we believe a quota formula including PPP GDP, which is simpler and more transparent, is the most effective way to raise the overall share of developing members" (Xiaoling 2007).

Despite the emerging economies' expressed desire for GDP PPP, pre-2008 IMF debates on the reform of the quota formula had by and large rejected the inclusion of this variable in a revised quota formula (e.g., IMF 2000b, 2001, 2003, 2005, 2006). This rejection primarily reflected the mood of the large advanced economies. Particularly, the US representative was clear in the same aforementioned 2003 meeting that GDP calculated at market exchange rates provided the "most robust indicator over time, given its central importance in reflecting the relative weight in the world economy, and ability to contribute to the Fund" (EBM/03/76 2003, p. 32). The Europeans concurred. For instance, the Italian Executive Director, Mr. Padoan, emphasized that GDP calculated at market exchange rates provided the best proxy for a "country's power to generate resources" (EBM/03/76 2003, p. 9). In short, the pre-reform discussions – at least as late as 2006 – did not show enough political momentum for the inclusion of GDP PPP in a revised formula. Before discussing what changed the dominant political mood by 2008, the other key factors that emerging economies preferred to see in the 2008 revision of the quota formula deserve attention.

The retention of the role of foreign exchange reserves in the formula also reflected one of the core preferences of the rising economies and its inclusion in the 2008 revision of the formula rendered the reform outcomes more in favor of these states than the reform proposals tabled earlier would have accomplished. Notably, reserves relate to both the potential of a member state to demand resources from the IMF (in which case, the higher the reserves, the lower their need to borrow from the institution), as well as their financial strength (higher reserves indicate greater financial strength). Unsurprisingly, given their build-up of reserves in the 2000s, the large emerging economies emphasized the latter role of reserves, thereby arguing that reserves should relate positively to quotas (see Chapter 5). In Executive Board discussions on members' foreign exchange reserves, members from the emerging economies expressed a variety of reasons for the retention of the reserves variable in the revamped formula: reserves provided an "an important indicator of members' financial strength"; they also "intended to capture the country's capacity to mobilize foreign exchange promptly and when needed"; and "reserve adequacy has been emphasized in the Fund's surveillance work" (EBM/03/76 2003, pp. 8, 10, 30). The representatives of the rising states also articulated these perspectives at the level of the Board of Governors. For instance, the Deputy Governor of the Central Bank of China emphasized the need to have reserves as a part of the new quota formula (e.g., Xiaoling 2007).

In contrast, many large advanced economies did not wish to preserve the variable on reserves in the quota formula. The American Executive Director articulated the US perspective unequivocally: "Reserves should not be included in the formula, as they play a much smaller role than in the past system of fixed exchange rates" (EBM/03/76 2003, p. 32). This logic, shared by other leading states, emphasized flexible exchange rates and access to private capital markets as obviating the need for states to rely on foreign exchange reserves. Further, the US Director and other advanced economy representatives emphasized the role of reserves as indicating the need to borrow from the institution, disagreeing directly with the notion that reserves indicated financial prowess. With most of the Directors being members from the advanced economies (Europeans, the American, and the Japanese representatives), the dominant political mood regarding reserves was negative in the reform discussions that preceded the 2008 quota formula change. Hence, the inclusion of reserves in the 2008 reform points to the relatively greater gains the rising states made through these reforms relative to preceding institutional discussions.

How did the institutionally dominant states ease their resistance to the inclusion of GDP PPP and reserves by 2008? Simply, by 2007, the political climate had changed remarkably. Critically, as indicated at the onset, the large emerging economies were rushing to end their entanglements with the IMF, paying back their loans. Also as previously indicated, that was the year in which the institution was laying off its staff. By that year, it had also become abundantly clear that the large emerging markets' build-up of reserves through the 2000s came to indicate this rising states' liquidity positions (as did these states' enhanced ability to borrow in international markets) (Cohen 2006; Helleiner and Pagliari 2011). And, given that the reserves indicated the liquidity position of these new set of potential creditors, by the onset of the 2008 changes, what was both politically acceptable and financially reasonable for the institution had changed. As the IMF (2001, p. 25) has long noted, "there are no rigorous criteria for the final selection of variables in a formula and for the choice of weights applied to these variables. These choices appropriately are, and indeed have been since the first formula was introduced, matters of judgment by and of political consensus among the membership." In this regard, there was never any illusion within the IMF that the objective economic criteria determined the selection of variables in the quota formula, but rather a mixture of economic rationale and political expediency and acceptance. By 2008, the political climate had changed.

To attribute the outcome of a relatively higher level of accommodation merely to the rising economic fortunes of large emerging markets, however, leaves the story sorely incomplete. It assumes a direct causal line from (a) "increased economic power of the rising states" to (b) "changed political climate" without explaining why and how (a) resulted in (b). There is no inherent and direct line between these two factors, and how the institutional setting facilitates that linkage remains crucial to analyze. The next section addresses this point.

Explaining the relatively higher level of accommodation

The book's adjusted power approach, in the preceding chapters, advanced three primary factors in explaining the relationship between (the changes in) the distribution of inter-state economic power and (the shifts in) formal political asymmetries within multilateral economic institutions: (1) the leading states' conceptualization of the functions and purposes of the institution; (2) the nature of the state financing of the institution; (3) the existing rules and conventions regarding the adjustment of formal political power. The adjusted power approach expects these three institutional factors to mediate the importance of the underlying distribution of economic power.

The description of the 2008 and 2010 changes above already reveal that factor 3 was at work. The adjusted power approach does not expect all institutional conventions to be followed at all times, but rather identifies them as an important dimension of the institutional flora, and as a potential factor for institutional inertia. In 2008, the quota adjustments across the membership occurred in the absence of a general quota increase (see Chapter 3). In this case, parting with the well-trodden method of shifting quotas in the presence of a total quota boost to the institution maintained the institutional momentum for quota adjustments to which the institution had committed itself as early as 1999. This exception aside, the 2008–2010 changes nonetheless conformed to previous institutional methods. The members, as they had always done, relied on the quota formula in a limited manner to attain the adjustments in members' relative position and manipulated all economic calculations to render them politically acceptable. Further, more extensive shifts could be achieved only when the members agreed to increase the institution's overall quota in 2010. This last factor points to a source of institutional inertia – if the political-economic climate does not necessitate an increase in the institution's overall quota, altering the relative position of member states will remain relatively politically contentious and thus difficult (see also Chapter 3). Instances such as 2006, when the members reluctantly agreed to boost the position of a small number of members, will remain few and far in between. In fact, between 1969 and 2000, there were only three ad hoc quota increases outside of a general quota increase (IMF 2000b).

Regarding factor 1, the book has argued that if the institutionally dominant states are undergoing a period of relative economic decline (which suggests the presence of rising states), then these states face both incentives to accommodate the rising states as well as motivations to limit this accommodation with a view to retaining their own position (Chapters 1 and 2). To reiterate, formal position in an institution such as the IMF provides both a source of control over the institution as well as prestige that both international actors and key domestic audiences value. The desire to retain formal political power will, thus, create a tendency for limited accommodation. Yet, at the same time, because relative economic decline increases the pressures for the declining states to burden share with the rising states as well as revise the distribution of power within the institution with a view to retaining the institution's legitimacy, the declining states also face incentives for accommodation. Hence the economically declining but institutionally dominant states face two contradictory impulses: accommodation and limited accommodation. Whether this tension gets resolved in favor of relatively more accommodation hinges upon the declining states' conceptualization of the rising states' importance to the institution's functions and purposes. To the extent that declining states consider the rising states' position enhancement (namely gains to their formal political power) as necessary for the fulfillment of their own priorities for the institution, then the declining states will concede to relatively higher levels of accommodation. In this context, the adjusted power approach also expects the leading states to engage in "cost shifting" among themselves – that is the most dominant state within the group will try to have other group members suffer relatively more costs from the redistribution of formal power away to the group of rising states (Chapter 2).

The declining states' tendency for accommodation

The economically declining states faced two primary inter-related reasons for the 2008–2010 changes, all of which had to do with their conceptualization of the core role of the IMF in governing the global economy: (a) position enhancement by the rising states would increase these states' accountability to the IMF both by enhancing multilateral attention on their policies and also by dissuading these rising states from "forum shopping"; (b) position enhancement by the rising states would increase their contributions to financial burden sharing (on accountability, see Grant and Keohane 2005; on forum shopping, see Drezner 2007). While the rising states' increasing importance for global financial and trade flows has underwritten both factors, their institutional manifestation was specific to the IMF. In other words, there is no reason to expect an increasing importance for the global economy to offer a generic set of implications across different institutional platforms.

Through the relatively higher levels of accommodation, the large advanced economies wished to bring greater multilateral scrutiny to the rising states' policies with a view to inducing policy change. Put differently, accommodation, the declining states reasoned, would increase the rising states' accountability to the institution. A number of representatives from the large advanced economies have indeed stated that giving the rising states more formal political power will allow these states' policies to be subjected to greater multilateral attention and even discipline. Consider the following remarks by the Canadian finance minister, James Flaherty (2006):

As the IMF reforms its governance structure to better reflect the global economic weight of its members, we must all remember that the IMF membership entails shared responsibilities and obligations. Indeed, as a member's role and voice in a global institution increases, it is reasonable to expect that the scrutiny placed on its responsibility to its partners and the stability of the international system will increase.

The Italian representative to the IMF, Tommaso Pado-Schioppa (2008), echoed these points: "After the quota increase, the most dynamic emerging economies will also bear a higher share of responsibility in ensuring a stable and well-functioning global economy and financial markets." Timothy Geithner (2010a), the US Secretary of the Treasury, also expressed similar sentiments in highlighting the American perspective on the issue of global imbalances (between surplus and deficit countries) and China's exchange rate:

We want to make sure these changes [quota reforms] go far enough in rebalancing both the rights and the responsibilities of member states of the institution. And for this reason, the agreement to modernize the governance of the IMF needs to be accompanied with more progress by countries, particularly the surplus countries, towards more market-oriented exchange rate policies and policies that will reduce reliance on exports and strengthen domestic demand.

Geithner's speech – through the emphasis on "rights and responsibilities" – specifically points to the strategy that the large emerging economies' position enhancement should enable greater scrutiny of these states' policies. China's managed exchange rate constitutes one of the areas where the USA and some other large advanced economies expect the fulfillment of "responsibilities" in exchange for greater "rights." Leaving aside for now the question of whether this strategy is well informed, the upshot of these representative examples is clear: greater stake in the institution comes from greater formal voice in the institution, and greater formal voice in the institution means greater accountability to the institution. As International Relations scholars have long noted, institutional frameworks are supposed to "bind" their members. The declining states have, thus, put forward a version of this binding argument in conceding to relatively higher accommodation (see also Chapter 2).

The impetus to bind the rising states within the IMF's platform makes sense given the institution is the only one of its kind with universal membership and the ability to carry out bilateral and multilateral surveillance of members' economies.[38] Also, it is the only institution that provides a global insurance mechanism for financial crises (because members can draw on funds during balance of payment crises). In these respects, even though the IMF is not the only platform where the large advanced economies and the large emerging markets could cooperate on global financial issues (the G20 is another setting, for instance), it is the only universal institution with a clear mandate for inter-state cooperation on global financial and monetary relations. Thus, the large advanced economies face a strong incentive to maintain the IMF as a viable platform and to retain the rising states' participation in the institution.

In this respect, the declining states also face an incentive to discourage the rising states from forum shopping. The rising states have long tied the unevenness of representation in the institution to the incentives they face for seeking alternative platforms. For instance, in discussing the political asymmetries in the IMF, the Argentinian representative to the International Monetary and Financial Committee (IMFC), Felisa Miceli, articulated in 2007 that: "This [the political asymmetries] makes very little sense. Moreover, it makes self-insurance policies and regional

---

[38] Bilateral surveillance means the IMF oversees the economic policies of individual member states, and multilateral surveillance indicates the IMF examines the external implications of members' policies and the inter-linkages between them. For studies on the IMF's changing role in surveillance, see for instance, Boughton (2001), Lombardi and Woods (2008), Pauly (2008). Some of the inadequacies of the IMF's surveillance include the institution's limited ability to carry out objective assessments of national economies and its limited ability to impose its recommendations on large economies.

pooling of reserves look more reliable than the Fund." The Brazilian representative to the IMFC, Guido Mantega, echoed these remarks forcefully the same year:

It has not escaped the attention of the United States – nor of anybody else, for that matter – that this reform process [the 2008 reforms] is crucial to ensuring the IMF's viability ... Developing countries, or many among them, would go their own way, were the perception to arise that reform will not happen or that we will be left with a purely cosmetic reform. We will seek self-insurance by building up high levels of international reserves, and we will participate in regional reserve-sharing pools and regional monetary institutions. The fragmentation of the multilateral financial system, which is already emerging, will accelerate. (Emphasis in the original removed)

And, the rising states have partially substantiated these threats. The foreign exchange reserves the emerging economies have accumulated not only increase their ability to have self-insurance mechanisms (though at a cost) during crises, they also enhance the ability of these states to create alternative platforms to the IMF. For instance, the Asian emerging markets have established the Chiang Mai Initiative, which includes regional financial surveillance and credit swap mechanisms, between the Association of Southeast Asian Nations (ASEAN) and China, Japan, and South Korea. During the writing of this book, Chinese officials announced the launch of the Asian Infrastructure Investment Bank, which would undertake the kind of lending, including for infrastructure, core to the World Bank's existence. While the effectiveness of these regional insurance mechanisms remains debatable, their existence suggests that the large emerging markets are already experimenting with systems alternative to the IMF.[39]

The rising states' intentions and their increased capabilities for forum shopping, as significant as they may be, do not by themselves explain the declining states' behavior. In the absence of the declining states' desire to bind the rising states to the platform of the IMF, it is not clear that the rising states' threats for forum shopping would have encouraged relatively greater accommodation. I return to this point later, both in the next chapter and in Chapter 8. For now, the bottom line is that consonant with the "greater voice, greater responsibility" argument, a desire to discourage the rising states from relying on alternative platforms also

---

[39] Self-insurance of grand proportions, as is the case with large reserves of most Asian states since the Asian financial crisis in 1997, means forgone spending. Additionally, although regional initiatives (such as the Chiang Mai Initiative) may pose fewer collective action problems than global ones, may dampen conditionality and be more sensitive to regional dynamics, collective action problems also beset these regional formations, which to date remain inadequate (Eichengreen 2009; Stiglitz 2010).

explains the declining states' relatively greater levels of accommodation of the rising states.

Finally, the declining states were looking to burden share financially, and the specific manner in which member states fund the IMF necessitated the rising states' position enhancement for the facilitation of these states' greater financial contributions to the institution. A number of declining states' representatives clearly linked position enhancement and burden sharing. For instance, in representing the common outlook of member states from the EU, a European finance minister explained: "EU member states remain committed to the goal of aligning members' quotas and voice to better reflect their relative weights in the global economy and *their capacity to support the Fund's work, with all countries taking their fair share in the financing burden*" (Saldago 2010; emphasis added). Similarly, the US Treasury Secretary, Timothy Geithner (2009), underscored the relationship between constrained financial resources at home and the funding of international financial institutions: "At a time when resources are at a premium here at home, the United States is carefully reviewing all options ... We are conducting a thorough review of how to best equip these [international financial] institutions for today's and tomorrow's challenges." Both the large emerging markets' increasing economic power and their high foreign exchange reserves have increased their capacity to contribute to the IMF's resources.

This desire to increase the role of the rising states in the financing of the IMF needs to be examined in interaction with two other variables. The first factor concerns the points just mentioned: the declining states' interest in binding the rising states to the IMF and the logic through which they are trying to motivate that binding ("greater voice, greater responsibility"). On the one hand, in the absence of this interest, whether the burden sharing rationale would motivate relatively higher degrees of accommodation remains uncertain. Hypothetically, if the large advanced economies had considered the rising states as an impediment to achieving institutional goals in accordance with their preferences, then they might have resisted the temptation to burden share, given increasing financial contributions in the IMF translate into increasing formal political power (through the quotas). In this case, however, the existing tendency of the declining states for relatively higher levels of accommodation eases the burden-sharing rationale.

The second factor is the manner in which the IMF is dependent on member states. The IMF remains a quota-driven institution with its other source of primary financing being credit lines (loans) from member states (Chapter 3). In the IMF, quotas, which designate a member's maximum financial contribution to the institution, enable the institution to make loans, and the institution earns interest on the loans it makes. The interest on the loans, in turn, provides the institution's operating income. The IMF's other source of funding, which constitutes a rather minuscule part of its income, concerns the sale of gold that the institution holds; however, since the Second Amendment to the IMF's Articles of Agreement, the IMF's ability to use gold in its operations has been strictly limited and remains contingent upon the Executive Board's (EB) approval with an 85 percent majority of the total voting power. Similarly, the IMF's ability to earn investment returns depends on member states' willingness to permit the usage of their quotas in investment ventures.

A Committee of Eminent Persons reviewed this financing structure for the IMF in 2008 and recommended the New Income Model (NIM) for the institution, but this model did not render the institution less member driven from a financial perspective (IMF 2007a). The Committee sought to minimize the variability in the IMF's income by diversifying the IMF's revenue sources, including the creation of a fund supplied with gains from the sale of gold and broadening the IMF's investment mandate. The Committee, however, ruled out financial independence for the IMF by rejecting a model where the IMF could borrow at below market rates and reinvest this debt at relatively higher rates. The NIM simultaneously tried to make the IMF less dependent on borrowers by diversifying the IMF's sources of funding, while retaining the key shareholders at the helm of the IMF's resources (see Woods 2010).

Essentially, as Chapter 3 emphasized, not only do quotas demand an upfront commitment, the IMF, unlike the World Bank, cannot raise its own funds in international markets by issuing bonds. An extension of this point is that members' shares in the institution (i.e. quotas), do not contain a "callable" aspect that the institution demands only in times of need, though the credit lines work in this fashion.

In this context, the increase of quotas has been contentious domestically, especially in the USA (e.g. Lavelle 2011). Congress requires an appropriations bill for US financial commitments to the institution (Boughton 2001, p. 858), and Congressional approval on IMF commitments has all along been prickly. As Broz (2005, p. 298) puts it: "Few aspects of the IMF are as contentious in the United States as requests for new resources." As Chapter 2 argued, during economic decline, the domestic scrutiny on financial commitments to multilateral institutions increases. The empirical evidence supports this point. In the 2010 increase to the IMF's quota, the USA and others members that provide credit lines to the IMF negotiated to offset their quota increases through reductions in their financial commitments to credit lines. In the case of the USA, the deal to reduce commitment to credit lines was intended to preserve the US commitment to the IMF to a total of about SDR 111 billion, more than 70 percent of which goes to the US quota commitments, with the rest constituting the credit lines (see also Truman 2013). A comparison between this number and the US paid-in capital to the 2010 World Bank capital boost – SDR 5.1 billion, which equaled about $3billion – underscores the differences in the kind and level of financial commitment to the two Bretton Woods institutions.[40]

The manner in which the IMF is state-funded, that is with a limited ability to raise its own funds and largely dependent on quotas, gives the large advanced economies strong incentives to accommodate the large emerging markets' position enhancement. At the same time, this kind of state financing also enhances the rising states' potential bargaining power. Aware of this point, the rising states have specifically tied their financial contributions to the IMF quota adjustment and its continuation. For instance, in 2012, when the IMF needed greater funds, these rising states were reported to have pledged more funds to the institution, but tied the delivery of these commitments to the institution continuing with its quota-related reforms.[41]

In sum, while the institutional design of the IMF's financing enhances both the declining states' tendency for burden sharing and the rising states' bargaining potential, the actual outcome of these variables in 2008–2010 was contingent upon their interaction with the other key variables emphasized – the institutionally dominant but economically declining states' conceptualization of the functions and purposes of the institution and existing institutional rules and conventions for adjusting asymmetries in formal political power.

---

[40] The issue of how states' financial commitments are recorded in national budgets is a distinct question. Although they do not alter the analysis at hand, the reader might appreciate the following details. Until 2009, the USA's financial commitments to the IMF required no "outlays" ("no estimated increase in the US budget deficit") (Congressional Budget Office 2009). This practice dated back to 1980, when the debates between the US Executive and Congress over US quota increases resulted in the latter continuing to authorize IMF financial commitments, though these commitments would be treated as an "exchange of assets" to avoid budgetary outlays (Sanford and Weiss 2009). With the reversal of this practice in 2009, the Congressional Budget Office treated IMF commitments as credit, thereby appropriating funds for the potential loss on these funds to the amount of five billion dollars (CBO 2009; Nelson et al. 2012). This new procedure will exacerbate the existing contentiousness of the quota increases in the USA. Notably, Congressional approval of IMF commitments has been contentious, despite the US Executive's emphasis on the financial and political gains the IMF and other multilateral financial institutions provide.

[41] For one of the many examples, see: "IMF Secures $430bn to boost firepower" in *The Financial Times* online, April 20, 2012.

Cost shifting within the group of declining states

The adjusted power approach advanced in this book also anticipates struggles over formal political power *within* the group of declining states, particularly when the declining states are conceding relatively greater degrees of accommodation. Here, the approach anticipates cost shifting within this group, where individual states within the group of declining states strive to achieve accommodation with minimum loss to their own position and thus have others within the group suffer the costs of a reduction in formal political power. This allows individual states within the group to more easily reconcile the appeal of accommodation and the tendency for limited accommodation.

A number of examples from the 2008–2010 changes to formal political asymmetries support this point about states' efforts for cost shifting. Prominently, the USA used its (de facto) veto power in the IMF to force the Europeans into agreeing to give up some seats on the EB (Lombardi 2010). According to IMF laws, the EB consists of only 20 Executive Directors, but Board of Governors' resolutions can allow this number to change by a special majority 85 percent of the total voting power. The recent practice in the IMF has been to have an EB of 24 Directors. The US preference has been to have a smaller EB without a reduction in the seats held by the emerging markets (Geithner 2010a). In October 2010, when the member states considered a proposal to keep the EB operating at 24, the USA vetoed this proposal with a view to compelling the Europeans to agree to a lower number of seats on the Board. The veto reached its aim, and as a part of the 2010 changes, the Europeans agreed to reduce their seats on the EB.

Conversely, the Europeans failed in their efforts to use the 2008–2010 changes as a platform for pursuing some of their preferences related to the governance of the IMF. For example, the EU preference was for lowering the threshold for special majorities. (e.g., Salgado 2010). As discussed earlier, critical decisions in the IMF, such as a change in the Articles of Agreement, require agreement among member states holding 85 percent of the voting power, giving the USA de facto veto power. Other sensitive decisions in the IMF, such as some financial decisions, also require special majorities at the lower threshold of 70 percent (Van Houten 2002). The Europeans justify wanting to lower the threshold for special majorities based on engendering a more "inclusive decision making process" (Saldago 2010), which would imply that such a change would benefit weaker states. However, the special majorities also offer benefits to weaker states, and were in fact demanded by them at the creation of the institution (see Schuler and Rosenberg 2012). Similarly, a recent IMF document indicates that there was no broad support for reducing the special majorities at the institution's EB because this would have affected not just the largest shareholder, but also the minorities that are able to form coalitions (IMF 2010c; also Van Houten 2002). In contrast, eliminating special majorities would enable Europeans to form blocking coalitions. The 2008–2010 reforms ended up not materializing the Europeans' wishes to lower thresholds for special majorities.

Finally, the within-group changes in voting power support the notion of cost shifting. Tables 5.2 and 5.4 show that the G20 European economies suffered about 66 percent of the total loss in voting power that the declining economies experienced. The same number for the USA was about 13 percent. The rate of change displayed in those tables also shows the distributional effects of the loss in voting power on the G20 advanced economies, with the G20's European members having experienced relatively more loss in voting power. The broad implication of some states being more on the losing end of the 2008–2010 changes in members' formal political power is that these states may be more resistant to future reforms that shift voting power further away from them (see Chapter 8). Certainly, the 2008–2010 shifts' distributional effects, both for the group of winners and losers, are worth examining more closely in future studies.

In sum, the evidence from the 2008–2010 shifts in members' formal political power in the IMF strongly supports the adjusted power approach. In order to bolster this point, I now turn to an examination of alternative explanations.

Alternative explanations

Alternative Explanation 1: The Great Recession's ramifications in the world economy explain the 2008–2010 changes to formal political power within the IMF.

While the 2008 global economic crisis may have plausibly affected the timing of the 2010 shifts in formal political power, the evidence suggests that it did not determine either the content or the timing of the 2008 changes. More importantly, the Great Recession impacted the institution because it was able to activate existing institutional conventions and not because it changed the institution's course.

The IMF documents clearly spelt out the 2008 shifts in members' formal political power in 2006, when four countries received ad hoc quota increases, and as this chapter emphasized, these changes had been in the works for almost a decade by that point. However, the IMF discussions merely foreshadowed the 2010 reforms without a specific date. For instance, in 2006, when discussing the 2008 reforms in clear terms, the

IMF documents do not mention any 2010 reforms by date, but only state: "in the context of the future general review of quotas, the Fund will seek to further realign quotas" (IMF 2006b, p. 7). In this regard, post-2008, quota (and thus voting) realignment hinged upon members' decision to boost the IMF's financial resources during the general quota reviews, which are assessments of the Fund's resource adequacy (liquidity position). The one major difference between 2008 and 2010 was the member states' decision to double the IMF quotas as a result of the Fourteenth General Quota Review, which was concluded in November 2010.

By virtue of compelling the member states to increase the IMF's total quota in 2010, which in turn made it politically feasible to undertake quota adjustments, the Great Recession ultimately impacted the timing of the 2010 reforms. As noted earlier, the *modus operandi* at the Fund has been to embed notable shifts in individual country standings within a general quota increase (see also Chapter 3). Recall that special or ad hoc quota adjustments, which denote increases to only some members' quotas, tend to be unpopular because they designate a select group of winners from quota shifts. Up to 2010, there had been no general quota increase since 1998. In fact, as late as April 2010, the EB of the IMF ruled out a general quota increase, which also made boosting the position of specific members politically difficult. By September 2010, however, the global economic situation had changed radically with the financial crisis still devastating European financial centers and renewing client interest in the IMF (e.g., Lavelle 2011). The lingering of the deep financial crisis necessitated an increase in the IMF's quota, thereby altering the position of members that were reluctant to provide a general quota increase up to that point (IMF 2010b). By animating an existing convention ("adjustments to members' quotas should occur during general quota reviews"), the ramifications of the Great Recession permitted the 2010 shifts in quotas. It is in this manner that the impact of the massive economic downturn got filtered through institutional layers (more on this point in Chapters 6 and 8).

Alternative Explanation 2: The IMF's staff's preferences explain the outcome of 2008–2010 changes to formal political asymmetries.

While the staff's role in the 2008–2010 shifts to members' formal political asymmetries cannot be overlooked, this role was severely restricted within the political parameters the member states provided (see also Woods 2006). The staff (a) undertook technical calculations and supplied advice on quota shifts; (b) acted as a repository of information about previous changes in formal political asymmetries; thereby, sustaining and voicing conventions.

On the first point, even though the staff presented numerous calculations of how different combinations of the four key variables in the quota formula would pan out for quota shifts, these calculations can be regarded more as reflecting the pulse of the political debates of the time than as innovative guideposts for member state discussions on quotas. The following remarks, all by different Directors, from a 2003 Executive Board meeting, where the primary topic of discussion was the revision of the quota formula, are typical: "The staff paper on quota distribution provides a good overview of the current state of our debate on this issue, including on alternative quota formulas"; "[The staff] have to contend with the inability of the Board to reach agreement on key issues, along with the imprecise and sometimes inconsistent requests for additional work"; "We thank the staff for their constructive paper on quota distribution, which confirms some of the early agreements on quota formulas, further investigates the feasibility of new variables, and presents some interesting alternatives" (EBM/03/76 2003). As the representative quotations make clear, the staff have room for autonomy and creativity – they can present new combinations of variables to the Directors. For instance, in the aforementioned meeting, the staff experimented with the idea of including a financial openness variable, for which the data is generally regarded as lacking. Given the openness of the American and European capital markets, the directors of those regions welcomed this potential addition, for which they had earlier expressed an interest. Ultimately, however, the tractability of the staff's suggestions remain dependent upon the political debates among the member states, both in the Executive Board and at the level of the Governors. In this regard, the nature as well as the impact of the staff's technical input cannot be analyzed independently from the member states' preferences; in fact, as one of the aforementioned quotes indicates, some of this technical input responds to member states' specific demands.[42]

Thus, the IMF staff's expressed perspectives cannot be understood as independent from the dominant member states' articulated preferences as far as the distribution of formal political power in the institution is concerned. For instance, the staff's views on both GDP PPP and reserves mirrored the views of the Directors from the advanced economies until these Directors had shifted their opinion. In a 2000 report, the IMF staff claimed that the inclusion of GDP PPP would have no solid economic rationale. While, the staff argued, GDP PPP was an appropriate measurement for cross-country comparisons of the real value of output, it was not

---

[42] The staff may have preferred certain calculations over others, but the point is about the content of what they presented.

a good indicator of the ability of a country to contribute to the IMF's resources (or the state's need to draw resources from the IMF) (IMF 2000b). Based on just this fact, one would think that the staff's perspective rested merely on technical grounds. Notably, the very same document admits that the quota formulae are based on political considerations and that the general acceptability of the formula by the membership is a necessary and often sufficient condition for ingredients in the formula. The same document acknowledges both that quota revisions are guided partially by economic rationale and partially by political rationale, while citing the former as the reason for proposing to exclude GDP PPP (see Chapter 3). Similarly, a staff document (2000) on reform discussions argued, "reserves are not a good measure of the ability to contribute resources for the subset of creditors that provide the bulk of the Fund's resources." Here, the subset of creditors refers to the G7 countries. Even though the staff paper justified this viewpoint again based on "economic sense" (2000, p. 15), it actually made political sense when the report was penned. As the same paper noted, the historical importance of reserves was that the large advanced economies, such as the USA, held them in gold at the IMF's creation. With financial globalization, however, the liquidity position of these states came to be defined by their ability to borrow in international markets (Cohen 2006), thereby reducing the rationale for the IMF to consider reserves as indicating advanced economies' liquidity positions. As just explained, with the key emerging economies' build-up of reserves, reserves have once again begun to signal liquidity. Overall, staff's earlier rejections of the inclusion of GDP PPP and reserves in the quota formula should not be taken to indicate some objective criteria and therefore as the IMF staff's scientific insight. Rather, as the various documents reveal, it reflected the dominant political mood of the time.

These discussions additionally suggest that the member state representatives appeared to have well understood the implications of the quota calculations (consider the non-elusive calculations of GDP PPP versus GDP market exchange rates) and resisted the technical advice that contradicted their interests. For instance, the Iranian Executive Director, Mr. Mirakhor, was exasperated that in a 2001 report, the staff had proposed the inclusion of market exchange rates. He noted: "the world has witnessed such large fluctuation in the exchange rates of the major currencies . . . as to throw into substantial doubt that we are opting for the best measure" (EBM/03/76 2003, p. 22). Such dismissal of some of the staff's views is not uncommon. That the member states' representatives grasped the implications of technical calculations undermines one of the critical ways in which the IMF staff can create room for independence – complex technical considerations that differentiate their expertise and compel the member states' significant delegation to them (e.g., Hawkins et al. 2006).

While the staff also acted as a conduit for institutional conventions, this role does not seem to show the staff independently affected the 2008–2010 shifts. The staff invoke prior actions and decisions taken in countless IMF documents, such as reminding the membership that the IMF quota increases tend to be more equally than unequally distributed among members – that is the number of countries getting special increases is limited. Similarly, the IMF staff act as the repository of past technical calculations, which can act as pseudo conventions if the institution relies on them repeatedly. Yet, evidence shows that members at times strategically contested these conventions. As a representative example, in the aforementioned 2003 meeting on quota changes, the Japanese Executive Director noted that "the past practice of giving much weight to the equiproportional element in quota increases [explain] should be changed" (EBM/03/76 2003, p. 18). This last point raises questions about the extent to which conventions are habitually accepted versus strategically embraced – a topic that extends well beyond the purposes of this book. The point is that the staff's different critical roles do not suggest the staff has an autonomous role in affecting the outcomes of formal political asymmetries.

These findings affirm the book's earlier discussions that given quota adjustments remain member-state driven, the room for maneuver the staff possesses is relatively little compared with instances where delegation from member states is extensive (Chapter 3).

Alternative Explanation 3: The member states acted based on a concern for the poorest states.

The most straightforward way of assessing this explanation is to explore the extent to which both the advanced economies and the large emerging economies voiced and pursued the position of low-income countries in the IMF in the 2008–2010 shifts.[43]

Prima facie, the 2008 reforms' tripling of the basic votes and fixing their share of member states' total voting power to about 5 percent suggests that Explanation 3 is a possibility. Given that all states receive the same number of basic votes, an increase in basic votes, all else being held constant, should benefit the poorest member states. The 2008 reforms also enabled Executive Directors representing seven or more members on

---

[43] To the extent that the relatively rich's advocacy of the poorest members' interests point to behavior that does not aim at self-returns, it could also be deemed as norm-driven behavior.

the IMF's EB to have a second Alternate ED after the 2012 elections. This reform is intended to ease the workload of Directors, particularly the African chairs, which represent many members.

However, upon closer look, the tripling of the basic votes fits with the existing explanation that the institutional rules and conventions necessitated the tripling of basic votes to move ahead with the 2008–2010 quota adjustments. Before explaining this point, the discussion focuses on whether or not the increase in basic votes was a primary concern for both the advanced and emerging economies.

The evidence from the Executive Board minute meetings in 2006 indicates that almost all members desired an increase in basic votes, but the large advanced and emerging economies generally preferred a more conservative increase. Based on Executive Board meeting minutes, Table 5.5 summarizes the positions of the EDs in 2006 on the issue of the increase in basic votes. The table shows that, in addition to a general willingness to increase basic votes, representatives of African states or non-emerging developing economies pushed for a relatively large increase, some of them explicitly expressing a return to the original 11 percent (basic votes as 11 percent of the total votes). Notably, while willing to boost basic votes, members from advanced and emerging economies on average expressed a preference for increases much more modest than restoring basic votes to their original importance. The general willingness to enhance basic votes is in line with the qualitative nature of the discussions within the institution that foresaw *some level* of gains for the poorest members given the IMF's role as a technical advisor and lender in these countries (IMF 2006a).

A desire to increase basic votes on its own, however, does not indicate enough about the relatively rich states' interests in boosting the position of low-income members. Crucially, the boost in basic votes also enabled easier negotiations among member states. This point, in turn, suggests that members' self-interested motivations in pursuing the reform of basic votes cannot be disregarded. As early as 2003, when reforms to the quota formulae were being discussed, IMF documents noted the rationale for embedding an increase in basic votes as part of an overall effort to bring up the actual shares of some countries:

The erosion of basic votes through quota increases has had negative side-effects on the quota adjustment process. Because the shares of many developing countries in actual quotas have been significantly larger than their shares based on the quota formulas (and the opposite has been the case for the advanced countries), there has been considerable opposition from many of these countries to raising the selective element of general quota increases as a means of closing the gap between members' shares in actual and calculated quotas. (IMF 2003, p. 20)

Table 5.5 *Executive Director positions*

Last name of the Executive Director	Constituency of the Executive Director	Preference on basic votes
Phang	**Indonesia,** (Brunei, Cambodia, Fiji, Laos, Malaysia, Myanmar, Nepal, Singapore, Thailand, Tonga, Vietnam)	11% (from 2%)
Fried and Jenkins	**Canada,** (Antigua and Barbuda, The Bahamas, Barbados, Belize, Dominica, Grenada, Ireland, Jamaica, St. Kitts and Nevis, St. Lucia, St. Vincent and the Grendines)	At least double
Misra and Bannerji	**India,** (Bangladesh, Bhutan, Sri Lanka)	Depends on the formula
Loyo and Steiner	**Brazil,** (Colombia, Dominican Republic, Ecuador, Guyana, Haiti, Panama, Suriname, Trinidad and Tobago)	Increase (unspecific)
Kashiwagi and Kihara	**Japan**	At least double
Shaalan	**Egypt** (Bahrain, Iraq, Jordan, Kuwait, Lebanon, Libya, Maldives, Oman, Qatar, Syria, United Arab Emirates, Yemen)	n/a
Saarenheimo and Hollensen	**Sweden,** (Denmark, Estonia, Finland, Iceland, Latvia, Lithuania, Norway)	At least double
Kremers	**Netherlands,** (Armenia, Bosnia and Herzegovina, Bulgaria, Croatia, Cyprus, Georgia, Israel, FYR Macedonia, Moldova, Romania, Ukraine)	At least double
Torres and Nador	**Argentina,** (Bolivia, Chile, Paraguay, Peru, Uruguay)	n/a
Sadun and Cipollone	**Italy,** (Albania, Greece, Malta, Portugal, San Marino, Timor-Leste)	Increase (unspecific)
Lundsager and Kaplan	**USA**	Double
Al-Turki	**Saudi Arabia**	Too early to discuss

Table 5.5 (cont.)

Last name of the Executive Director	Constituency of the Executive Director	Preference on basic votes
Mirakhor and Rouai	**Iran**, (Afghanistan, Algeria, Ghana, Morocco, Pakistan, Tunisia)	At least double
von Stenglin and Brinkman	**Germany**	Increase (unspecific)
Larsen and Gregory	**United Kingdom**	At least triple (preference for returning to 11%)
Moser and Lanz	**Switzerland**, (Azerbaijan, Kyrgyz Republic, Poland, Serbia and Montenegro, Tajikistan, Turkmenistan, Uzbekistan)	Size of increase depends on formula
Ngumbullu	**South Africa**, (Angola, Botswana, Burundi, Eritrea, Ethiopia, The Gambia, Kenya, Lesotho, Malawi, Mozambique, Namibia, Nigeria, Sierra Leone, Sudan, Swaziland, Tanzania, Uganda, Zambia)	At least triple (preference for returning to 11%)
Schwartz and Calderon-Colin	**Spain**, (Colombia, Costa Rica, El Salvador, Guatemala, Honduras, Mexico, Venezuela)	n/a
Ge and Xu	**China**	At least double
Mane	**Democratic Republic of the Congo**, (Benin, Burkina Faso, Cameroon, Central African Republic, Chad, Comoros, Republic of the Congo, Cote d'Ivoire, Djibouti, Equatorial Guinea, Gabon, Guinea, Mali, Mauritania, Mauritius, Niger, Rwanda, Sao Tome and Principe, Senegal, Togo)	At least triple, and eventually return to 11.3%
Oh and Murray	**Korea**, (Australia, Kiribati, Marshall Islands, Federated States of Micronesia, Mongolia, New Zealand, Palau, Papua New Guinea, Samoa, Seychelles, Solomon Islands, Tuvalu, Uzbekistan, Vanuatu)	At least double
Kiekens	**Austria**, (Belarus, Czech Republic, Hungary, Kosovo, Slovak Republic, Slovenia, Turkey)	At least double

Source: Author's own compilation from EBM 06/78–1 2006.

Because quota changes require 85 percent of the total voting power of the IMF's member states as well as three-fifths of the membership, widespread acceptance to quota changes are necessary. Further, in order to change a member state's quota (upward or downward), that state's consent is necessary. In these respects, poorest members' support for the quota shifts was essential. While for the poorest members the gap between actual and calculated quotas was generally in favor of the actual quotas, for many large emerging economies, the opposite was true. Thus, the large emerging economies, such as Brazil and China, stood to gain from quota adjustments. Yet, as the above quote explains, the poorest states had no interest in aligning actual and calculated quotas, as the former was already in their favor. Given the rules of quota adjustments, sweetening the deal for the poorest countries was necessary in drumming up their support for quota realignment.

The analysis of whether the relatively rich member states would have been content with increasing basic votes in the absence of any other type of shift in members' formal standing in the institution further corroborates this point. Did the EDs prefer a "package deal," where basic votes would be increased only in the case of other quota changes, or did they prefer an increase in basic votes followed by further changes? This point was discussed in the 2003 Executive Board Meeting on quota changes (EBM/03/76 2003). In that meeting, only one of the representative for Sub-Saharan African states and the representative from the Netherlands, who contained a number of small and slow-growing European member states in its constituency, including Armenia, Bosnia-Herzegovina, and Moldova, preferred to have basic votes increase first. All other EDs preferred either a simultaneous increase in basic votes and boosts to certain member states' voting power, or having the latter before a change in basic votes. The notion of the package deal gives further credence to the perspective that the poorest members' consent to the increase in the voting of the relatively rich members would have eased political negotiations.

At the same time, as Bhattacharya (2012) points out, the non-emerging developing economies made no gains, or even suffered some losses, in terms of their quotas at the end of the 2008–2010 shifts.[44] Figure 5.3 shows the shifts in the share of quotas for the poorest states, again differentiating them into three different categories. Because Bhattacharya includes both low-income economies and some emerging economies in his discussions, I provide my own calculations in the figure. As this figure shows, the poorest

[44] Bhattacharya, A. 2012. Overview and Summary Assessment of the 2006–2010 IMF Quota and Voting Reforms: G-24. Personal Communication.

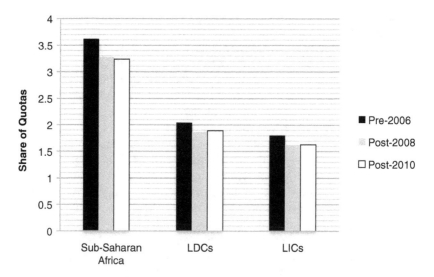

Figure 5.3 Changes in low-income countries' share of quotas(%).
Source: Author's own calculations from IMF sources.

states' share of quotas, as a group, will be lower as a result of the 2010 reforms compared to their position prior to the 2008–2010 changes. Quotas, as previously noted, determine the basis for states' access to funds from the IMF in case of an emergency or an impending balance of payments problem. Given that states with strong economic performance can access private international capital, the poorest members need public funds (whether from other states or multilateral institutions) relatively more, especially during crises. For instance, the 2008 crisis sapped the flow of capital into the whole developing world. But, as Griffith-Jones and Ocampo (2011) point out, by 2010, emerging markets, unlike the poorest countries, were facing the problem of regulating capital inflows to moderate volatility, not starving for capital flows. That the IMF quota has recently been growing, but the poorest states' share of it has declined does not necessarily mean that these countries do not have access to adequate funds – the size of the funds needed by each country depends on a number of factors.[45] Figure 5.3 does, however, call into question any argument about concerns for the poorest states' position significantly explaining the motivation for the 2008–2010 changes.

---

[45] The Conclusion of the book returns to this point by discussing the poorest states' access to IMF facilities (loans).

In short, while the considerations for the voice of the poorest states were not absent in the reform of the basic votes, such considerations were neither central nor completely void of self-interested calculations. In this regard, the possible alternative explanation of the shifts in formal political power being motivated by normative concerns for the weakest members does not hold up well against the evidence.

Conclusion: reforms and discontent

While the 2008–2010 changes have provided more position enhancement for the large emerging markets, namely the rising states, than envisioned by earlier reform discussions, these reforms also leave some of the key preferences of the rising states unfulfilled. Also, the large advanced economies are likely mistaken in their view that the rising states' greater formal political power will accompany greater pressure and scrutiny on these states' policies. After addressing these points, the chapter ends with possibilities for further research.

The rising states' discontent

The 2008–2010 changes, as many large emerging market representatives have indicated, were merely sufficient for the moment from the perspective of these states. As a Chinese official put it, the 2008–2010 reforms were "not the end, not even the beginning of the end, but the end of the beginning."[46] Put differently, these rising states consented to reform outcomes that enhanced their formal political power in the institution, but they did not hold up the 2008–2010 institutional changes with a view to maximizing their gains (pursuing all their core preferences) during the reforms. As discussed in Chapter 2, a number of reasons can plausibly explain their strategy. Particularly, holding up the reform process would not only endanger the gains these states would stand to make, it would also make them vulnerable to accusations of being reform-blockers. Nonetheless, the reforms failed to fulfill some of the key preferences of the rising states.

One source of discontent has been the quota formula. The rising states, generally, found the 2008 formula to contain variables that gave "large quotas for small and medium advanced open economies, especially in Europe" (Mantega 2011). While the inclusion of GDP PPP and reserves

---

[46] Remark by Cui Tiankai, Vice Foreign Minister, quoted in "Voting Power Shift Just the Start of IMF Reform," www.china.org.cn, November 6, 2010 (Last accessed: February 21, 2011).

met the demands of large emerging markets, the rest of the formula was in keeping with the Europeans' preferences. Particularly, the weights of different variables in the new quota formula were in line with European expectations. As the Chairman of the EU Council of Economic and Finance Ministers indicated prior to the reforms: "[EU members] consider a factor of no less than 30% for openness, and a weight of variability of no more than 15% and 5% respectively" (dos Santos 2007). These weights ended up being the actual weights in the post-reform formula, which magnifies the voting power of relatively smaller European economies. Notably, current formula calculations treat intra-EU trade as external trade (e.g., Cooper and Truman 2007). Hence the openness variable provides a huge boost to the European economies' relative economic, thus political, weight within the IMF. Also, the compression factor (the formula was raised to the power of 0.95) advantages small economies regardless of whether they are advanced or not because the way in which the compression factor is applied to the formula reduces the difference between the quotas (and hence the voting power) of large and small economies. In this regard, it disadvantages the large emerging markets, among other large economies, while benefitting small European economies.

Some large emerging markets have already voiced their preference for greater inclusion of GDP PPP in the formula (e.g., Subbarao 2010). And, some of these rising states found that the new quota formula lacked any good criterion for determining a country's need to borrow from the IMF (Lousteau 2008). Moreover, although some of these rising states have been more vocal about it than others, the fact that all under-represented countries, including most advanced economies, received a boost during the 2008–2010 changes is a potential source of discontent for these countries (see previous discussions). As IMF documents emphasize (2010b), there was opposition to all under-represented nations receiving a boost. In this regard, it was not just the underlying formula that was problematic for the rising states, but also how the formula was politically utilized to engender quota (voting) realignment in the institution. Because the large emerging markets found the new quota formula inadequate for future reform in the IMF, the member states are in the process of re-reviewing this formula. In fact, the rising states conceded to the 2010 reforms only with the understanding that a comprehensive reform of the IMF's quota formula, which was revised in 2008, would be undertaken by January 2013 but that deadline was missed (Mantega 2011; see Chapter 6).

The large emerging markets can reference "objective" indicators as the basis for their discontent with the reform outcomes. Surely, different

Table 5.6 *GDP–voting power ratios*

G20 emerging market economies	Voting power:GDP ratio
Argentina	1.02
Brazil	0.81
China	0.64
India	0.79
Indonesia	0.90
South Korea	0.99
Mexico	0.93
Russia	0.95
Saudi Arabia	2.63
South Africa	1.08
Turkey	0.79
Average	0.85
Small, Advanced European Economies	
Belgium	1.84
Netherlands	1.45
Luxembourg	3.76
Switzerland	1.78
Average	1.71

Source: Author's own calculations from WDI and IMF sources.

states will pursue different conceptualizations of what is a fair distribution of voting power in the IMF, and criteria that seem objective to one group will seem subjective to another group. Still, one has to consider the kind of quantitative criteria that the large emerging markets might consult in voicing discontent in the future based on what the reform discussions at the IMF have already considered. One such criterion is voting power to GDP ratios, even when GDP is calculated as the 2008 formula does (60 percent at market exchange rates and 40 percent at PPP). Table 5.6 provides comparisons between the voting power to GDP ratio of large emerging markets and some selective small, advanced European economies – Benelux countries and Switzerland. Notably, these European economies have often been taken as a point of reference in arguments for boosting developing countries' formal political power. The table shows that with the exception of Saudi Arabia, the Benelux countries and Switzerland are all over-represented compared to G20 emerging market economies by the criterion of voting power to GDP ratios.[47] Interestingly, a comparison of the voting power to GDP ratio of G20

---

[47] Vestergaard (2011) applies the same technique for an analysis on the World Bank.

Table 5.7 *Members' calculated versus actual quota shares*

Countries	Calculated quota share	Post-2010 quota share
G20 advanced		
Australia	1.4	1.38
Canada	2.30	2.31
France	3.79	4.23
Germany	5.68	5.59
Italy	2.99	3.16
Japan	6.49	6.46
UK	4.66	4.23
USA	16.99	17.41
G20 emerging		
Argentina	0.60	0.67
Brazil	2.15	2.32
China	7.92	6.39
India	2.40	2.75
Indonesia	0.90	0.98
South Korea	2.11	1.8
Mexico	1.79	1.87
Russia	2.94	2.71
Saudi Arabia	1.34	2.1
South Africa	0.58	0.64
Turkey	1.15	0.98

Sources: Author's own calculations from WDI and IMF sources. Numbers are rounded.

advanced economies versus G20 emerging economies shows very similar average ratios – 0.86 for the first group and 0.85 for the second group. This similarity, however, does not negate the point that the large emerging markets can find sensible data in pushing for further position enhancement in the IMF.

Finally, pure calculations of quotas based on the 2008 formula would have granted some of the rising states a higher share of the overall quota than what they have as a result of the reforms. Table 5.7 shows the G20 members' calculated quotas – based on the 2008 formula – versus actual quota shares after the 2010 reforms. This table shows that a number of the rising states' calculated quota shares were higher than their actual quota shares. These countries include China, South Korea, Russia, and Turkey. In contrast, many of the declining states had higher actual than calculated quotas, with Australia and Japan being exceptions.[48] One reason for the discrepancies between the calculations and the actual outcome has to do with how the

---

[48] Assuming calculated quotas to be a better proxy for importance in the global economy, this point suggests that even when the rising states' "exit" option was becoming more

gains/losses were distributed within the groups. The discrepancy is also attributable to the way in which the reforms did not solely follow the quota formula and many adjustments to the results were sought to make the reforms politically acceptable (see above). Overall, these outcomes of the quota adjustment point to another potential source of discontent for the rising states and another potential point of contention between them and the declining states in future quota reviews.[49]

The declining states' miscalculations?

A different type of tension between the large advanced economies and the large emerging markets is likely to be due to the former's miscalculations regarding how position enhancement will affect the latter's behavior. As emphasized in this chapter, the large advanced economies are hoping that the increased formal political power of the large emerging markets will enable the rising states' policies to come under greater multilateral scrutiny, which can potentially compel policy change. This strategy is more likely to fail than succeed.

As studies have shown, the higher a member's formal position within the IMF, the greater that state's autonomy from the institution. For instance, as Woods and Lombardi (2008, p. 714) emphasize, "[e]ffective surveillance is seen as depending upon the asymmetric and hierarchical power relationship between the IMF and member countries that are more likely to be structurally or situationally dependent on it." Put differently, as a state moves up the formal hierarchy at the IMF, the less leverage the institution has over that state. And, as the chapter also discussed, the rising states are not dependent on IMF credit. Rather, the institution needs their financial contributions.

Position enhancement by the rising states promises these states greater autonomy from and influence over the institution – the opposite of what the large advanced economies are trying to achieve. For instance, China has been increasingly vocal about modifying the basket of currencies that make up the IMF's reserve asset, the SDR, with a view to eventually including the renminbi.[50] Senior Chinese officials have also indicated their desire to debate the appropriateness of having national currencies

---

probable, the dominant states did not incentivize these states to not forum shop by closing the gap between actual and calculated quotas (on exit, see Stone 2011).

[49] France and the UK requested their quota shares to be the same, so this explains the quota share for the UK. And, the difference between its actual and calculated quota share was minuscule for Japan.

[50] See, also, "China's senior banker wants IMF reform before EU aid" in www.euractiv. com, November 9, 2011 (Last accessed: February 21, 2011).

as reserve currencies (Xiaochuan 2009). Similarly, some of the rising states have resisted the pressure to construct multilateral rules to govern capital controls, given that many of these states, such as China and Brazil, have exercised capital controls. Until recently, the standard IMF advice, which was influenced by G7 policies, was against capital controls.[51] I elaborate upon these points in the book's conclusion.

Moreover, the rising states generally do not see the reforms as ameliorating all of their existing grievances with the institution, which only further reform can achieve. For instance, the following statement by the Brazilian representative is emblematic of the rising states' approach to the IMF:

The institution should strive to foster more balanced decision-making so as to eradicate the widespread perception that the major developed countries often subordinate the Fund to their own national and regional agendas. We realize of course that this crucially depends on further distribution of quotas and voting power in favor of developing countries. (Mantega 2011)

The fourth summit of the BRICs also noted the need to re-adjust the quotas in favor of reflecting the underlying shifts in inter-state economic power and emphasized the rising states' increasing contributions to the IMF's finances.[52] In sum, the rising states do not see the reforms as a reason to bind themselves more strongly to the institution; rather, they are using their enhanced formal political power to exert more control over it. Thus, the large advanced economies' strategy for accommodating the position enhancement of large emerging markets – to extract change in the rising states' policies – is likely to fail (see Chapter 8).

Future research

Insufficient space exists to discuss a number of points that are outside the scope of this analysis. Some issues surfacing in the discussion of political asymmetries are worth the analysis, but their substantive implications for the issues at hand are hard to ascertain. For instance, the issue of staff diversity and the choice of the IMF's Managing Director (MD) are important issues. After all, the informal deal between the USA and the Europeans to split the top management positions of the international financial institutions (with the World Bank president having always been an American and the IMF MD being a European) is an anachronism. Staff diversity in these institutions matters, but studies have also shown that despite their specific backgrounds, the heads of the financial institutions have successfully carved out independence from their

---

[51] For a history of this issue, see Chwieroth (2010).

[52] See, for instance, www.brics5.co.za/about-brics/summit-declaration/fourth-summit/.

putative national masters (e.g., Van Houten 2002; Mason and Ascher 1973). And the training of the staff might matter more for generating different perspectives within the institution than staff diversity (Barnett and Finnemore 1999; Evans and Finnemore 2001). Given that the main shareholders in the institution staff the key positions, the rise of the large emerging economies promises further change in the composition of the IMF staff. Informally, staff diversity is tied to quotas, which points to yet another significance of formal political power.

Further research could also explore in greater detail the implications of within-group divisions for the IMF's future. For instance, cost shifting implies tensions within the group of the large advanced economies, such as the disagreements between the Europeans and the Americans. Potential tensions can also mark the group of the rising states – some of these states display a greater potential to borrow from the IMF in the future than other members of the group.[53] For instance, in the context of the 2008 quota adjustment, the Argentinian representative referred to these reforms as "giving more votes to a few emerging economies that seem to be 'graduating' from potential use of Fund support, at the expense of other developing countries that remain to be potential borrowers," likely considering Argentina's economic prospects as not strong as those of other emerging markets (Miceli 2007). These within-group tensions suggest that in-house divisions will likely not be only between the rising states and the declining states, but also among them. More importantly, the changes in formal political power discussed in this chapter are likely foretelling of other changes in the IMF.

---

[53] One cannot say with certainty whether any member of the IMF, who has already ceased to be a borrower from the IMF, will resume such a relationship with the institution.

6   Shifts in political power in the World Bank in 2008–2010

> Concerns by Bank shareholders and other stakeholders about inequities in representation at the Board and in the voting power of shareholders challenge the appropriateness and fairness of the World Bank Group's most senior governance bodies. The Bank's legitimacy, credibility and accountability could suffer without tangible and timely progress on the Voice and Participation agenda.   (DC2008 – November 25, p. 23)

The 2008–2010 shifts in members' formal political power in the World Bank were necessitated by the institution's credibility crisis in the eyes of both stakeholders and shareholders (e.g., see also DC2008-0013, p. 2). As the then president of the World Bank, Robert Zoellick, put it in no uncertain terms in 2010, the World Bank faced an imperative to move past the domination of American influence in the institution: "This is no longer about the Washington Consensus. One cannot have a consensus about political economy from one city applying to all. This is about experience regarding what is working – in New Delhi, in Sao Paolo, in Beijing, in Cairo, and Accra" (Zoellick 2010a). While Zoellick's pronouncement of the death of the Washington Consensus and his nod to the development policies of the emerging economies are significant, of particular relevance to this discussion are his remarks about the new era in which the institution cannot afford to preserve the asymmetric control of the USA and a handful of other rich economies over it.[1] Bank documentation has consistently foreshadowed this new era. For instance, since 2002, various Bank documents have referenced the United Nations Monterrey Conference's statement that a critical goal for the Bank is to "enhance participation of all developing countries and countries with economies in transition ... in [its] decision making" (e.g., DC2010-0006/1). External reports on the Bank also focused on political asymmetries among member states. Particularly, the report of

---

[1] Babb (2009) provides a detailed history of the Consensus, which basically prescribed privatization, deregulation, and liberalization in developing economies. For a critical assessment of the Consensus' success in engendering economic development, see Rodrik (2008), and for opposing perspectives, see Dollar (2007) and Wolf (2004).

the High Level Commission (2009), chaired by former Mexican president Ernesto Zedillo, pinpoints the link between the asymmetries in the governance of the institution and the institution's acceptability to various shareholders as well as stakeholders as a key area for reform.

The shifts in members' formal political power in 2008–2010 aimed to tackle these grievances with the Bank. In 2008, with the aim of bolstering developing countries' representation in the organization, the members doubled the share of basic votes and fixed its amount in the members' total voting power.[2] This move – the fixing of the basic votes – was a first since the institution's inception, when the basic votes hovered around 11 percent of a member's total voting power. In April 2010, the Bank's member states agreed to an increase in its capital for the first time in about two decades. That same month they also agreed to reforms to the Bank's governance structure and realigned different (groups of) members' shares and thus voting power in the institution. These 2010 shifts in members' formal political power also advanced a new method for calculating shareholding, for the first time in the institution's history officially parting with the tradition of following the IMF quota formula as the basis of determining members' shares in the Bank. An additional 2010 reform created a new, elected chair for Sub-Saharan Africa on the institution's Executive Board (EB).[3]

What do these changes indicate about the relationship between the shifts in the distribution of economic power among states and the distribution of formal political power in multilateral economic institutions? To what extent do the shifts reflect the rise of large emerging economies? How did the poorest states fare in the 2008–2010 changes? These last two questions are not only central to this book's analyses, they also remain directly relevant to the Bank's professed goals for the 2008–2010 shareholding realignment. Bank documents expressed these goals as follows: (1) to "make progress in the overall adjustment of voting rights and shareholding in light of members' evolving economic weight in the global economy"; (2) to "strengthen [v]oice and [p]articipation for countries, whose weight in the global economy may be small, but for whom the Bank plays an important financing and advisory role" (DC2008-0013).

---

[2] Voting in the World Bank consists of two components – basic votes (also often referred to as membership votes) and subscription votes, namely one vote for each share of stock held by the member state. Basic votes, as discussed later in the Chapter, comprise a much smaller percentage of the total voting than subscription votes. Simply, voting in the World Bank is weighted.

[3] The Bank's EB runs its day-to-day activities and it is comprised of elected or appointed government representatives. These representatives have dual roles – they represent the country/ies that appointed/elected them as well as being Bank officials (e.g., Lister 1984).

In this respect, the examination of the 2008–2010 changes offers insights into the Bank's success in meeting its self-determined target for reform.

This chapter argues that both compared to earlier reform discussions at the Bank and in relation to the expressed preferences of developing countries (both emerging and low-income), the 2008–2010 changes point to the institutionally dominant but economically declining states' relatively limited accommodation of the rising states. And, this limited accommodation cannot be explained with reference to the modest gains the low-income countries have made in the 2008–2010 reforms. Overall, while some level of accommodation was necessary to appease concerns regarding the Bank's credibility, very little redistribution away from the declining states occurred.[4]

What explains this relatively limited accommodation? The chapter claims the adjusted power approach advanced in this book accounts for the majority of the process of change as well as the outcomes of the 2008–2010 changes. First, accommodation was limited because the large advanced economies (the declining states) and the large emerging markets (the rising states) have come into conflict regarding the primary purpose of the International Bank for Reconstruction and Development (IBRD), the non-concessional lending arm of the Bank. The former would like to see the Bank as serving increasingly only its poorest members, thereby discouraging the rising states from relying on the institution's resources. In this context, greater position enhancement by the rising states would only increase the ease with which these members could rely on the IBRD's relatively inexpensive loans.

Second, the burden-sharing rationale was relatively muted in the World Bank. The adjusted power approach advanced in this book expects that the declining states should look to burden share the financing of the institution (Chapter 2). However, the approach also cautions that the burden-sharing impetus should be analyzed in conjunction with both the declining states' conceptualization of the role of the rising states in the institution, and the specific manner in which the member states fund the institution.

In the case of the IBRD, relatively greater position enhancement would have conflicted with the large advanced economies' steering the

---

[4] Throughout, the chapter refers to two institutions of the World Bank Group: the International Bank for Reconstruction and Development (IBRD) and the International Development Association (IDA). IBRD provides loans to middle-income countries at non-concessional rates, whereas the IDA is reserved for the world's poorest countries and provides credits (loans) at concessional (low) rates as well as grants. Unless otherwise indicated, the numbers refer to the IBRD. The Bank is used synonymously with the World Bank.

institution in accordance with their own vision (of serving the poorest states). While a strong desire to burden share could have, in theory, counteracted this incentive for limited accommodation, the IBRD relies relatively little on upfront capital infusions from member states. Instead, the institution can raise debt on international markets and largely requires callable capital from its members. Hence, in the case of the IBRD, a strong force toward higher accommodation spurred by a pressing need to reduce financial commitments was absent. Moreover, the declining states managed to shift more of the burden of the financing of the institution toward the rising states by increasing the loan prices for IBRD borrowers – that is, they managed to achieve a greater financial contribution by the rising states without needing to boost these states' formal political power.

The situation in the International Development Association (IDA) was more complicated. Although the dominant but the economically declining states pushed for greater donations by the rising states, that demand for increased burden sharing was not tied to an interest in revising the governance of the organization with a view to granting the rising states greater influence. This lack of interest in giving the rising states greater influence undermined a potential incentive the rising states would have in making greater financial contributions to the institution. Further, in keeping with their preferences over the IBRD, the declining states would like to increasingly have the IBRD transfer resources to the IDA. This alternative avenue for IDA financing eases any potential pressure to alter the IDA's governance structure in order to persuade the rising states to make greater IDA contributions. In short, the conflict in how the large advanced economies and the large emerging markets envision the core purposes and functions of the two key constituent parts of the Bank limited the former's pursuit for burden sharing.

Third, the Bank's relevant existing rules and conventions help one understand the 2008–2010 shifts. Even though in 2010 the Bank parted – for the first time – with the tradition of calculating shares based on IMF quotas, the 2008–2010 changes were nonetheless path dependent on the IMF changes in the same period. Particularly, the Bank members specifically waited for the results of the IMF quota shifts before deciding on share adjustments in the Bank, as they had repeatedly done in the institution's history (Chapter 3). Further, the doubling of the basic votes in the Bank imitated the IMF's decisions. While not void of political rationale, the Bank's continued following of IMF quota adjustments affected the nature of the 2008–2010 shifts in the member states' formal political power in the institution.

The chapter considers alternative approaches to these three factors the adjusted power approach advances (Chapter 2). Can a lack of interest by the rising states in their own position enhancement explain the process and outcome of the 2008–2010 shifts (e.g., Kahler 2013)? Good evidence suggests that the rising states' push for increases in their formal political power depends on the accommodation space provided by the declining states. Did the staff significantly influence the outcome of the 2008–2010 shifts? While the staff, as in the case of the IMF, provided critical technical guidance, the core states' demands and preferences heavily circumscribed the staff's work. Similarly, the demands of the poorest member states also fail to account significantly for the 2008–2010 shifts.

The rest of the chapter begins with an overview of the 2008–2010 changes, followed by a discussion of why these shifts point to limited accommodation. The analysis then moves to explanations for limited accommodation. In its conclusion, the chapter discusses the implications of the 2008–2010 changes for the World Bank's foreseeable future.

Overview of the 2008–2010 shifts

This section summarizes the 2008–2010 reforms to formal political asymmetries in the World Bank, focusing on their descriptive characteristics.

The 2008 reforms

The 2008 reforms to members' political power in the institution doubled the number of basic votes with a view to propping up the formal political power of the institution's poorest members (see footnote 2; also Chapter 3). While the original share (1944) of basic votes in the Bank (IBRD) was 10.78 percent, this amount had fallen to 2.8 percent prior to 2008. The 2008 reforms brought the share of basic votes up to 5.55 percent and fixed it at that percentage. Basic votes matter both symbolically and in the practice of membership at the Bank (e.g., Gold 1972; Chapters 3 and 4). They represent the putative equality of member states, which is related to notions of sovereign equality in international law. They also aim to give the poorest states higher representation than they would get, judged simply by their relative importance in the global economy (see Chapter 3). In this respect, in practice the share of basic votes as a percentage of overall voting power determines the extent to which the poorest states have a say in the Bank's decision-making.

The doubling of the basic votes boosted the voting power of the smallest member states. For instance, by my calculations, taking the Sub-Saharan African states as a group (minus South Africa), pre-2008, this group's voting power was approximately 4.7 percent in the institution, while post-2008, the group's voting power exceeded 5 percent. Similarly, if we take the Least Developed Countries (LDCs), pre-2008 the group's voting power was approximately 3.8 percent, while its post-2008 voting power was approximately 4.4 percent (see discussions below).[5]

The 2010 reforms

The 2010 reforms to the Bank, through capital increases, primarily aimed to boost the emerging economies' formal political power. At the 2010 Spring Meetings, the members agreed to a general capital increase (GCI) of $58.4 billion and a selective capital increase (SCI) of $27.8 billion for the World Bank. This total capital increase represented about a 30 percent addition to the institution's capital (Moss et al. 2010). While a GCI incurs responsibilities on all shareholders of the Bank, the SCI incurs costs, and hence enhanced voting privileges, to a select number of members. Thus, the SCI component of the 2010 capital boost allowed for adjustments in the distribution of voting power across Bank members, specifically the position enhancement of the rising states.[6]

Table 6.1 presents all previous increases to the Bank's capital. The table is more useful in getting a sense of the previous changes in the Bank's capital than showing the 2010 change in a comparative light. While the absolute number of the shares added to the institution in 2010 appears staggering, one has to take into account that the Bank was a much larger institution than ever in its history in 2010. In this respect, the relative (to the existing capital stock) importance of the capital increases matters. Not shown in the table, the average increase in the Bank's shares through general or selective increases was 36 percent in 1959–1988, with the highest increases doubling or more the Bank's existing stock (in 1979 and 1988). In this context, the 2010 increase was just below the preceding average capital increase in the institution. The 2010 increase, nonetheless, deserves close scrutiny because it was the first general increase since 1988.

Further, in 2010 the Bank members agreed on a new formula for calculating shares in the institution for the first time since the institution's inception. Previously, shareholding at the Bank was linked to the IMF

---

[5] I exclude South Africa from the group of Sub-Saharan states because it is an emerging economy.

[6] In 1998, the Bank had an SCI through which Brazil, Denmark, Spain, South Korea, and Turkey increased their voting power. The total voting increase for all these countries was 1.49 percent.

Table 6.1 *Capital increases to the Bank*

Year	Nature of increase	Number of shares added	Expressed rationale for increase
1959	GCI	110,000	Expansion of operations
1963	Increase	10,000	Accommodation of new members
1965	SCI	20,000	To follow IMF changes
1970	SCI	30,000	To follow IMF changes
1976	SCI	70,000	To follow IMF changes
1979	GCI	365,000	Expansion of operations
1981	Increase	11,500	Accommodation of new members
1984	SCI	70,000	To follow IMF changes
1987	SCI	19,376	Change in economic size
1988	SCI	9,858	Change in economic size
1988	GCI	620,000	Expansion of operations
1987	SCI	19,376	Change in economic size
1998	SCI	23,246	Change in economic size
2010	SCI	230,374	Change in economic size
2010	GCI	484,102	Expansion of operations

Source: Bank documents. GCI = General Capital Increase; SCI = Special Capital Increase.

quota formula and thus representation at the IMF.[7] In addition to a country's economic weight, the IMF formula also takes into consideration other economic variables, such as the country's level of exports and imports and the level of its foreign exchange reserves (Chapters 3 and 5). The Bank's new shareholding formula includes three components in calculating shares and thus voting power in the institution: (1) economic weight (75 percent weight in the formula), (2) contributions to IDA (20 percent weight in the formula), and (3) development contributions, which is a generic term for a member's contributions to the Bank's core mandate of economic development (5 percent weight). This formula constituted the basis for the redistribution of shareholding, and thus voting power, in 2010.

Table 6.2 presents the shifts in voting power that the 2008 and 2010 reforms engendered. In addition to showing states' pre-2008, post-2008, and post-2010 voting power, the table displays the "rate of change" for each of these groups.[8] For instance, the rate of change for China was larger

---

[7] The institution did not consistently adhere to this linkage (Chapter 3).

[8] The rate of change is the difference between the post-reform (post-2010) voting power and the pre-reform voting power (pre-2008) divided by the latter and multiplied by 100.

Table 6.2 *States' voting power (%) before and after the reforms*

Group/state	Pre-2008	Post-2008	Post-2010	Rate of change
G20 Advanced	44.37	43.07	40.59	−8.52
USA	16.36	15.85	15.85	−3.12
G20 European	15.86	15.4	14.14	−10.84
Japan	7.85	7.62	6.84	−12.87
G20 Emerging	18.8	18.73	22.3	18.62
China	2.78	2.77	4.42	58.99
Sub-Saharan Africa	4.72	5.29	5.07	7.42
LDCs	3.78	4.37	4.3	13.76
LICs	3	3.44	3.35	11.67

Source: Author's own calculations from World Bank sources.

than any other state. The table also shows that the selective redistribution in voting power at the Bank resulted in the G20 emerging economies increasing their voting power from just below 19 percent before 2008 to over 22 percent post-2010. While the G20 emerging economies had lost some voting power in the 2008 reforms, which had on the whole benefitted the poorest states in the developing world, their gains in 2010 exceeded their preceding losses. In contrast, the G20 advanced economies experienced a 3.8 percent decrease in their voting power as a result of the 2008–2010 changes. Within this group some states experienced relatively higher losses than others, Japan being the key example.

Table 6.2 also presents three different classifications as a reference for the position of the poorest member states – the Sub-Saharan African countries (minus South Africa); countries that are classified as low-income countries by the World Bank (LICs); and the UN's classification of Least Developed Economies (LDCs).[9] The table shows declines in the poorest members' voting power across all three of these classifications from 2008 to 2010. Also, as the table indicates, the rate of change for the poorest states (comparing pre-2008 to post-2010), again across all three classifications, was lower than the gains made by other groups of states. For instance, the rate of change for the Sub-Saharan African states was 7.4; whereas, the same number for the G20 emerging economies was close to 19. And, since the 2008 reform had fixed the percentage of basic votes in members' total voting power, there was no opportunity in the 2010 shifts to boost the poorest states' position through another revision

---

[9] In the chapter, the LICs refer to the poorest members of the Bank in general and not to the Bank's classification.

of the basic votes. Although the 2010 reforms added a third chair for Sub-Saharan Africa (SSA) on the Bank's EB, the significance of this chair, as discussed below, remains unclear.

Key outcome of the 2008–2010 shifts: limited accommodation

Comparing the 2008–2010 changes to members' formal political power in the Bank to earlier reform discussions in the institution, as well as to the changes in the IMF within the same period, reveals the institutionally dominant but economically declining states' limited accommodation of the rising states (the large emerging economies).

The significance of the Bank parting with the IMF's quota formula and the effects of this on the position of large emerging economies cannot be ignored. By including a country's economic weight as the most important variable, the formula enabled the fast-growing emerging economies to boost their formal political power in the institution. Importantly, just as the IMF did in 2008–2010, the Bank agreed to calculate a member's economic size based on a blend of GDP calculated at purchasing power parity (PPP) and GDP calculated at market exchange rates, with the former constituting 40 percent of the blend (hence the latter is 60 percent of the blend).[10] The inclusion of GDP at PPP had long been the preference of emerging markets, whose economies are relatively larger by that measure (Chapter 5). Also, the member states inserted some dynamism into voting realignment in the institution by agreeing to update shareholding every five years, in a manner that the IMF's Articles of Agreement foresees for that institution. Such a commitment to regular revision of shareholding was previously absent from the Bank. From the perspective of the rising states, this dynamism provides them with the potential for further position enhancement in the future.

Despite these innovations, the 2010 shareholding formula reform left the large emerging economies' preferences unfulfilled in a number of critical ways. These states preferred the GDP blend in the 2010 shareholding formula to consist more of GDP calculated at PPP rates than GDP calculated at market exchange rates (e.g., Chidambaram 2008; Chawla 2009; Indrawati 2009; Mantega 2008). Table 6.3 presents the differences between these countries' GDPs at PPP versus market exchange rates. EW1 (economic weight 1) in this table calculates the

---

[10] PPP exchange rate is the rate at which a similar bundle of goods and services can be purchased in different countries.

Table 6.3 *Country GDPs – different calculations*

	GDP (2006–2008 average) at ME	GDP (2006–2008 average) at PPP	EW1 (60ME-40PPP)	EW2 (40ME-60PP)
Brazil	1,375.59	1,850.87	1,565.70	1,660.76
China	3,575.70	7,263.53	5,050.83	5,788.40
India	1,104.22	3,079.10	1,894.17	2,289.15
Russia	1,316.83	2,095.40	1,628.26	1,783.97

Source: Author's calculations based on the WDI. ME is at current prices, US$. PPP is current international US$. The numbers are in billions.

economic weight (GDP) of the emerging market based on the 2010 World Bank formula: the 60–40 blend of, respectively, GDP at market exchange rates and GDP at PPP. EW2 reverses these respective weights to be 40–60. Like the World Bank formula, the table takes the 2006–2008 averages. The differences between EW1 and EW2 for these leading emerging markets are non-negligible. Hence, a number of rising states' representatives repeatedly pushed for an emphasis on GDP PPP in the formula. In a representative statement, the Indian official to the Development Committee remarked: "any blend should be overwhelmingly weighted in favor of GDP-PPP" (Mukherjee 2009). The Brazilian representative underscored that "reform should fully embrace the PPP methodology (which the World Bank itself helped design) to assess the relative weight of countries in the global economy" (Mantega 2008). In the same manner, the Russian representative discussed the role of the Russian economy in the world based on GDP-PPP and expressed that the voting power should consider this measurement (Kudrin 2009).

Another area where large emerging markets' preferences were not reflected concerns the small role "development contributions" play in the Bank's new shareholding formula (weighted as 5 percent of the new formula). The notion of development contributions is an all-encompassing concept with which the Bank aims to tackle numerous concerns in calculations of shareholding (and thus voting power). As the Bank puts it, "the term can encompass the move to equitable voting power, incentives for future DTC [developing country] IDA contributions, protection of voting power of the smallest poor members and client shares" (DC2010-0006/1). This last item in the Bank's list – client shares – denote the shares of those that rely on the World Bank loans (both concessional and non-concessional).

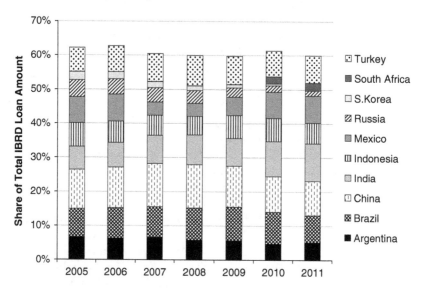

Figure 6.1 IBRD loans to G20 emerging economies. *Source:* Author's own calculations from IBRD Financial Statements 2005–2011. Y-axis presents the loans as a percentage of the amount of total loans approved.

A focus on client shares helps one understand why the formula fell short of the rising states' expectations from the reforms. Client shares are important for the large emerging markets because they continue to borrow from the IBRD. Figure 6.1 demonstrates the extent to which the emerging economies in the G20 have recently relied on the Bank. This figure shows that these states received about 60 percent or more of the loan amounts the IBRD dispersed in 2005–2011. The figure also shows that, during these years, China received 10 percent or more of the total IBRD loan amount. Other high recipients include Brazil, Turkey, and Mexico. The Bank documents indicate that client shares were excluded from the 2010 formula revision simply because the members' views on it diverged (e.g., DC2010-0006). Other documents also emphasize that the contribution of the loan charges to the IBRD's finances is unclear, and that the asymmetries between small and large borrowers make client shares a slippery concept (DC2009-0011, p. 6). These points indicate that some members rejected the inclusion of client shares because they found the contribution of the interest the institution earns from lending as insignificant to the institution's expenses. Whether or not this point represents the truth is less important than its implicit implication that the advanced economies, which are lenders to the Bank, did not find the large borrowers' financial contributions justified the inclusion of client shares.[11]

In contrast, leading up to the 2010 reforms, a number of emerging economies emphasized the necessity to give borrowers an enhanced voice in the governance of the Bank. In a representative statement, the Brazilian delegate to the Development Committee (Mantega 2009) emphasized that "[b]orrowers' contributions should be recognized for the purposes of shareholder realignment" (see also Chawla 2010; Chidambaram 2008; Yong 2008). A number of officials from the rising states directly tied their demands for increasing voice to their increasing financial contributions, not just in terms of their enhanced contributions to the IDA, but also in terms of their contributions as borrowers from the institution (e.g., Mantega 2008; Mukherjee 2009). The rising states consider their reliance on IBRD loans to serve the interests of the World Bank group in important ways (also Pincus and Winters 2002; Weaver 2007). Financially, the interest from these loans contributes to the IBRD's income directly. According to one count, in the fiscal year 2008, income from IBRD loans constituted 25 percent of the IBRD's gross income (Zedillo 2009, p. 26, footnote 42). Because the IBRD transfers resources to the IDA, the large emerging markets also consider themselves to contribute indirectly to the IDA. Non-financially, borrowers contribute to the Bank by being sources of new development knowledge.[12] These types of arguments, however, did not have enough traction with the advanced economies in 2008–2010.

In accordance with the large advanced economies' preferences and adding to the grievances of the rising states, amid the reforms in 2010, the Bank increased its IBRD loan pricing, overturning a reduction instituted in 2007. Here, remarks by Christine Lagarde (2008), who is the former French finance minister and the current head of the IMF, are telling: "The IBRD is facing a deterioration of its medium term financial outlook and a downward trend in its net income ... The decline of the Bank's net income is partly attributable to the falling interest rates but has clearly been compounded by measures taken [in 2007] to lower the pricing of IBRD loans." In gaining a sense of the counter-perspective, consider the following remark by China's delegate to the Development Committee: "we object to shifting the burden and cost to developing countries through initiatives such as IBRD increases" (Xuren 2009). The Russian representative echoed the same viewpoint: "we have to express our serious opposition to an emerging

---

[11] The only exception here was the German representative, who expressed a preference for the formula to include the Bank's clients' voice more systematically (Wieczorek-Zeul 2009).

[12] From a more critical perspective, they act as laboratories for the Bank's work.

idea of continuous [p]rice [i]ncreases as the major method for achieving certain pre-determined income generation benchmarks" (Kudrin 2009). The increase in loan pricing without an explicit acknowledgement of borrower contributions in the new shareholding formula suggests again the limited nature of the accommodation.

Further, the rising states' expectations for parity in voting power between developed and developing member states of the Bank also did not materialize in the 2008–2010 reforms. Many emerging markets, including Argentina, Brazil, China, and Saudi Arabia, emphasized the importance of parity pre- and post-reform (e.g., Al-Assaf 2009; Bodou 2009; Yong 2007a, 2007b, 2009). At the end of the 2008–2010 changes, however, the advanced economies still ended up retaining the majority shares in the institution. The notion of parity is not a helpful concept in guiding voting power reform at the Bank (for the opposite perspective see Zedillo 2009). It distracts from the disparities within each of the groupings (developed and developing), especially at a time when the large emerging economies are increasingly differentiating themselves from the rest of the developing world. Further, meaningful parity among countries at different levels of development can only be achieved with the redefinition of those levels of development – the categories of developed and developing are too generic. These normative assessments aside, by sidelining the issue of parity, the 2008–2010 shifts fell short of the large emerging markets' expectations.

Another reform that featured in institutional discussions in the lead up to the 2008–2010 changes, but not in the outcome of these changes, to the dismay of the rising states, was transformations to the IDA's decision-making processes (DC2007-0024). The IDA can be best characterized as a donor-dependent institution, with the large advanced economies as its primary donors. More than 70 percent of the IDA's financial capacity comes from Bank member states' donations. The representatives of donor countries, known as the IDA Deputies, make the core decisions of the IDA. The identities of the IDA Deputies are not disclosed, and consensus, and not voting, is the method of decision-making, which further decreases transparency and enhances accountability problems, both internally (within the institution) and externally (to the outside world) (Zedillo 2009).[13] While the Bank reports that the recipient countries have increased their participation in recent years in these negotiations, the donors continue to hold sway over decisions.[14]

---

[13] On internal and external accountability, see Keohane (2003).

[14] For instance, in the latest replenishment of the IDA (IDA 16), twelve representatives from borrower countries were present at the negotiations.

Because the top donors to the institution remain the large advanced economies, the rising states, such as China, wanted this donor-dominated decision-making of the institution to be reformed (Yong 2007b). At the same time, the rising states justify seeking changes to the governance of the IDA based on their contributions to the IBRD's income, given the IBRD transfers funds to the IDA (e.g., Yong 2007b). Yet, the 2008–2010 changes left the governance of the IDA intact.

Also, related to the IDA, the key rising states had serious reservations with the recognition of donations to this concessional lending arm of the Bank in the new IBRD shareholding formula. This new shareholding formula, as noted earlier, counts IDA donations in a cumulative, not marginal, manner. And, from the start of the IDA to IDA15, which provided the funds for the institution from 2008 to 2011, the G20 large advanced economies provided approximately 75 percent of the IDA's funds; whereas, the G20 large emerging markets provided only about 3 percent of these funds, despite the fact that these states have recently increased their contributions to the institution (author's own calculations).[15] As these numbers suggest, counting IDA contributions in a cumulative manner increases the importance of the declining states for the institution; hence the rising states' objections to it. For instance, the former Brazilian Minister of Finance, Guido Mantega, rejected the idea that development assistance "should become a precondition for enhancing the voting power" of developing countries (Mantega 2008). The Chinese representative repeated the same point: "We have a strong reservation on the ODA [official development assistance, namely foreign aid] linkage" (Yong 2008). More directly on the issue of cumulative versus marginal and future contributions, the Saudi Arabian representative also advanced the notion that "contributions should be measured in terms of not only ability, but also willingness" in the context of voice reform (Al-Assaf 2009). In contrast, representatives from the declining states either did not engage with these requests, or explicitly stated a preference for calculating contributions to the IDA on a cumulative basis (e.g., Minekazi 2009). While one could advance arguments to defend the position of either the rising or the declining states, the upshot here is the cumulative counting of IDA contributions in the Bank's new shareholding formula ran contrary to the rising states' demands.

---

[15] Out of the BRICs, India continues to be a recipient only from the IDA, and the other members of the group are all small contributors to it. By my calculations, China has increased its share of the total contribution to the institution from being 0.1 percent in IDA15 to 0.48 percent of total contributions in IDA16. Brazil's and Russia's contributions to IDA 15 (IDA16) are, respectively, 0.62 (0.30) percent and 0.35 (0.50) percent of the total contributions.

Overall, while the 2008–2010 reforms boosted the formal political power of the large emerging markets in the World Bank, they fell short of meeting some of their key preferences and hence point to the declining states' limited accommodation of the rising states.

Outcomes in the World Bank compared to the outcomes in the IMF

Comparing the shifts in formal political power within the Bank in 2008–2010 with the results of the shifts in formal political power at the IMF in the same time period affirms the limited nature of the accommodation in the Bank. Table 6.4 supports this point. The table again displays the rate of change for the voting power of different groups of states. The rates of change show that, generally, in terms of redistributing voting power away from the declining states to the rising states, the reforms went deeper in the IMF than in the World Bank. For instance, the rate of change for the G20 emerging economies was about 19 percent in the Bank; whereas, this number was approximately 28 percent in the IMF. The differences in the gains of some individual states are stark: the rate of change for China was about 59 percent in the Bank compared to 107 percent in the IMF. In turn, the losses for some declining states were less extensive in the Bank than in the IMF. For instance, the rate of change for the G20 European economies was less than negative 11 percent in the Bank, but it was more than negative 14 percent in the IMF.

Table 6.4 also shows that the USA's post-reform position in the two institutions is comparable to its pre-reform position, despite losses to its voting power. As the table shows, compared to the other members of the group of large advanced economies, the USA suffered the least amount of losses to its formal political power. Also, as in the previous (1988) capital increase, the USA retained its veto power. In the 1988 capital increase, the US contributions translated into the US voting power decreasing to 18.75 per cent of the total vote, thereby undercutting the USA's then ability to veto the changes to the Bank's Articles of Agreement. In order to retain the US veto, the Bank Board increased the requirement of the 80 percent majority to 85 percent (Babb 2009, p. 137). Although no such change to the 85 percent threshold was necessary this time around, voting realignment was in all likelihood done with consideration to the US veto power, given key US domestic audiences' emphasis on retaining the veto (US Senate 2010).

Table 6.4 also shows the gains the poorest shareholders made in the World Bank versus the IMF as a result of the reforms. Judging by

Table 6.4 *States' post-reform voting power (%) in the World Bank and the IMF*

Group/state	World Bank			
	Pre-2008	Post-2008	Post-2010	Rate of change
G20 advanced	44.37	43.07	40.59	−8.52
USA	16.36	15.85	15.85	−3.12
G20 European	15.86	15.4	14.14	−10.84
Japan	7.85	7.62	6.84	−12.87
G20 emerging	18.8	18.73	22.3	18.62
China	2.78	2.77	4.42	58.99
Sub-Saharan Africa	4.72	5.29	5.07	7.42
LDCs	3.78	4.37	4.3	13.76
LICs	3	3.44	3.35	11.67

Group/state	IMF			
	Pre-2006	Post-2008	Post-2010	Rate of change
G20 advanced	46.621	44.347	42.535	−8.76
USA	*17.023*	*16.727*	*16.479*	−3.20
G20 European	19.068	17.529	16.372	−14.14
Japan	*6.108*	*6.225*	*6.138*	0.49
G20 emerging	17.411	18.973	22.241	27.74
China	*2.928*	*3.806*	*6.071*	107.34
Sub-Saharan Africa	4.083	4.477	4.252	4.14
LDCs	3.025	3.5787	3.6312	20.04
LICs	2.435	2.7759	2.7869	14.45

Source: Author's calculations from Bank and IMF sources.

the rate of change, the Sub-Saharan African economies made relatively larger gains in the World Bank than in the IMF. However, the other two classifications for the poorest states (the LDC and LIC classifications) show greater gains for these states in the IMF than in the World Bank. Had the 2010 reform not occurred, the Bank reforms would have been more advantageous to the poorest states than the IMF reforms in terms of voting power (see above). However, when the poorest states are broadly considered, it is not possible to reach a conclusion that the 2008–2010 shifts in members' formal political power benefitted these states more in the World Bank than in the IMF.

Explaining the outcome of limited accommodation

The three factors at the center of the adjusted power approach explain the primary outcome of limited accommodation well: (1) the large advanced economies' conceptualizations of the role the large emerging markets play in the provision of the World Bank's intended global good of economic development; (2) these rising states' role in the financing of the World Bank (the IBRD and the IDA); (3) the rules and conventions regarding the adjustments of members' formal political power within the institution. Because (1) and (2) are interlinked, I will analyze them together.

Tensions over the IBRD

Although the large emerging markets are crucial for the Bank's mission of economic development, they rely on the Bank less as a "development agency" and more as a "bank" – a situation that the large advanced economies find unpalatable.[16] The large emerging economies, by definition, have managed to engender economic growth. They have also done so in ways that have often contradicted the Bank's advice (e.g., Rodrik 2008; for opposing perspectives see Dollar 2007; Wolf 2004). Thus, their reliance on the Bank as a development agency has diminished (Einhorn 2006). Yet, these states not only continue to be major borrowers from the IBRD, they also would like to continue to rely on it.

The supply side – why the Bank is loaning to large emerging economies – is self-explanatory. The World Bank, as a bank, is driven by the necessity to make loans. The large emerging markets need larger loans and have lower levels of risk of not being able to repay them, though default on Bank loans has in general not been an issue even with poorer states. The empirical literature on the determinants of multilateral aid also point to the large emerging economies as the likely receivers of loans through the Bank (e.g., Burnside and Dollar 2000; Alesina and Dollar 2000; Fleck and Kilby 2006; Neumayer 2003; Winters 2010). This literature shows, for instance, that more funds go to more populous countries (e.g. Fleck and Kilby), and that less poor countries receive more aid than poorer countries (see Neumayer). These findings from the literature on the determinants of foreign aid reinforce the point that factors other than the economic need of the recipient governs aid giving.

Furthermore, maintaining the large emerging markets as borrowers serves the Bank's self-preservation. Simply, as a former official of the Bank has emphasized, whether or not the IBRD survives as an institution

---

[16] See Gutner (2005) for this distinction in a different context.

depends on middle-income countries, such as the rising states examined in this book (Einhorn 2006). If the IBRD is completely displaced by private capital flows, which the rising states can access relatively easily, then it will cease to exist. Additionally, as Birdsall and Subramanian (2007) report, the Bank's lending to low-income countries has declined significantly over time. The Bank's lending to countries that are eligible to borrow from the IDA dropped to less than 8 percent of the total external resources received by these countries in 2005 from about 17 percent in 1995. In this context, the Bank's lending to the relatively larger economies increasingly matters in maintaining a client base. During the writing of this book, the BRIC countries have been in the process of setting up their own bank for financing development projects. Such a forum-shift by these rising states would threaten the World Bank's livelihood. As Robert Zoellick noted, letting the large emerging markets displace the Bank with alternative institutions would be a "mistake of historic proportions" for the Bank and its institutionally dominant members.[17]

Non-financially, the IBRD loans allow for a two-way transfer of knowledge, including expertise building in specific issue-areas. The Bank's close working relationship with borrowers, such as China, serves the purpose of expanding the Bank's knowledge capacity. In fact, the Bank emphasizes in various documents the important role countries like China play in providing development experience to others (e.g., Annual Report 2008). In sum, the Bank not only relies on the large emerging markets to keep the IBRD financially alive, but its reputation as a development agency rests on it maintaining good relations with these countries and learning from their experience.[18] This point, however, does not change the overall picture that these rising states count on the Bank more as a bank than a development agency; it merely suggests that the Bank's role as a development agency may not be completely diminished.

The demand side of the large emerging markets' reliance on loans from the IBRD is less self-explanatory than the supply-side of these loans because the private capital flows to these countries minuscule the public funds from the IBRD. Still, there are financial reasons as to why a country might prefer funds from the IBRD and not from private capital markets. IBRD loans tend to be slightly below market rates with relatively longer maturity terms. Also, members can borrow in their own currencies. At the same time, the importance of counter-cyclical funds suggests that during economic downturns, public funds through the Bank are important. And,

---

[17] Quoted in "Zoellick throws support behind Brics bank," *The Financial Times,* April 1, 2012, online.

[18] This last point relates to previous discussions on the necessity for the Bank to move away from the Washington Consensus.

it is not always the case that the private sector would be willing to provide capital for any type of project, necessitating Bank funds for some projects. An example here is investment projects with no obvious immediate pay-offs (Rajan 2008). Additionally, the Bank loans do not necessarily displace private capital as they can often complement and enable it, such as through the facilitation of private-public partnerships.[19] Furthermore, if we accept the plausible assumption that "even in the absence of external loans, governments would fund the best projects from their own resources," then funds through the IBRD permit governments to pursue non-core projects without devoting immediate resources to them (Pincus and Winters 2002, p. 11). In sum, the rising states' reliance on the Bank as a bank has a number of plausible explanations.

In this context, the large emerging markets would like to continue to rely on IBRD loans and would in fact like the IBRD to better tailor its instruments for the middle-income countries (e.g., Boudou 2010; Guangyao 2010; Kudrin 2011; Mantega 2011; Mukherjee 2011). The following two statements, by Chinese and Indian representatives, support this point:

The World Bank has acquired from MICs net income and development experiences which have become the Bank's direct financial and knowledge resources for the low-income countries. Meanwhile, MICs face enormous development needs and require the Bank's long-term and effective assistance. Such cooperation features a new development partnership based on equality and mutual benefit. (Yong 2007b)

Since the Bank's comparative advantage as a knowledge institution derives primarily from its operational presence in a large number of countries through its lending program, in our view, the main task for the Bank should be to ease access to IBRD and design more customized and innovative products to address the specific needs of middle income countries. (Chidambaram 2007)

In addition to keeping the IBRD loan pricing at relatively low levels, an example to how the Bank, from the rising states' perspective, can better tailor its services for IBRD countries concerns the use of "country systems." Although the Bank has traditionally relied on "special project implementation units" (PIUs) when it funds projects in a country, it has over time switched to country systems, namely reliance on the existing national or sub-national institutions and laws of a country. Bank documents indicate that the reliance on country systems increases the role of country ownership and helps build capacity in the country. It also reduces

---

[19] More generally, the Bank loans can grant credibility to specific projects and ease, if not enable, the flow of private capital. It is not clear, however, how much this signaling effect of Bank loans is needed for the large emerging markets. It is likely more important for the poorer countries.

the costs for the state implementing the project because the state does not have to create and monitor additional institutions for Bank projects.[20] Large emerging markets would, for instance, like the country systems approach to be strengthened to reduce the non-financial costs of borrowing from the IBRD (e.g., Kudrin 2007).

The tensions between the two key sets of shareholders – the rising and the declining states – over how the IBRD should be utilized manifests itself in different ways. The USA prefers the Bank to primarily serve the poorest states. US Secretary of the Treasury, Timothy Geithner, has expressed the American vision for the Bank in clear terms: "the United States continues to view the World Bank as the leading global institution focused on supporting the development needs of the poorest countries, and we rely on the Bank to remain squarely focused on programs and policies to help the most fragile nations grow" (Geithner 2010c, p. 3).[21] His emphasis on serving the poorest countries and his reference to the most fragile nations is intended to disagree with the notion of the Bank as providing funds and services to the middle-income countries in a significant way. Importantly, Geithner's point is consonant with the general US preference for the emerging markets to access financing from the private capital markets and predates his administration (see Bird and Rowlands 2006, p. 156). Further, the conservative political opinion in the USA is particularly (but not exclusively) skeptical of the emerging markets' usage of IBRD resources. The following testimony made to Congress by a member of a conservative think-tank, the American Enterprise Institute, is emblematic:

When China buys a $3billion stake in private equity giant Blackstone, with the expectation of a 25% annual return, the World Bank is busy lending to China at a 5% interest rate which does not even cover the Bank's real cost of borrowing. The Bank should not be lending to the world's third [now second] largest economy. (Lerrick 2007, p. 2)

As this quote suggests, the rising states' borrowing from the IBRD is domestically a hard sell in the USA, which contributes to explaining the US position on the IBRD, though the rationale for that position is less important for the purposes of this study than the position itself. At the same time, other members of the large advanced economy grouping also share the US perspective. The aforementioned tensions between the large advanced economies and large emerging economies over loan pricing are effectively about whether or not the large emerging economies should be accessing relatively cheap loans from the Bank. To the extent that other

---

[20] A representative document that discusses these points is Operations Policy and Country Services (2005).

[21] US Senate (2010) confirms this view.

states support the increases in loan pricing, they are implicitly supporting increasing the emerging economies' costs of access from the IBRD.

In short, the declining and rising states do not converge on their expectations of how the Bank should pursue its goal of global economic development and where institutional priorities lie. In turn, the tension between the two sides regarding the Bank's pursuit of its intended global good encourages the declining states to limit the rising states' position enhancement. Relatively greater position enhancement by the rising states would give them greater voice within the IBRD thereby, in all likelihood, affecting the trajectory of the institution in a manner contrary to the declining states' priorities. At the same time, the tensions between the declining and the rising states regarding the core functioning of the IBRD help understand their attitudes toward the financing of the institution.

The impact of the Bank's financing

The nature of the Bank's financing segues into the tensions between the rising states and the declining states regarding institutional priorities in two primary ways. First, the two sides do not agree on whether and the extent to which the IBRD should finance the IDA. As noted earlier, part of the IDA's financing comes from the IBRD. Large advanced economies have expressed their preference to have the IBRD resources to continue to finance the IDA and at increasing levels (see, e.g., Geither 2011). Following directly from the US preference to have Bank funds serve the poorest states, the US representatives have also pursued to have IBRD funds service the IDA: "we have pushed for … more effective use of the capital we provide by transferring more of the resources from the middle income 'hard loan' windows to the poorest countries …" (Geithner 2011). Some representatives from other declining states have even introduced the idea for IDA-only countries to be considered for access to financing from the IBRD, which would effectively channel the funds available for middle-income countries to poorer ones (Shinohara 2008).

In contrast, the large emerging markets are unhappy about the push to transfer more funds from the IBRD to the IDA. The rising states not only wish to limit their contributions to the IDA, seeing the institution as the richer countries' responsibility, they also wish to retain the funds available to them through the IBRD (see above). As the Indian representative to the Development Committee puts it, "And to those who see an IBRD-IDA trade-off, they may note that 70% of the world's poor live in middle income countries which are IBRD clients" (Mukherjee 2009). In other words, the Bank should continue to assist middle-income countries.[22] Similarly, the Brazilian Finance Minister, Guido Mantega, underscores: "We cannot shift the burden of replenishing IDA to the World Bank Group or else we will put to risk the financial health of this institution as a whole" (Mantega 2007b). This last point about different sides' preferences over how the various constituent parts of the Bank should be financed is ultimately about a tension regarding the core functions and purposes of the Bank – with the large emerging economies preferring to have an IBRD with a strong lending capacity.

The second primary way in which the nature of the Bank's financing relates to tensions between the rising states and the declining states concerns the fact that the manner in which the IBRD is financed lowers any tendency the declining states might have for burden sharing. Particularly, the IBRD relies relatively little on large, immediate capital infusions from member states. The IBRD raises most of its funds through the sale of its triple-A rated bonds. Because of this ability to raise funds in international markets, the Bank relies on little paid-in capital from the member states, even though the members states determine its gearing ratio, thereby deciding on how leveraged the institution can be. An example from the 2010 capital boost to the Bank is instructive here. The 2010 capital boost of $86.2 billion to the Bank came mostly in the form of callable, and not paid-in, capital. The paid-in portion of this $86.2 billion was $5.1 billion in total (for both the GCI and the SCI). This small paid-in portion affirms the long-term trend that "the influence that comes with ownership has become less expensive" over time (Kapur 2002, 348). Additionally, the chances of callable capital being drawn are low. In fact, the Bank has never demanded its callable capital, which contributes to the Bank's triple-A rated status (Kapur 2002).[23] Despite the limitations on the Bank's financial independence – the gearing ratio and its triple-A status being at least partially underwritten by its callable capital – the Bank is nonetheless leveraged. Thus, compared to the IMF, which remains a quota-driven institution, the Bank relies less on upfront capital infusions from member states (see Chapters 3 and 5). For these reasons, the large emerging markets are less immediately needed for the institution's funding than they are for that of the IMF's, though their importance for bolstering the IBRD's capital (paid-in and callable) cannot be overlooked.

---

[22] The intensity with which the large emerging economies would like to continue to utilize the IBRD's resources varies – some states, such as India, are relatively keener to continue relying on it (Interviews).

[23] The Bank's status as a preferred creditor with very low default rates from borrowers also contributes to its high rating.

To sum, in the case of the World Bank, there was not a strong enough impetus for financial burden sharing that could have motivated relatively higher position enhancement. The manner in which the members fund the IBRD dampens the declining states' tendency for burden sharing. Thus, compared to the IMF, the IBRD's funding structure creates a weaker rationale for the declining states to concede to greater position enhancement by the rising states. Plausibly, in the absence of tensions between the rising and declining states over the Bank's institutional priorities, the burden sharing rationale could have had a different impact on the 2008–2010 shifts. Also reasonably, had the Bank's financing completely depended on immediate financial infusions from members, the financial burden-sharing rationale could have worked differently. In reality, however, the relatively lower pressure for financial burden sharing reinforced the declining states' already existing tendency for limited accommodation. These points beg the question of whether the burden-sharing impetus worked differently in the IDA, which is a donor-funded institution.

While the institutionally dominant but economically declining states aimed to shift some of the burden of the financing to the IDA, their status quo-oriented approach regarding the governance of the IDA and the linkage between the IDA and the IBRD did not provide an incentive to encourage greater burden sharing by the rising states. Numerous documents indicate that the declining states preferred the rising states to increase their IDA contributions. Nonetheless, they were not willing to alter the existing governance structure to realign the rising states' incentives. Prominently, as already noted, during the 2008–2010 changes to the governance of the Bank, change over the structure of the IDA was generally off the table. Additionally, the manner in which IDA contributions have been linked to the IBRD disincentivizes the rising states from making large increases in their financial contributions to the institution. The declining states regard cumulative IDA contributions as a significant determinant of economic weight in the Bank (through the formula). In this context, Christine Lagarde claimed that was it was "inconceivable that the same small group of shareholders, particularly the Europeans, should continue to shoulder responsibility for IDA, while their voting rights are being reduced [in the Bank's shareholding] as a consequence of their diminished economic weight" (Lagarde 2009). If, for instance, the declining states had entertained the idea of counting in the low but nonetheless increasing contributions of the rising states to the IDA, or their "willingness to contribute" as one representative had suggested, then more room for altering dynamics could have potentially opened up. Yet, the cumulative nature of counting IDA contributions ruled out this scenario. Simultaneously, the declining states' pursuit of a stronger IBRD-IDA financing connection effectively aimed to enhance the rising states' role in the financing of the institution without increasing their importance as donors per se (because they would not be directly contributing to the institution). In sum, the large advanced economies' desire to maintain their control over the IDA countervailed their desire to increase the large emerging economies' financial contributions to the institution.

Effects of existing rules and conventions

During the 2008–2010 reforms, the member states only partially broke with the institution's tradition of mirroring IMF quota changes. As noted earlier, 2008 was the first time that the Bank devised its own formula for calculating shareholding (and hence voting power) in the institution. The Bank has followed the IMF in a number of ways, including relying (in different ways) on the calculations that resulted from the IMF quota formulae. The Bank has also had "parallel share adjustments" to follow shifts in members' formal political power in the IMF, though this parallelism has neither been one-to-one, nor has it been consistently pursued.[24]

In addition to the absence of the Bank's own formula for shareholding (until 2008), political convenience explains this particular linkage between the two institutions. Bank documents, for instance, emphasize that when the negotiations in the Bank follow those in the IMF, the Bank can inherit the political convergences already forged by the lengthy IMF negotiations. Bank documents pertaining to the 2008–2010 changes specifically underscore this point by emphasizing that the IMF quota shifts signaled political consensus among the same set of member states that would have to agree to similar changes at the Bank (e.g., DC2007-0024). Although going as far back as 1975 the members as well as the staff questioned the advisability of this linkage between the two institutions, this connection was not addressed until 2008 (World Bank 1975, p. 17).

The 2008–2010 changes, however, only partially broke with the Bank's convention of following IMF quota adjustments. The Bank's new formula directly borrows the IMF's specific GDP blend (see Chapter 5). A World Bank document (and not the only one to do so) details the IMF's rationale for the GDP blend:

---

[24] Available documents suggest there was not a single way in which the Bank used the IMF quota formula as a benchmark, and Bank share adjustments after 1984 did not follow the IMF.

This approach [the specific blend of market exchange rates and PPP] captures the central role of quotas in the Fund's financial operations, for which GDP at market exchange rates is the most relevant, as well as the Fund's non-financial activities, where PPP GDP can be viewed as a relevant way to capture the relative volume of goods and services produced by economies. (DC2009-0011, p. 5)

These institutional considerations implicitly suggest that during the 2008–2010 reforms the linkage between the two institutions was once again on the table. It also hints at doubts about following the IMF GDP blend within the institution. Indeed, as another document noted, "the Bank has an independent need to deal with the Voice issue and the considerations that it needs to take into account are different from the Fund. Of particular importance, the Bank needs to give special consideration to the representation of the poorest countries and to the role of the IDA" (DC2007-0009/1, p. 5). Although the suitability of the formula to the Bank's specific institutional features was on the table during 2008–2010, following in the IMF's footsteps in terms of the measurement of the GDP effectively removed from the agenda a discussion of alternative measurements. For instance, the Indian representative had put forward a proposal to include poverty measures and infrastructure needs in order to assess members' potential need for Bank resources, but such proposals were not pursued (Chidambaram 2007). Regardless of the merits of alternatives, the convention of following the IMF narrowed the paths available in the Bank.[25]

Moreover, the Bank followed the IMF's lead on the question of basic votes, which are distributed equally to member states. In 2008, the IMF member states tripled the share of basic votes and fixed their portion as 5.502 percent of the total votes (Chapter 5). The Bank mirrored this very shift at the IMF. The relatively more ambitious scenarios were ruled out because "a number of key donors … indicated that an increase in basic votes should be linked to parallel action at the Fund" and thus it was "considered unlikely that support could be obtained for an increase higher than the one being proposed at the Fund" (DC2007-0024). Notably, however, this same change offers different implications for the two institutions. In the Bank, the basic votes were doubled, but not tripled as in the IMF. More crucially, as numerous Bank documentation including the ones cited in this Chapter highlight, the Bank's self-professed mission concerns the poorest states; therefore, on an issue that directly and significantly concerns the poorest members of the institution, the Bank's following of the IMF's lead suggests that the actual outcome potentially differed from one that could have been obtained, had the

---

[25] On path dependence, see Chapter 2.

member states considered and followed an institutional logic unique to the Bank.

Taken together, the tensions between the rising and the declining states' priorities for the Bank, the specific manner in which the members finance the IBRD with little paid-in capital, and the Bank's tradition of following the IMF in adjusting members' formal political power explain well why the declining states' accommodation of the rising states was limited in the Bank.

Alternative explanations

In this section, I consider alternative explanations with a view to assessing their potential contribution to the 2008–2010 changes in the Bank. I find these alternatives to hold relatively less explanatory power than those advanced in the previous section.

Alternative Explanation 1: The ramifications of the Great Recession explain the 2008–2010 changes to formal political asymmetries.

As in the case of the IMF, the 2008 financial crisis does a better job of explaining the timing of the 2010 reforms but not their content (see Chapters 1 and 5 on the crisis). The credit crunch caused by the Great Recession facilitated a politically opportune environment for a share-holding increase in the Bank, thereby contributing to the understanding of the timing of the 2010 changes, though not their content. The 2008–2010 changes to formal political asymmetries in the Bank are known in the institution's discourse as "structural reforms." Even though these structural reforms had long been in the making, the political support necessary for them had previously been lacking (e.g., DC2008-0013). As in the IMF, since at least the 2002 Monterrey Conference, increasing the formal political power of developing countries had been on the Bank's agenda. Yet, given the lack of adequate support from the membership, earlier efforts to increase the voice of developing countries at the Bank focused on reforms upon which the membership could easily converge. For instance, earlier changes provided the Sub-Saharan African constituencies on the EB with additional advisors and created a Voice Secondment Program for the training of civil servants from developing countries.

Yet, the opportunity for "structural reform" hinged upon the Bank getting a capital increase, so that the political climate could be more permissive of shareholding realignment. Just a year before the 2008 financial crisis, the members could not forge a consensus on the need for capital increases (selective or general). As a 2007 document noted, "some may see the SCI [selective capital increase] as an inefficient

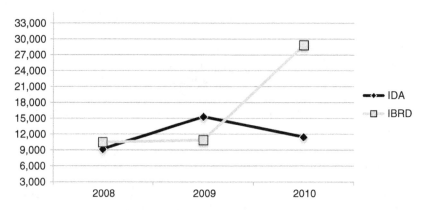

Figure 6.2 IBRD and IDA disbursements (in million USD). *Source:* Author's calculations from World Bank Annual Reports.

instrument for adjusting the relative shares among members, especially when the Bank has sufficient capital to meet the foreseeable borrowing needs of its clients" (DC2007-0024, p. 14). In other words, shareholding realignment had to wait for a general capital increase. The 2008 crisis provided that window of opportunity for the Bank members and staff to seek capital increases. Figure 6.2 shows the Bank's lending during the Great Recession. For now, ignoring the differences between the IBRD and the IDA, the figure displays the rising demands on the Bank's resources, which compelled the members to converge on boosting the institution's capital. The capital increases, in turn, generated political momentum for the structural reforms that had long been on the institution's agenda. In other words, while the members had long recognized the need to adjust relative shares (and thus voting power) in the institution, prior to the crisis there was no political consensus on a capital increase that would have facilitated such shareholding realignment.

Even in this case, however, the Bank's tradition of following the IMF may have been more important than the crisis in explaining the outcome. As a Bank document explicitly put it, "[a]dvances on structural elements of reform ... have awaited the results from discussions on Quota and Voice Reform at the Fund [the IMF]" (DC2008-0013, p. 1). To the extent that the IMF changes to formal political asymmetries underwrote the same kind of changes in the World Bank, then the Great Recession's contribution to the *timing* (but again not the content) of the 2010 shifts in the IMF are worthwhile to mention (see Chapter 5). In any case, perhaps the question of "did the Great Recession have an effect?" is less interesting than the question of "why did the Great Recession impact the IMF and the World Bank differently?" Providing an answer to this second question, in turn, demands the kind of analysis that this chapter already provided.

Alternative Explanation 2: The World Bank's staff's preferences explain the 2008–2010 shifts in formal political asymmetries.

A number of different points militate against this point, although the staff/management's role in the 2008–2010 changes cannot be ignored. They not only provided the technical analyses that discussed how the numbers (on members' shares and voting power) would pan out under different kinds of scenarios, but they also communicated the institutional conventions. For instance, even a brief perusal of the Bank documents returns common references to "here is how we have done it in the past" type statements, including the Bank's manner of relating to IMF quota adjustments. Yet, the evidence is not strong on the Bank's preference affecting the 2008–2010 changes.

First, based on analyses of bureaucratic politics, one can safely assume the staff would have preferred a larger increase than the 2010 boost, given their interest in extending loans and thus keeping themselves in business (e.g., Vaubel 1991; Weaver 2008). Yet, as already noted, the 2010 increase was in line with the Bank's historical average, even though it occurred during a watershed, the deepest crisis since the Great Depression. In this context, the staff appear not to have been able to leverage a historical opportunity. For instance, the 1988 increase had doubled the Bank's capital, whereas the 2010 increase constituted about a 30 percent raise. This point suggests the members were in the driving seat. In fact, there have been accounts of the then Bank president Zoellick needing to visit four continents to generate enough support for the capital increase, with the institutionally leading states being especially reluctant.[26] Evidence from the Bank's history also suggests that the Bank management usually had to settle for smaller increases than their initial ask (see Kapur et al. 1997).

Second, many of the cases that previous research identifies as reflecting a high level of staff influence designate issue areas, where members have delegated to the staff relatively more extensively, such as the drafting of loan agreements.[27] In contrast, the change in Bank's shares and members' voting power remain under the control of member states, namely delegation to the staff is close to non-existent beyond the kind of technical input discussed. The reasons for this member-driven process have already

---

[26] See, for instance, "World Bank President Zoellick Said to be Near Securing Capital Increase," Bloomberg online, April 1, 2010. (Last accessed: October 31, 2013).

[27] See, for instance, discussions in Chwieroth (2008); Hawkins et al. (2006); Weaver (2008).

been highlighted and include prominently the formal rules surrounding share and voting power changes (Chapter 3). Specifically, not only do the share adjustments require a special majority, but also the member's standing in the institution cannot be altered without that member's consent. Generally, the political sensitivity of share adjustments means the members scrutinize and debate these changes extensively. For instance, in 2007, the Executive Board spent 65 percent of its time on topics related to "policy," which includes big picture issues regarding the Bank's general direction including questions of shareholding.[28] In contrast, it spent only 16 percent of its time on lending. Put simply, when delegation occurs, there is little Board contemplation, while the opposite holds true when little delegation occurs. Hence, virtually every document that discusses shareholding within the Bank, regardless of whether they are written by staff or not, includes the word "political consensus" because when member states are not in agreement, the management faces limited room for maneuver.

Alternative Explanation 3: The rising states were not interested in relatively higher levels of position enhancement in the Bank.

This alternative explanation explores whether or not the preferences of the rising states explain the outcome (e.g., Kahler 2013). While the preferences of the rising states regarding the increases in their formal political power cannot be overlooked in any institution, the rising states' expressed preferences relate closely to the room for accommodation the institutionally dominant but economically declining states provide. Put differently, the parameters for the level of position enhancement the rising states can push for is limited by institutionally leading states' willingness for accommodation. If the leading states were willing for greater levels of accommodation, would the rising states bother to achieve higher position enhancement? The plausible answer is the affirmative one.

Emerging economy representatives have consistently expressed a desire to increase the voice of developing countries in the World Bank (e.g., Mantega 2008, 2011a, 2011b; Xuren 2011). At one point, the Chinese representative emphasized that they did not want a selective capital increase in the absence of a redistribution of voting power away from the declining states, and, more importantly, called for "developed countries to demonstrate political will" for shifting the asymmetries in formal political power in the Bank (Yong 2008). Yet, these demands ran into the declining states' low political will for relatively higher levels of accommodation. The following comments by Christine Lagarde are

---

[28] These numbers were calculated based on Annex V of World Bank (2008).

representative: "whereas the reform of the IMF was logically aimed at achieving better representation of the new balance in the world economy, reform of the World Bank should not aim at this objective exclusively" (Lagarde 2008). Higher levels of position enhancement would allow the rising states to more effectively pursue their preferences, including their desire to shape the IBRD loans after their own interests on the cheap, given there is little paid-in capital to the institution.

While it is true that the rising states did not express much interest in increasing their commitments to the IDA, this lack of interest cannot be analyzed in isolation from the declining states' preference for the status quo (see above). Although key rising states, particularly Brazil and China, did make contributions to this concessional lending arm of the Bank, they nonetheless regarded IDA replenishment as the declining states' responsibility. On this point, the Chinese Vice Minister of Finance, Zhu Guangyao, explained:

We call on developed countries to heighten their political will and take concrete actions to honor their commitments to ODA [official development assistance], thereby ensuring a substantial increase of funding to IDA-16. Developing countries, on the other hand, may supplement IDA-16 funding according to their own capacity ... As a developing country with a large population, China has on its shoulders an arduous task of handling its own domestic poverty reduction. Nevertheless, China is willing to support, within its capacity, to IDA funding. (Guangyao 2010, emphasis added)

The Brazilian perspective did not differ significantly from this stance (e.g., Mantega 2007). On its own, the rising states' lack of willingness to take on greater responsibilities at the IDA might be read as their lack of interest in the institution. But, such a reading is incomplete and potentially misleading. The rising states consider themselves to be contributing to the IDA through their borrowing relationship with the IBRD, given the transfers from the latter to the former. Further, because the declining states did not look favorably upon altering governance in the IDA, the rising states did not face a situation in which their greater financial contributions to the IDA would have translated into greater voice either there or in the IBRD. In short, the rising states' expressed preferences cannot be understood in isolation from the room for accommodation the declining states provided.

Explanation 4: The 2008–2010 changes can be explained with the institution's (member states' and the staff's) concern with the position of the poorest states.

Did the 2008–2010 changes primarily target the institutional position of the poorest member states, which helps understand the rising states' limited position enhancement? This question comes down to whether the gains the low-income countries made account for the rising states' limited position enhancement. The 2008–2010 changes on paper embraced two goals – to prop up the formal position of the low-income countries and to reflect the enhanced importance of emerging economies in the global economy. In this regard, the 2008–2010 reforms to formal political power should have been expected to garner some gains for the poorest states.

The rising states' limited accommodation cannot, however, be explained with the gains the poorest states made. The G20 advanced economies (i.e. the institutionally dominant, but economically declining states) lost 3.78 percentage points in voting power, and the G20 emerging economies (i.e. the rising states) gained 3.5 percentage points in voting power, while the least developed economies (LDCs), which made the biggest gains out of the poorest states, made a gain of 0.52 percentage points in voting power (see Table 6.2). These numbers suggest that most of the losses in voting power experienced by the declining states were redistributed to the rising states. It is, thus, difficult to argue that the Bank's concern with poorest states can explain the outcome of the 2008–2010 changes in members' formal political power.

Other evidence also confirms this point. The doubling of the basic votes was conservative in comparison to previous reform discussions at the Bank. Prior to the 2008 reform, the Bank member states had considered tripling the portion of basic votes in total voting power (8.10 percent) or even restoring it to its original level (10.78 percent) (e.g., DC2008-0013; DC2007-0009; DC2007-0024). As already noted, the IMF members tripled, not doubled, the percentage of basic votes because they mirrored the IMF's decision. Put differently, the large advanced economies ("key donors") were reluctant for a significant increase in the basic votes.

Further, the 2010 share realignment eroded some of the gains the smallest members of the Bank made through the doubling of the basic votes (see Table 6.2). There is no doubt that, on average, these countries made gains in 2008–2010. If we take Sub-Saharan African states as a group, pre-2008, this group's voting power was approximately 4.7 in the institution, while post-2008, the group's voting power exceeded 5 percent. Similarly, if we take the Least Developed Countries (LDCs), pre-2008, the group's voting power was approximately 3.8 percent, while its post-2008 voting power was approximately 4.4 percent (see the tables above). Still, with the 2010 shifts, the Sub-Saharan countries and the LDCs shares dropped by, respectively, 0.25 and 0.07 percentage points. Given how minuscule these countries' voting shares already are, these numbers are worth noting. More importantly, as Table 6.4 shows, the rate of change for the poorest states was not generally higher than it was in the IMF.

Finally, although the 2010 reforms added a third chair for Sub-Saharan Africa (SSA) on the Bank's EB, this reform was again not ambitious compared to prior institutional discussions. The addition of the third chair raised the total number of EDs to 25. During the reform process members had considered "a reduction in the number of EDs appointed or elected by industrial countries," but given that this reform was not followed through, representation on the Board still looks skewed against the poorest members (DC2007-0009/1, p. 11). In the absence of a reduction in the number of other Board seats, only three EDs will serve 47 Sub-Saharan African countries. By contrast, three European countries (France, Germany, and the United Kingdom) have their own appointed EDs, and there are four other constituencies that are heavily dominated by EU members. Furthermore, the addition of a Board chair offered legal and budgetary feasibility compared to alternative changes, which would have enhanced the position of the poorest states relatively more. The addition of the Board chair did not require an amendment to the institution's Articles of Agreement and was considered as relatively "budget neutral," as the other two SSA EDs were willing to release advisors for the creation of the third ED and share a travel budget across the three constituencies (DC2008-0013). These discussions reveal that the formal political power of the poorest states in the Bank ended up being a marginal aspect of the 2008–2010 reforms.

Conclusions

The finding that the 2008–2010 shifts in members' formal political power in the World Bank garnered relatively little gains for the rising states – when compared to prior reform discussions in the Bank and when compared to the outcomes of similar changes in the IMF – supports the adjusted power approach advanced in this book. The adjusted power approach expects that the tension between the rising states' desire for position enhancement and the declining states' desire to limit this position enhancement (namely, engage in limited accommodation) to be resolved in favor of the former if the declining states reason that position enhancement will contribute to the fulfillment of the institution's intended global good in accordance with their own expectations. In the case of the IBRD, however, the large advanced economies and the large emerging economies disagree on how the institution's intended global good should be achieved. In this respect, increasing the formal political power of the rising states at higher rather than lower degrees can distract from the declining states' vision for the institution.

At the same time, in accordance with the expectations of the adjusted power approach, because the rising states are relatively less important for the Bank's financial resources, compared to the IMF, the declining states' willingness to boost the position of the large emerging economies was limited. Two features of the Bank's funding help explain this outcome. One, the Bank, compared to the IMF, is relatively less reliant on upfront capital infusions from states, given its ability to raise debt on international financial markets. Two, the IDA remains donor-dependent, and the large advanced economies remain as its primary donors. While the large advanced economies wish to have the rising states increase their share of the IDA's funding, they are not willing to abandon their control over the institution. For instance, discussions about the IDA's governance structure, which is also donor-dominated, were off the table during the 2008–2010 changes, despite the rising states' expressed discontent with that structure. So was a shift in the way in which IDA contributions are calculated – the current way of putting an emphasis on cumulative calculations retains the declining states' control over the IDA. In short, the financing of the Bank (both the IBRD and the IDA) reinforced the dominant states' tendency for limited position enhancement.

The chapter also noted the importance of existing rules and conventions in explaining the 2008–2010 shifts in members' formal political power. Particularly, while the 2008 changes marked a departure from the Bank's tradition of changing shareholding in accordance with quota shifts in the IMF (Chapter 4), this break was only partial. The Bank, despite coming up with its own shareholding formula and integrating non-IMF-based criteria into calculations of shareholding, nonetheless waited for the results of IMF changes before proceeding with its own set of similar reforms to formal political power. Further, the doubling of the basic votes in the Bank mirrored the IMF change. This final point is of particular importance not only in highlighting the Bank's path dependence on the IMF, but it is also indicative that a pure institutional logic was not pursued in the Bank. Had the 2008–2010 changes been based only on the Bank's institutional purpose and rationale, there could have been a case made for a different level of basic votes. Put simply, the analysis of the intersection of power and institutions provides different outcomes than expectations based merely on institutionalist reasons.

Beyond these points, the analysis here offers some insights into the possible future direction of the Bank and questions about its legitimacy, which motivated the 2008–2010 changes in the first place, as discussed at the onset. The 2008–2010 reforms have left intact some of the key tensions between the declining and rising states. For instance, the chapter argued that the two sides diverge on their preferences regarding how the

IBRD's resources should be utilized. The rising states wish to continue relying on IBRD funds and want the institution to refine its instruments and decrease the costs of accessing its loans. But, the large advanced economies, at the very least, want to increase the cost of access for the large emerging markets (as illustrated by the example of loan price increases in 2010), better yet dissuade these states from using the Bank's resources. This disagreement over the IBRD's resources also illuminates a divergence about how the Bank should pursue its intended global good of economic development. While the rising states regard their borrowing from the institution as an important aspect of the institution's pursuit of global economic development, the declining states prefer the institution's resources to be primarily devoted to the poorest states.

The chapter's discussions also reveal tensions over the IDA. The IDA, as shown, remains donor-dependent with the majority of the donors from the large advanced economies. These declining states would like the rising states to increase their contributions to the IDA. But, this would alter the declining states' hold over the institution and, most likely, increase the pressure on them to agree to reform the governance of the IDA. For instance, the rising states would likely press to have the IDA EDs exert more influence over the institution, instead of the IDA Deputies (see above). At the same time, given that the IDA remains the province of the advanced economies, it is not clear what motivations the rising states have in investing more resources into it until they know such investment also comes with influence. Thus, the declining states' expectations might be self-contradictory – they want to remain in charge of the institution and share the burden of financing it with the rising states, but the latter is more feasible only with their declining influence over the institution.

Although the reforms left the declining states at the helm of the institution, they nonetheless represent the slow beginning to long-term change, as the recent process of the selection of the Bank's new president shows. After the 2008–2010 changes, the Bank membership set out to select a new head to fill the position after Robert Zoellick's departure. The process of the election of the president has long been a contested issue because the USA has always had the informal privilege of "selecting" an American to the position. Despite widespread calls within and outside of the institution, the new Bank president also ended up being an American, Jim Yong Kim. Given that the Americans and the Europeans have the majority of voting on the Bank's EB, their support sealed the American candidate's selection. While the ending was familiar, the process of Dr. Kim's selection was not. For the first time in the Bank's history, developing nations put forward two candidates, the Nigerian Ngozi

Okonjo-Iweala and the Colombian José Antonio Ocampo. The fact that the developing nations challenged the selection process points to the slow beginning of long-term change. It may be tempting to write off the 2008–2010 shifts as merely incremental. Yet, their importance is best judged not by their putative incrementality, but rather their contribution to our understanding of the institution's evolution, including critical features of the declining and rising states' interactions with the institution.

7   The G20: a delegatory institution

Under the leadership of the heads of state of a number of large advanced economies, including the USA, the UK, and France, the G20 reformed itself from being a forum for finance ministers and central bank governors to one for heads of state with its inaugural summit on Financial Markets and the World Economy on November 15, 2008, in Washington, DC.[1] The same advanced economies, along with Canada, had formed the G20 in 1999 with a view to addressing issues of international financial stability in the aftermath of the 1997 Asian financial crisis.[2] Less than a decade later, the inaugural summit of the reformed group came roughly a month after the collapse of Lehman Brothers in the USA, which many scholars mark as the beginning of the greatest global financial and economic crisis since the Great Depression.[3] In this respect, while a crisis among the emerging markets led to the creation of the G20, a crisis among the developed economies facilitated its upgrade.

The reformed G20 did not end up as a momentary by-product of the 2008 global financial crisis. In their Pittsburgh Summit in September 2009, the G20 members declared their designation of the group as "the premier forum for [their] international economic cooperation" (G20 Pittsburg 2009). This elevation of the G20 meant the supplanting of the G7. Various leaders from the G20 member states have expressed the significance of the G20 for global economic cooperation. For instance, President Obama called the 2009 London Summit a "turning point in our pursuit of global economic recovery."[4] Russian president Medvedev remarked, "it currently is the only forum where we can discuss issues of

---

[1] Member states of the G20 are: Argentina, Australia, Brazil, Canada, China, France, Germany, India, Indonesia, Italy, Japan, Mexico, Russia, Saudi Arabia, South Africa, South Korea, Turkey, the United Kingdom, the United States. The EU, as a union, is the twentieth member.

[2] For a detailed history of the G20 meetings, see Bradford and Lim (2011).

[3] This 2008 global economic crisis is now commonly referred to as the Great Recession. For comparisons between the two crises, see, e.g. Frankel and Saravelos (2010) and Eichengreen and O'Rourke (2010).

[4] CBS News online, April 2, 2009.

the world economic order openly, directly and quite efficiently."[5] Hu Jintao, the Chinese president, similarly noted that coordination through the G20 has been effective.[6] Since its new beginnings in 2008, the G20 has scheduled its tenth summit for heads of state at the time of the writing of this book. Given that the upgrading of the G20 has also meant the demotion of the G7, the G20's assent is one of the most important reforms to global economic governance in recent history (e.g., Eichengreen 2009).[7]

Since its first summit for heads of state, the G20 has tackled a range of issues regarding global economic governance, including the reform of multilateral economic institutions, particularly the IMF and the World Bank, the regulation of the global financial industries, efforts to engender global economic growth and ensure global food security. The upgrade of the G20 also directly facilitated the expansion of the Financial Stability Forum (FSF) into the Financial Stability Board (FSB). FSB includes the G20 emerging economies, and the G20 has mandated it to act as an umbrella institution for the coordination of financial standards and policies (Helleiner 2012; Lombardi 2011). At the same time, other standard-setting bodies reformed to expand their membership to include the emerging economies of the G20, as the inaugural meeting of the G20 declared standard-setting bodies to "review their membership" (Lombardi 2011, p. 5). The reform of these other sub-global institutions was a by-product of the enhanced status of the G20. The G20 has, thus, become a central institution in the governance of the global economy.

The case of the G20, *prima facie*, appears to contradict one of the core findings of the preceding chapters of this book: the shift in formal political asymmetries, namely the (economically) declining states' accommodation of the rising states is a contentious process. While the claim of the book has been that the declining states face a number of reasons for accommodating the rising states in institutional platforms, the book has also postulated and shown that these declining states will, by and large, aim for limited accommodation (Chapters 2, 5, and 6).[8] In the case of the G20, however, key leaders from advanced economies seem to have recognized the shifting distribution of power and responded to it by revamping the G20. Consider the following explanations by Gordon

---

[5] BBC, "Russian President says negative trends persist in global economy, praises G20", June 22, 2010.

[6] http://news.xinhuanet.com. October 10, 2010.

[7] The G7/8 meetings have continued in addition to G20 summits. The Interviews I conducted also suggested the G7's demotion. For a detailed analysis of the G7, see Baker (2006).

[8] The book has consistently defined declining states as those that are in economic, but not necessarily in institutional decline (Chapters 1 and 2).

Brown, the British prime minister at the time of the reforms, and George W. Bush:

For forty years after the Second World War the G7 was responsible for around 70 percent of all world economic activity. Only in the past twenty years has the G7's share of world output fallen dramatically, from above 70 percent in the early 1990s to around 40 percent on the eve of the world-wide recession in 2008. . . . this mean[s] we could not simply rely on the G7 to deal with the crisis [the Great Recession]. (Brown 2011, p. 115)

The financial crisis was global in scale, and one major decision was how to deal with it in the international arena ... Nicholas Sarkozy, the dynamic French President ... urged me to host an international summit. The question was which countries to invite. I heard that some European leaders preferred that we convene the G-7 ... But the G-7 included only about two thirds of the global economy. I decided to make the summit a gathering of the G-20, a group that included China, Russia, Brazil, Mexico, India, Australia, South Korea, Saudi Arabia, and other dynamic economies.[9] (Bush 2010, pp. 465–6)

To explain the upgrade of the G20 with mere reference to the shifting inter-state distribution of economic power, however, leaves out key questions. Particularly, that simple explanation does not account for why that very distribution elicited frictionless accommodation in the case of the G20, but not in the two Bretton Woods institutions.

The case of the G20 contrasts with the IMF and the World Bank in other ways. In the G20, the rising states seem to have made no demands regarding either the formation or the upgrade of the G20 (Kirton 2011). In contrast, in the IMF and the World Bank, pressures on the legitimacy of the institutions and the rising states' demands for change in formal governance prompted the process of the reform of formal political asymmetries (Chapters 5 and 6). In this respect, in the case of the G20, the declining states' accommodation of the rising states was not just voluntary but also discretionary. Further, the declining states' designation of the G20 as a "premier forum" after 2008 deepened that accommodation, which can be seen as an extension of that discretionary move. Also, in the Bretton Woods institutions, the declining states conceded to accommodation under formal asymmetry, given the presence of weighted voting and its ramifications; whereas, in the case of the G20 the declining states led accommodation under a decision-making system that is relatively egalitarian.[10] Thus, not

---

[9] As Martinez-Diaz (2007) notes, the US actors preferred to revamp the G20 (as opposed to another institution) because of its inter-governmental nature, namely the lack of participation by non-state actors, be they the staff of international financial institutions or financial actors.

[10] I do not use "egalitarian" to suggest actual equality in decision-making, but rather symmetric decision-making rules (regardless of whether or not these rules are codified).

only did the rising states engage in discretionary accommodation, but they also specifically pursued it in an institution that gave more or less equal formal voice to the rising states.

Given the lack of demand for change from the rising states, the declining states could have reasonably gotten away without upgrading the G20, and they could have also avoided solidifying that upgrade in subsequent G20 meetings. Instead, they chose to take a different route – the route of discretionary accommodation that was also (relatively) frictionless. What explains this puzzle?

The book has throughout suggested that the specifics of different institutional settings mediate the importance of the underlying inter-state distribution in economic power. This claim invites a close look at the G20's institutional design and setting. This chapter argues that the G20 can best be described as a "delegatory" informal institution: the G20 delegates specific tasks concerning the global economy to more formalized international economic institutions, such as the IMF and the World Bank. The delegatory nature of the G20's informality helps explain the low "sovereignty costs," namely the "surrender of national discretion," associated with the institution (Moravcsik 2000, p. 227; also Abbott and Snidal 2000). Low sovereignty costs, in turn, lessen the importance of the asymmetries in members' formal political power.

The rest of the chapter begins with the institutional design of the G20 and then proceeds to examine the functions and purposes of the institution, which remain crucial to both validating and examining its status as an informal delegatory institution.[11] In arguing that the G20's delegatory informality contributed to the declining states' discretionary accommodation of the rising states, the chapter also addresses alternative explanations, including both explanations that focus on power *or* institutions, but not the intersection of the two.

The G20's institutional design

Although the upgrading of the G20 has triggered a rich literature, much of the literature does not provide a comprehensive understanding of the institutional features and functions of the G20. Rather, the emphasis

---

[11] Given the paucity of *comprehensive* information about the G20, the researcher has to piece together disparate pieces of information in many different documents. For instance, as of September 15, 2011, the G20 website (www.g20.org) did not even list the G20 working groups (there is an empty page for it). In this respect, this chapter also contributes to the literature in the most basic way of making information available. An exception here that I came across after completing this chapter is Kharas and Lombardi (2012), which discusses the institutional features of the G20 but still focuses mostly on issues of representativeness and effectiveness.

concerns how the G20 deals with specific issue areas (e.g., compilations by Brookings 2010; Bradford and Lim 2011). This chapter fills in this gap regarding the G20's institutional design, highlighting its relatively egalitarian features of decision-making.

Relative equality of decision-making within the G20

Figure 7.1 presents the basic structure of the G20. The chair of the group belongs to one of the member states, and the chairmanship rotates every year. The chair cooperates with the most recent past chair and the forthcoming chair in a troika. The troika format aims to ensure continuity across different Presidencies. As omitted from Figure 7.1, the G20 does not yet have a permanent Secretariat for the coordination of its activities, namely a permanent office for executive functions. Yet, both the Korean (2010) and the French (2011) Chairs have expressed support for establishing one.[12] Crucial to G20 summits are the role of sherpas, the member states' primary representatives and negotiators. The meetings of the sherpas facilitate states' convergence on an agenda and its negotiation. The G20 also meets in the form of finance ministers and central bank governors (usually) on an annual basis. Although the sherpas are in charge of the broad coordination of the G20's work, the financial and economic matters with technical content tend to be negotiated through representatives from finance ministries (Lesage and Kacar 2010). The working groups, which have increased in number since the 2009 London Summit, carry out the substantive work of the G20. Figure 7.1 displays a sampling of these working groups, which are fixed neither in number nor content. A team of advanced economy and emerging market member states chair the working groups.[13]

Three features of the G20 permit a relatively egalitarian (namely, equality in formal political power) decision-making process: (1) its emphasis on consensus building underwritten by formal equality; (2) the rotational chairmanship; (3) the chairing of the working groups by a team of advanced and emerging economies.

The G20 decision-making process emphasizes the equality of each member. As an unwritten rule, the decision-making procedure rests on consensus building underlined by equality of membership. As the G20 indicates, "[w]ithout a charter, votes, or legally binding decisions, members interact as equals. Emphasis is given to reaching consensus on

---

[12] See, e.g., "G20 to discuss establishment of secretariat" in the *Korea Herald,* October 28, 2010, accessed online.
[13] For a summary of the G20 summits see Kharas and Lombardi (2012).

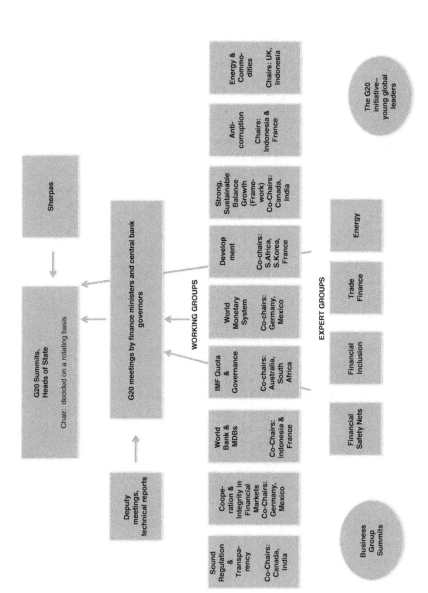

Figure 7.1 The G20's institutional structure

important issues" (G20 History 2008, p. 24). The notion of equality in formal political power should not be taken to suggest that in practice all interactions within the G20 are of equal consequence for the decisions taken, or that every country's agreement with specific agenda items is of identical import. Rather, the expectation of membership is for equal input. In practice, the emphasis on equality means that members of the G20 that are relatively small players (sometimes referred to as "middle powers"), such as Turkey, consider the G20 as a valuable outlet for international influence (Lesage and Kacar 2011).

Another feature that makes the decision-making of the G20 relatively egalitarian is the rotating chairmanship of the institution. When the G20 was established as a group of finance ministers and central bank governors, the member state consensus was that "there should be an equitable annual rotation among all regions and between countries at different levels of development" (G20 History 2008, p. 23). The chairmanship of the institution can give the chair state an enhanced profile in international relations as well as leverage for being able to shape the group's agenda in accordance with that state's priorities. The implication of this point is that when the large emerging markets chair the G20, they are able to insert some of their preferences into the summits. Prominently, the South Korean chair made an effort to get the G20 to produce a document on economic development, known as the "Seoul Consensus on Development." Indeed, as discussed below, the Seoul Consensus on Development reflected many of the priorities of large emerging markets regarding economic development.

The final feature of the G20 that makes the decision-making within the institution relatively egalitarian is that a team of large advanced economies and large emerging economies chairs the working groups (Figure 7.1). The working groups undertake the substantive work of the G20 and the chairs coordinate and oversee that work. For instance, the work on the quota reform in the IMF benefitted from the output of one of these working groups. The 2005 *G20 Statement on Reforming the Bretton Woods Institutions* provided the background for the 2006 voting changes at the IMF and subsequent reforms in 2008 and 2010 (Chapter 5). The chairing of the working group does not facilitate the kind of influence that the chairmanship of the G20 as a whole can engender. Nevertheless, that a team of advanced economies and emerging markets are in charge of steering the work of a single working group suggests the non-hierarchal organization of the G20's affairs.

G20's relative egalitarianism in practice   While some have called into question the relatively egalitarian features of the G20 on grounds that the two heavyweights, the USA and China, dominate the grouping, the evidence does not support this criticism. Schneider and Wilson (2010), for instance, assert that "[t]here may be many seats at the table, but the central debate revolves around the 'G-2'." Although there is no denying the importance of the USA and China and the agreement between the two for the G20, the reduction of the G20 to G2 is an over-simplification of the institution.[14] It is plausible that the G20 could become dysfunctional if the USA and China refuse to negotiate on any core issues. Also, the G20 provides the USA and China with another multilateral platform to scrutinize and place pressure on each other's policies, such as China's putatively under-valued currency. These points do not, however, mean that G20 equals the G2. As an expert familiar with G20 negotiations notes, "[t]here is no evidence of the G20 being a substitute for U.S. hegemonic control" (Cooper 2012). Chinese and US negotiations within the context of the G20 promise to be different than outside the context of the G20, given that other states can weigh in and affect the negotiations. Moreover, the G20 constitutes the collective grouping necessary for addressing spillover issues, such as the negative spillovers that arise during a global financial crisis. For instance, even if the USA and China were to agree on how much capital banks should hold (namely, how leveraged they can be), other major international bank-originating countries, including those in Europe, would be necessary for international coordination on this issue. In sum, equating the G20 with the G2 is an over-simplification.

Further, the content of the G20 discussions is marked more by fluid coalitions based on issue area than a power struggle between the advanced and emerging economies (Patrick 2011; Schirm 2011). When it comes to global imbalances between surplus and deficit countries, for instance, the surplus countries, specifically Germany and China, opposed the US Treasury Secretary Timothy Geithner's proposal to have specific targets for addressing imbalances. Another example concerns the topic of bankers' remuneration, which put the Americans along with the British and continental Europeans on opposing ends. While some issues, such as the extension of the agenda to economic development, discussed below, unite the emerging market members of the G20, generally, coalitions within the G20 shift based on issue area. And, more often than not, these groups involve coalitions of advanced economies and emerging markets. The presence of fluid coalitions also suggests that dominance

---

[14] Baker's study (2006) reaches a similar conclusion regarding the role of the USA in the G7.

by a select group of great powers over the decision-making processes of the group is not easy.[15]

The previous points about the relatively egalitarian nature of the institution can also be criticized on grounds that the G20 has followed the G7's path on a number of key areas, including some central financial issues such as standards and codes (e.g., Martinez-Diaz 2007).[16] This criticism, in effect, would suggest that while the G20 might be relatively equal in giving representation to member states, the large advanced economies still dominate the institution to the point that the rising states, namely the large emerging economies, are not able to use the relatively egalitarian features of the institution to shape the agenda in accordance with their own preferences, even when they have relatively homogenous preferences. If one could show that the rising states were able to affect (or shape) the G20's agenda, then this criticism would be invalidated.

Indeed, the emerging economies within the institution have affected the content of the G20's agenda and actions. For one, the emerging economies have been the primary members of the G20 pushing for the inclusion of development issues into the group's agenda to the contrary of the advanced economies' preferences.[17] Since the G20's inception, with the exception of Australia, the group has ventured into development issues under the chairmanship of emerging markets.[18] For instance, India (2002) and Mexico (2003) oversaw the inclusion of development issues for the first time into the agenda of the G20 finance ministers and central bank governors' meetings, and China (2005) also pursued this topic during its chairmanship. Similarly, the reform of the Bretton Woods institutions was put on the agenda during the Chinese chairmanship (2005) and was later pursued by South Africa (2007) (G20 2008).

Since the upgrading of the G20, many emerging economy members have pushed for the expansion of the G20 agenda to address issues beyond those of a strictly financial nature, including economic development. As already noted, the Korean chairmanship played a critical role in producing the Seoul Development Consensus. At the same time, the Turkish ambassador to the Seoul Summit highlighted the G20's expansion into development issues as a requirement for the group: "Its agenda should be expanded in a phased manner to cover other

---

[15] Baker's analysis (2006, Chapter 2) on the G7 also suggests the importance of non-power based coalitions in consensus decision-making.

[16] Yet, Martinez-Diaz agrees that the non-advanced members of the G20 are indeed able to affect the G20 agenda.

[17] This does not mean the G20 works toward the benefit of the poorest countries, who are non-members.

[18] Given that Australia is not a member of the G7, it has consistently supported the notion of the G20 and the inclusion of emerging markets as a key aspect of its legitimacy.

related topics, such as the development issues, food security, poverty eradication, climate change, energy security, etc."[19] Along the same lines, the Chinese vice-foreign minister expressed "[Developing countries'] demands and development needs should be fully reflected at G20 through various channels."[20] Similarly, the Chinese president Hu Jintao underlined the importance of addressing North-South issues within the group in numerous instances.[21] The Mexican president advanced a comparable rationale in discussing development issues during the Seoul Summit: "Promoting worldwide development from a broad and cross-cutting perspective should be the G20's ultimate goal."[22] Overall, emerging economies in the G20 have successfully pushed the group to address economic development.

The large emerging markets have also, disputably, made a substantive difference to the G20's development agenda by emphasizing the importance of a diverse set of approaches to economic development. For instance, under the Chinese leadership (2005), the G20 documents have advanced the importance of various models of economic development in their communiqué: "With regard to the diversity of growth models and development approaches, we are committed to strengthening the dialogue on varying development philosophies, strategies, and policies, from which all countries can benefit" (G20 Communiqué 2005). Of relevance, Wonhyuk Lim (2011) of the Korean Development Institute differentiates the advanced economy approach to development as the "endowment" view and argues that East Asian countries embrace the "bootstrapping-ingredients" perspective on development. The former focuses on the government setting up the "framework," namely institutions, and ensuring these are the appropriate institutions before letting the market work toward development. In contrast, the latter model emphasizes a constant government role in fine-tuning the institutions and removing bottlenecks in development. Having identified these two different paradigms, Lim suggests a central role for the G20 in creating a platform for knowledge sharing on successful development strategies. As this example from Lim's essay shows, the G20 has the potential to widen the perspectives on development, though this widening might not necessarily meet the demands of the poorest states, as Chapter 8 discusses.

[19] Quoted in "G20 is legitimate, effective response to global challenges" in *The Korea Herald*, November 9, 2010.
[20] "Chinese official urges G20 members to 'help each other in the same boat' on November 7, 2010.
[21] See, e.g., "Hu Jintao answers South Korean media's questions on G20 ... " on www.bbc. co.uk on November 12, 2010.
[22] Quoted in "G20 will be a lever for enhancing global development" in *The Korea Herald*, November 8, 2010.

Overall, the large emerging markets have led the inclusion of economic development in the G20's agenda.

Crucially, this agenda expansion has occurred against the wishes of the advanced economies in the G20. Specifically, the Europeans, the USA, and Canada have expressed their desire to restrict the G20 to "economic issues," which they understand narrowly as financial issues.[23] These members prefer for cooperation at the G20 to primarily center around global finance. The Europeans justify an opposition to the expansion of the G20 by worries about it replacing already existing multilateral plat-forms, such as the World Bank and the IMF. Yet, others note that the G20 "dilutes" the influence of Europe, which likely explains European resistance to the expansion of the G20's responsibilities.[24] In short, then, existing evidence suggests that the rising states have managed to utilize the relatively egalitarian structure of the institution to exert some influ-ence over its agenda.

Given the G20's relatively equal decision-making procedures, it becomes even more puzzling that the declining states would take the G20 – a marginal forum for finance ministers – and upgrade it to a central forum for heads of states, without any demand from the rising states (i.e. the large emerging economies). As Chapter 2 noted, while the declining states confront a plethora of reasons for accommodation, they also face a number of reasons for limited accommodation. Thus, probing the expla-nations behind the declining states' discretionary accommodation of the rising states in the context of an institution with relatively egalitarian features is important.

Explanations: G20 as an informal, delegatory institution

The rest of this chapter argues the nature of G20's informality helps understand this smooth accommodation. Informal institutions often involve un-written documents, and even when written, they tend to contain vague terms of cooperation and unclear levels of commitment by states (Lipson 1991). At the same time, Executives of states tend to negotiate informal institutions, as Lipson emphasizes, without domestic ratification procedures and in a speedy manner. The G20 displays these

---

[23] For instance, see statements by Edward Lipman, ambassador of Canada to the G20, quoted by the *Korea Herald* in "Ambassadors divided over role of G20" on May 26, 2010, versus statements by his Turkish counterpart, Erdogan Iscan, and his South African and Mexican counterparts.

[24] The quote is by Edwin Truman in "Old world fault lines evident at G20" in *The Gazette* (Montreal) on September 25, 2009; see also statement by the Head of the European Commission, Jose Manuel Barroso, in the same piece.

different qualities. When the large advanced economies created the G20 in 1999, they bestowed it with the imprecise purpose of addressing challenges to international financial stability. This core function is not only broad, but also remains open to interpretation. Similarly, when the leading advanced economies reformed the G20 into a forum for heads of state, they left its institutional objectives general. Consider the following explanation from the erstwhile US president, George W. Bush:

> On November 15, every leader at the summit signed on to a joint statement that read, "Our work will be guided by a shared belief that market principles, open trade, and investment regimes, and effectively regulated financial markets foster the dynamism, innovation and entrepreneurship that are essential for economic growth, employment, and poverty reduction ... " It sent a powerful signal to have countries representing nearly 90 percent of the world economy agree on principles to solve the crisis. (Bush 2010, p. 466)

This passage indicates a vague purpose for the institution – the addressing of the 2008 global financial crisis through a commitment to generally liberal markets. Other leaders' recollections affirm this lack of specificity during the institution's upgrade in 2008 (e.g., Brown 2010; Darling 2011). This is not to deny the G20 undertaking of important tasks, such as the provision of coordinated fiscal stimuli in key economies during the crisis. But, the members did not deliberate or articulate such specific functions in advance.

Another point relevant to the G20's informality is the group's unspecified selection process for membership, though there are latent criteria for membership. Initially, the USA and Canada invited the original members of the G20 in the lead up to 1999. Some commentators thus criticize the G20 for having membership "handpicked" by the USA (e.g., Aslund 2009). The G20 does, however, consist of economies that are "systemically important." The members of the G20 are not only among the largest economies of the world, measured by GDP, they are also central to trade and financial flows (see Chapter 5). In 2000–2009, the total economic output of the G20 members, excluding the EU as a whole, was approximately 80 percent of the world's economic output.[25] Additionally, the G20 contains some of the most important energy exporters (Russia, Saudi Arabia) and energy importers (China).

But, the G20 does not include all of the world's largest economies. Some economies that could be included based purely on GDP criteria are left out. Wright (2010, p. 182), for instance, notes the absence of Spain as the world's ninth largest economy. Eichengreen (2009) notes the absence of Iran in the group, which, he emphasizes, is a larger economy than

---

[25] Author's own calculations from WDI, GDP measured at constant 2000 US$.

Argentina. The fact that the G20 does not exactly correspond to the list of the world's largest economies can be explained by both the fact that the USA decided on its initial membership, predictably leaving out Iran for instance, and by the importance of regional representation in the group.[26]

Geographical representation evidently constitutes another feature of G20 membership, as the grouping contains some of the most important economies from the Americas, Europe, and Asia. Yet again some have criticized the membership of the G20 both on the grounds of over- and under-representation of certain regions (e.g., Cooper 2010; Fues and Wolff 2010, p. 21; Shorr and Wright 2010; Bradford and Lim 2011). As widely noted, while South Africa is the only member from the African continent, there are four states that are members of the EU, and the EU is additionally counted as the twentieth member (see footnote 196).

At the same time, non-member states and organizations also participate in G20 meetings on an *ex-officio* or non-permanent basis. Spain, for example, is a "permanent guest" (*ex-officio* member). So are the leaders of the IMF and the World Bank. The chairs of the International Monetary and Financial Committee (IMFC) and the Financial Stability Board, the general-secretary of the World Trade Organization, as well as the general secretary of the United Nations, also regularly attend the G20 meetings. At the G20 Leaders' Summit in Seoul in November 2010, member states reached a "broad consensus" that no more than five non-members can be invited to G20 summits, and out of these invitees two will be African states (see Seoul Summit Document 2010). Limiting the number of invitees to G20 summits reflects concerns about the effectiveness of the group, while the invitation of two African states is a direct attempt to address concerns about the under-representation of the African continent and the absence of low-income states altogether.[27] It can also be interpreted as creating another criterion for unofficial membership. In short, while the G20 documents do not clearly articulate the criterion of membership in the G20, subterranean requirements for membership in the group have emerged, including economic size and regionalism.

To sum, the G20 carries a number of the hallmarks of informal institutions. Although it has been defined in broad strokes (the institution has a general direction as well as latent guidelines for membership), the members have not delineated its institutional functions in a detailed fashion. Even a quick comparative perusal between G20 documents

---

[26] Having said this, the exclusion of Iran can also be justified based on its lack of membership in key economic forums, such as the World Trade Organization.

[27] These discussions of membership in the G20 should not be taken to suggest that all informal institutions lack clear guidelines for membership; rather, one of the informalities of the G20 lies in its non-existent rules for membership.

and the Bretton Woods' Articles of Agreement makes this point clear. Further, the creation as well as the evolution of the institution has remained in the hands of state Executives, away from the checks and balances or interference national legislatives tend to provide (Lipson 1991).

The delegatory nature of informality

Informal institutions, however, can vary in their design and function. Thus, how the G20 fulfills its vague but existent agenda, and what kind of an informal institution it is, deserves further probing. The G20, in my words, is a delegatory informal institution. Since the previous discussions have established the informal aspect of the institution, the delegatory dimension deserves exposition.

In tackling the global financial crisis and aiming toward reducing the risks of another crisis, the G20 has delegated various responsibilities to numerous multilateral bodies in a diverse set of areas, ranging from global accounting standards to the surveillance of the G20 economies to rules on banking. Table 7.1, with data gathered from all G20 summits up to September 2011, provides an overview of the major institutions to which the G20 has made delegations. Because the table is lengthy, I will not repeat all the information it contains here. As a key example, the G20 has tasked the IMF with the Mutual Assessment Process (MAP). Through the MAP, the IMF evaluates the G20 members' economies, explores the external implications of national policies, produces these results in reports, and makes policy recommendations. While the IMF provides reports on the state of the global economy, such as the Global Financial Stability Report, toward fulfilling its surveillance function, Article IV reports, which the IMF conducts bilaterally with members, constitute the core product of its surveillance efforts. The MAP, then, essentially enables the IMF to have another instrument toward undertaking multilateral surveillance. Similarly, as Table 7.1 indicates, the G20 states have tasked the IMF and the World Bank with carrying out Financial Sector Assessment evaluations. The effectiveness of these assessments aside, the G20 has again delegated a specific task and enabled the IMF and the World Bank with a tool for it. In another example, the G20 has delegated the mission of examining food security to other multilateral institutions, including the World Bank, the Food Agricultural Organization, and the IMF.

As these examples suggest, the notion of a delegatory institution differs from the common understanding of the G20 as an agenda-setter (e.g., Woods 2011). An agenda-setter might provide broad guidelines for

Table 7.1 *G20's delegation to other institutions*

Multilateral institution acting as an agent of the G20	Delegated tasks of the institution (major ones are listed)
Financial Stability Board	– surveillance of the global financial system with a view to assessing vulnerabilities, including Early Warning Exercises with the IMF
	– review the work of Standard-Setting Bodies
	– improve cross-border crisis management, including establishment and oversight of supervisory colleges for cross-border financial firms
	– development of macro-prudential tools, alongside the Bank on International Settlements
	– guidance on financial firms deemed as "systemically important," alongside the IMF
	– assist states with the surveillance of hedge fund activities
	– compensation mechanisms at banks
Basel Committee on Banking Supervision (BCBS)	– prudential regulation, including capital requirements for banks, strengthening of risk management in banks, harmonization of the meaning of capital across countries, the role of external rating in prudential regulation
International Organization of Securities Commissions (IOSCO)	– oversight of Credit Rating Agencies
	– review of regulation of banking, securities, insurance sectors (along with International Association of Insurance Supervisors) to assist cross-border cooperation
	– assistance with oversight of commodity futures markets through the recommendations
	– assist with hedge fund oversight

Table 7.1 (*cont.*)

Multilateral institution acting as an agent of the G20	Delegated tasks of the institution (major ones are listed)
International Accounting Standards Board and Financial Accounting Standards Board (IASB)	– improve accounting standards for the valuation in securities, transparency for off-balance sheet exposures, disclosure of financial instruments – IASB now has an "external monitoring" body, which includes the IOSCO and BCBS, to oversee cross-border cooperation in accounting standards
Various institutions, including the Global Forum on Transparency and Exchange of Information	– tax transparency and avoidance of tax havens – anti-money laundering and terror financing instruments
IMF	– Review SDR currency basket by 2015 to reflect currencies' changing roles, based on existing criteria – Creation of a new single facility to fulfill the emergency assistance needs of its members (beyond the Precautionary and Liquidity Line, which is case by case) – Further progress toward "even-handed" bilateral and multilateral surveillance – Calling on international organizations (UN, WTO, ILO, IMF, OECD, WB) in general to enhance dialogue and cooperation and intensify coordination – Assess the prospects for external sustainability and reducing current account imbalances worldwide as part of the Mutual Assessment Process (MAP) – More effective supervision of the financial sector, in support of the Financial Stability Board – Support the Financial Sector Assessment Program (FSAP) through activities such as assessing tax havens, terrorist financing and implementing macroprudential standards – Report on Debt Sustainability framework

World Bank

– Support the Financial Sector Assessment Program (FSAP) alongside the IMF

– Lead response to problems like climate change and food security (problems whose nature requires globally coordinated action)

– In that vein, develop new trust fund to support new Food Security Initiative for low-income countries

– Strengthen coordination with regional banks, allow recipient countries to have policy space

– Help analyze scope of energy subsidies and support energy security initiatives, along with IEA, OPEC, OECD

– New crisis support facility in IDA

– Work with donors and organizations to create multilateral trust fund to scale-up agricultural assistance to LICs; coordinate efforts with UN, African Development Bank, Food and Agricultural Organization, International Fund for Agricultural Development, World Food Program, etc.

– Report on Debt Sustainability framework

desired outcomes, but the G20 has provided specific aims, and instruments that go with these aims, for various multilateral institutions. Thus, the G20 is, currently, one of the most important principals in the governance of the global economy, and its primary function is to delegate tasks to various agents, which are other multilateral institutions with relatively more precise goals.[28]

The implications of delegatory informality

How does the G20's delegatory informality explain the rising states' discretionary accommodation? While the notion of formal political power, namely as a state's voice and representation within an institution, can be ascertained within the G20, this formal political power has different implications in the G20 as compared to the more formalized settings of the Bretton Woods institutions. Formal political power can be identified through written or unwritten rules and procedures of that institution (Chapter 1). In the case of the G20, the institution's documents and customs emphasize the relatively equal decision-making procedures of the institution. However, this formal political power works differently than it would work under a more formal institutional setting.

Specifically, the differentials in formal political power (or lack thereof) have mattered relatively less in the informal setting of the G20 than in the Bretton Woods institutions because the G20 imposes relatively lower "sovereignty costs" on its members. In turn, lower sovereignty costs translate into less focus on the differences in members' formal political power. Because the G20 does not spell out states' commitments clearly, its ability to circumscribe a state's national autonomy is generally relatively limited. Further, because the G20 executes by delegation, it itself does not impose high sovereignty costs on members. It can delegate to other institutional settings that can generate high sovereignty costs, but in that case those other institutional settings matter relatively more both for the execution of tasks and for differentials in formal political power. Overall, in contrast to the Bretton Woods institutions, in the G20 there is less bang (ability to influence the institution or have autonomy from the institution) for the buck (formal political power) for the member.

Additionally, while the G20 has tasked other institutions with holdings its members accountable, these other institutions do not have any

---

[28] Principal-agent relations include "substantive actors of principals in granting conditional authority and designing institutions to control opportunism by agents" (Hawkins et al. 2006, p. 7).

mechanisms to sanction the G20 or pressure change in members' policies, which again suggests low sovereignty costs. For instance, regarding
the MAP process, the IMF's ability to get the G20 states to agree to its
recommendations remains circumscribed. The more economically
powerful the state the IMF is dealing with, the lower the leverage the
institution has over that state (e.g., Woods and Lombardi 2006). Given
that the most economically powerful states are members of the G20, in
addition to being the core shareholders of the IMF, the IMF cannot be
expected to hold the G20 accountable. Similar points hold for the IMF-
World Bank Financial Sector Assessment program. Although this evaluation program was started in 1999, it was only after the 2008 crisis and in
keeping with the G20 declarations that the USA agreed to undergo its first
financial sector assessment. The US officials' were, however, dismissive
toward the results of the report (Kaya 2012). In a similar vein, the G20
has tasked the Financial Stability Board with "thematic peer reviews" to
ensure the consistent implementation of financial regulation across
borders, but the FSB also lacks the ability to impose its recommendations
on the G20. Consider the following statement from the June 2010
Toronto Summit Declaration (item 35, emphasis added):

We welcomed the FSB's first thematic peer review report on compensation,
which showed progress in the implementation of FSB's standards for sound
compensation, but full implementation is far from complete. We encouraged all
countries and financial institutions to fully implement FSB principles and standards by year-end. *We call on the FSB to undertake ongoing monitoring in this area
and conduct a second thorough peer-review.*

As this quote captures, the task of determining whether or not the recommendations that the G20 has demanded is implemented by the G20
member states (that is holding the G20 accountable) falls on the organization tasked with the recommendations in the first place.

Likewise, when it comes to food security, the G20 members have
ignored some of the key recommendations contained in the report for
which they commissioned a group of multilateral institutions. This 2011
report called for G20 members to phase out export restrictions in agriculture and to roll back biofuel subsidies, indicating that "as long as
governments impose mandates (obligations to blend fixed proportions
of biofuels with fossil fuels, or binding targets for share of biofuels in
energy use), biofuel production will aggravate the price inelasticity of
demand that contributes to volatility in agricultural prices" (Interagency
Report 2011, p. 10). Despite these clear policy recommendations, the
subsequent 2011 G20 Action Plan on Food Price Volatility and
Agriculture did not include trade restrictions in food and biofuel

subsidies as a strategic objective of the G20. And, the relevant G20 communiqué simply responded to the multilateral report, claiming the involved organizations had more work to do before convincing the G20 members: "[we] call for further work on strategies to implement these recommendations in their final report" (Communiqué 2011). The G20 has, thus, easily bypassed these multilateral institutions' policy recommendations, which it has sought in the first place, on food security.

All these examples go to show the low sovereignty costs associated with the G20, which in turn makes the distribution of formal political power in the institution relatively less important compared to a setting that imposes higher sovereignty costs. This point should not be generalized as an all-encompassing statement regarding informal versus formal institutions. Rather, the G20's particular informality in this case goes toward explaining why differentials in formal political power did not matter significantly in the institution. Specifically, the G20 acts a delegatory institution, as opposed to undertaking important initiatives on its own. At the same time, the institutions to which the G20 has delegated key issues, such as financial sector assessment and food security, do not have a way to hold the G20 accountable.

These discussions do not suggest informality goes hand in hand with relatively egalitarian decision-making structures. As Chapter 4 demonstrated, the International Trade Organization, which the US actors planned as the third key multilateral economic institution alongside the Bretton Woods institutions, would endorse voting equality, even though it would have been a highly formalized institution. In that case, even though the members ended up embracing voting equality, they nonetheless worried about the distribution of formal political power in the institution and debated it at length. Different formal institutions may raise different concerns about differentials in formal political power. And, the same point holds for informal institutions too.

As this book has argued, the importance of the inter-state distribution of economic power is contingent upon the specifics of the institutional setting. In this case, the G20's delegatory nature lessened states' potential but plausible concerns about differentials in formal political power through its effects on sovereignty costs. In other words, members had relatively low sensitivity to the underlying distribution in inter-state economic power. Counter-intuitively, while the G20 appears as the poster child of a causal link between "changing economic distribution" and "changing institution," the shifting economic power dynamics among states, namely the rise of emerging economies, could be so easily reflected to the G20 precisely because in the context of the G20's delegatory informality, the distribution of formal political power mattered relatively less.

Alternative explanations

Some of the plausible alternative explanations regarding the declining states' puzzling discretionary accommodation of the rising states have already been addressed. For instance, one alternative idea could be that there was no accommodation of the rising states by the declining states in the case of the G20, since the G20 is an irrelevant forum. In this scenario, the accommodation can be deemed as a fake accommodation of sorts. The evidence already presented suggests that this perspective is not viable, as the G20 has evolved into more than a platform gathered during the 2008 crisis and has become the "premier forum."

Another alternative explanation could be that the G20 may physically exist, but it remains inconsequential to the global agenda. The chapter has also refuted this point. It showed that the rising states have been able to shape its agenda, for instance placing development issues on it. In this regard, the revamped G20 does actually alter the agenda of the global economy. The entire discussion on the G20 as a delegatory actor also shows that the G20 has been able to affect the agenda of other institutional institutions, giving them new tasks such as the Mutual Assessment Process. By the same token, the chapter discussed how reducing the G20 to the G2 does not do justice to the institution. The bottom line is that the evidence does not support the case of the G20 as a fake or an immaterial accommodation.

Further, a power-based explanation alone does not aid in the answering of crucial questions. While a power-based approach foresees that declining states might accommodate the rising states' demands for more influence, there is no reason within that framework as to why the declining states would engage in the kind of discretionary engagement that this chapter discussed (e.g., Gilpin 1981; see Chapter 2).[29] More importantly, saying that the G20 is a byproduct of changing economic power dynamics does not do much in the way of explaining its institutional features. While some have identified the G20 as a concert of great powers (Gahr Store 2010), the institutional features of concerts of great powers can take different shapes and forms. The United Nations Security Council is of a radically different make-up than the Vienna Conference despite also being identified as a concert of great powers (Voeten 2005).

At the same time, however, the chapter's findings do not support existing institutionalist accounts (Chapter 2). Some of the most elaborate

---

[29] While some power-based accounts point to legitimacy concerns as a reason why the declining states should revise the institutions, within their frameworks, the legitimacy concerns are intrinsically related to perceptions of the institution as being outdated (Brooks and Wohlforth 2009).

explanations within this literature identify institutional design features as deliberate attempts to deal with specific collective action problems (e.g., Koremenos et al. 2001a, 2001b). In this framework, state actors take pains to devise institutional features that will handle different collective problems, ranging from uncertainty to distributional problems. This chapter suggests that states may, in certain cases, predetermine the broad policy objectives of institutions, but leave unclear how institutions will reach those objectives. Both in origin and upgrade, the leading states tasked the G20 with the handling of global financial stability, but how the group would achieve this broad objective appears not to have been subject to much careful deliberation. Instead of asserting the landscape of institutional design is replete with state actors' unintentional reactions, this point rather suggests there is great variation in how deliberately state actors approach institutional design and the levels of intentionality may be more broad-stroked than fine-brushed.

Likewise, the survival of the G20's existing institutional features during its upgrade in 2008, including its relatively egalitarian decision-making, appears to have more to do with state designers' lack of sensitivity to power differentials in the institution than their contemplations about how redesign would serve different collective ends. Plausibly, the G20's revamped version was path-dependent on its earlier form: in 2008, the leading states neither changed the membership of the G20 that was decided in 1999, nor tweaked its decision-making rules. In this respect, the 2008 G20 was based on the chassis of the 1999 model. The question of why the leading states did not worry about power differentials in revamping the 1999 model, however, cannot be explained with reliance on path dependence of this sort.[30] It was the particular informality of the G20 that reduced sovereignty costs and thereby concerns about power differentials in the G20. Overall, the understanding of the dynamics of the G20 requires analysis that lies at the nexus of power and institutional features.

Conclusions

While the chapter, following the book, approached the G20 with a focus on the relationship between the inter-state distribution of economic power and members' formal political power within multilateral economic institutions, the chapter's discussions could be extended beyond these points to conjecture about the future of the G20.

---

[30] I do not deny existing institutional frameworks are prone to survival (e.g., Thelen and Mahoney 2010). Still, that tendency for survival does not explain the declining states' discretionary accommodation of the rising states through the transformation of the G20.

The chapter's discussions about the G20 as a delegatory institution –
where the G20 delegates tasks to other institutions some of which are
tasked with generating guidelines and policy recommendations toward
the G20's pursuit of global financial stability – imply that the G20 has low
accountability. For instance, the chapter has discussed how the institutions that made recommendations to the G20 on food security had no
traction with the G20 members.

The G20's informal setting does not provide a tool beyond "peer
accountability," at best, for compliance and enforcement (Grant and
Keohane 2005). The G20 publishes periodic "progress reports" to facilitate both external and peer accountability, but the impact of these
reforms on the G20's members remains unclear. These reports have
been, until recently, too broad to facilitate the monitoring of the G20.
For instance, on the Basel II recommendations on banking laws and
regulations by the Basel Committee on Banking Supervision, the G20
progress report in July 2010 did not provide enough transparency regarding the member states' implementation of these recommendations.[31]
It simply indicated: "G20 countries have either implemented or are taking
steps to implement Basel II into national regulatory frameworks"
(G20 Progress Report 2010). More recently, in the 2012 Mexico
Summit, the G20 members have improved upon the progress reports,
which now outline individual member state commitments by issue area.
This improved version of the progress reports collates public information,
such as whether a specific country has implemented the Basel recommendations, in a single space. In this regard, it contributes to the creation
and dissemination of information, which is the first necessary step
for monitoring the G20. Nonetheless, there is no mechanism for addressing the lack of substantive progress under certain commitments.
Furthermore, individualizing member state commitments does not
facilitate an understanding of the group's actions as a whole.

The low accountability of the G20 also relates to concerns about the
group's lack of representativeness. As noted earlier, the existing literature
has criticized the G20's representativeness based on its membership (e.g.,
Aslund 2009). For instance, articulating the sentiments of many other
spectators, Eichengreen (2009) asks, "Who … appointed the G20 to
represent 190 countries of the world?" At their core, arguments about
representativeness are concerned with the group's responsiveness to
external stakeholders. The link between representativeness and responsiveness is established because the exclusion of certain members can

---

[31] The relevant G20 declaration from the 2009 G20 Pittsburgh summit was: "All major G-20
financial centers commit to have adopted the Basel II capital framework by 2011."

easily suggest the exclusion of certain interests. In this respect, the existing literature largely approaches the issue of the G20's accountability through a discussion of the representativeness of its membership (see also the review in Kharas and Lombardi 2012).

Ultimately, discussions on accountability in this chapter imply a concern with responsiveness to external stakeholders. Low levels of external accountability can easily translate into low levels of responsiveness to outside actors for a number of reasons. Low external accountability, to some extent, suggests insularity. It also means that outside actors may not have a viable way of transforming their concerns with the G20 agenda/policies into influence over the group. It is plausible that some non-members may have more say in multilateral institutions that produce policy recommendations for the G20 by virtue of their participation in those institutions, but given that the G20 can ignore those policy recommendations at its behest, those non-members lack influence over the group. In these respects, the discussions on accountability here also raise concerns about whether the G20 can represent the interests of non-members effectively. I return to this point in the next chapter.

8 Conclusions

In this book, I analyzed the relationship between the inter-state distribution of economic power and the states' formal political power in multilateral economic institutions. When state actors create or redesign different multilateral economic institutions in the same era, they arrange the distribution of formal political power differently across them. The book centralized the investigation and the explanation of this variation in formal political power and its relation to the underlying distribution of economic power. Overall, the book has argued that institutional settings mediate (adjust) the importance of the underlying inter-state distribution of economic power.

In explaining the relationship between states' economic power and their formal political power in multilateral economic institutions, this framework (the adjusted power approach) highlighted three primary factors: (1) the institutionally dominant states' approach to institutional priorities, (2) the manner in which states fund the institution and how that funding intersects with factor 1, and (3) the existing rules and conventions for adjusting formal political power within the institution. The book showed these factors moderate the importance of the underlying asymmetries in inter-state economic power. Hence while they render some institutions relatively more sensitive to the shifts in inter-state economic power, they lessen the importance of those shifts in other institutions. I applied this analytical framework to two historical cases – the emergence of the IMF/World Bank and the ITO – and three contemporary cases – shifts in member states' formal political power in the IMF, the World Bank, and the G20 in 2008–2010.

The rest of this concluding chapter discusses the book's broad implications, continues the book's engagement with alternative perspectives, and outlines future research possibilities based on questions that the book leaves under-explored. The chapter, finally, focuses on the policy implications of the book for the governance of the global economy.[1]

---

[1] This is understandable given how the field has evolved, e.g. see Cohen (2008).

Broad implications

The book has utilized a rich literature, both on the multilateral economic institutions studied here and International Relations theory, in advancing different conclusions than those offered in these existing literatures. The dominant tendency within International Relations has been to analyze the two realms of interest in this book – the distribution of inter-state power (power) and institutional design features (institutions), specifically the distribution of formal political power within institutions – as alternative frameworks. Based on competing motivations, while power-based approaches tell us that multilateral institutions do and should reflect the inter-state distribution of economic power, the institutionalist literatures inform us that institutions constrain and tame power asymmetries among states. While both power-based and institutionalist explanations provide some of this book's necessary ingredients, the book's focus on the inter-section of power and institutions advances significantly different claims than those found in the existing literatures.

By way of example, what explains the gains China has made in the 2008–2010 changes to members' formal political power in the IMF and in the World Bank? The adjusted power approach's focus on the variation in how economic power manifests itself differently across different multi-lateral economic institutions (in the same period) invites reiterating that question along the following lines: What explains the differences in the gains China made to its formal political power in the IMF and the World Bank in 2008–2010? This question in and of itself does not easily emerge out of existing frameworks because of these frameworks' under-articulation of the said variation.

The question has a simple answer in a variety of power-based approaches: China's economic rise, and its implications, whether they be China's increasing prestige or capacities, explain the changes China's formal political power has experienced in multilateral economic institutions (Chapter 2). Yet, the book has shown that China's economic rise was more pronounced in the institutional setting of the IMF than in the World Bank. There is little in the power-based approaches that motivate a focus on this kind of institutional variation and its explanations.

From various institutionalist perspectives, the answers to the question about China's rise and its ramifications for the IMF and the World Bank are not clear, as these accounts remain ambiguous on how power and institutions interact. Based on an institutionalist perspective that sees multilateral institutions as providing a "constitutional order" that con-strains great powers (e.g., Ikenberry 2000), there is no clear answer as to why different institutions within the same order would adapt differently to

China's rise. One possibility is that US power has been constrained differently across the IMF and the World Bank, hence the differences across them regarding the relationship between China's economic rise and its institutional gains in formal power. But, especially in these two institutions, American influence has been almost identical – it was limited, or unrestrained as some might argue, to the same degree (see Chapter 3). In this respect, the answers have to be found elsewhere than the degrees of restrictions the institutions place on power.

From a different institutionalist perspective – the rational design theory of institutions – it is also not clear why China's economic rise manifests itself in different degrees of formal political power in the IMF and the World Bank. As I already mentioned, the interaction of power and institutions remains unclear in the approach, but beyond this point, the theory's essential ingredients do not clearly guide in understanding China's differential gains in formal political power in the two institutions. Let's start with the four central explanatory factors in this literature – distribution, enforcement, the number of actors, and uncertainty – that are key to understanding the design and redesign of institutions (Chapter 2; see Koremenos et al. 2001a, 2001b). Based on rational design theory, it is difficult to ascertain the variation in enforcement or uncertainty across the IMF and the World Bank that would matter for the varied treatment of China across the two institutions.[2] At the same time, undoubtedly, there are distributional issues in the IMF and the World Bank, and plausibly these distributional issues could differ significantly across the two institutions, but how exactly they impact upon the manner in which institutions respond to China's economic rise remains indeterminate (see also Chapter 2). The numbers of actors do not differ significantly across the two Bretton Woods institutions. The bottom line is while rational design theory has advanced the literature in pointing to possibilities for state actors' deliberate design, it does not provide the necessary mechanisms for drawing the implications of power for the theory's core explanatory variables without over-stretching the theory.[3] More critically, as I emphasized in Chapter 2, it omits a meaningful discussion on how (economic and/or military) power differentials and institutional design features relate.

This book's analysis, in contrast, has specifically highlighted how institutional settings affect power dynamics. Which of the myriad of institutional factors affect the relationship between the inter-state

---

[2] To recall, "a distribution problem refers to selecting one outcome from a range of known possible outcomes" (Koremenos et al. 2001b, p. 775).

[3] Additionally, in Chapter 2, I discussed how deliberate design may be less deliberate than suggested by the rational design theory.

distribution of economic power and formal political power within multi-lateral institutions? The adjusted power approach has posed three critical factors in explaining how institutions mediate the inter-state distribution of economic power, as I just reiterated. It has shown how institutions, and not other factors, affect states' abilities to turn economic power into political power in multilateral economic institutions. In other words, showing institutions affect the fungibility of economic power contributes greatly to understanding how institutions and power interact.

The adjusted power approach demonstrates, for instance, how existing institutional rules and conventions impede or ease states' ability to get more formal political power for their increased economic prowess, or conversely to maintain the same level of formal political power in the face of declining economic power. For instance, existing rules and con-ventions regarding the issue of the adjustment of the distribution of formal political power among members affected significantly the contem-porary shifts in members' formal political power within the IMF (2008–2010). As Chapter 5 explained, in 2008–2010, existing institutional features inclined the institution toward giving everyone a little quota increase and reserving special quota increases (beyond what every mem-ber gets) only for a select number of members (selective recognition is institutionally politically contentious). In this regard, existing institu-tional rules and conventions impact how the institutional setting responds to shifts in the distribution of economic power.

This kind of focus on the details of institutions contributes to resolving any remaining uncertainties concerning the impact of institutions upon inter-state power dynamics. Power-based approaches have suggested that there are a number of different institutional outcomes that are Pareto-efficient, thereby suggesting indeterminacy in institutionalist approaches (e.g., Krasner 1991). However, the same could perhaps be said about power-based approaches – there are a number of different outcomes that are consistent with power dynamics (consider the differences in how the rise of China got reflected in the World Bank versus the IMF). Showing the contribution of institutional settings to that outcome demands the kind of close-up analysis provided here.

Bureaucratic staff and member states

The discussions here also offer insights into the notion of the technocratic and the bureaucratic staffs of the IMF and the World Bank as autono-mous actors. This autonomy can be understood from the principal-agent perspective as "agency slack," while it can also be interpreted as organiza-tional culture, the expertise of the staff, and "institutional pathologies" having lives of their own (on the former, see Hawkins et al. 2006; on the latter see Barnett and Finnemore 1999; Chwieroth 2010; Weaver 2008).[4] The book both vindicates and complicates the conception of staff autonomy.

On the one hand, the book finds that the technocratic staff of the IMF and the World Bank has played a number of important roles in the 2008–2010 changes to members' formal political power. Crucially, the staff prepared the technical calculations that provided the background for the discussions of quota shifts at the IMF and shareholding reform at the World Bank, though the Executive Directors specifically requested some of these technical calculations. The staff also provided the Directors with technical possibilities, namely alternative calculations for consideration. Further, while executing this technical role, the staff also sustained or resuscitated institutional conventions. For instance, in 2008–2010, through various reports the staff reminded the Executive Boards, and through them the Governors, how the institution had handled previous adjustments in members' formal political power. The staff can also lead to the creation of new conventions, not just the evocation of old ones. Importantly, these rules and conventions might have a life of their own.

On the other hand, the book finds that the staff's views are significantly connected with their perception of where the key member states stand, when adjustments in formal political power are concerned. The book shows that the staff craft technical calculations generally within the parameters of possibility the political climate permits. Prior to making their technical calculations, through their interactions with the Executive Directors, the staff have a reasonable idea of the bounds of political feasibility, and the reports they produce reflect those possibilities. Although the staff also try to push their own preferences through, such as aiming for the highest possible increase to the institution's resources, in the absence of adequate support from the Directors, the chances of the staff getting their way remains unlikely.

These findings, on the whole, suggest the importance of the political limitations the Directors and the Governors of the institutions impose. To recall, quota adjustments remain member state centered with little delegation to the staff. In comparison, loan decisions, the study of which the existing literature on the Bretton Woods institutions centralizes, involve a significant deal of delegation to the staff (Stone 2011). In this respect, the points here raise caution, at least when little delegation is involved,

---

[4] There are important distinctions between these approaches, but for the purposes of the current analysis these frameworks' convergence on institutional autonomy (and not whether the sources of that autonomy is rooted in rational principal-agent action or non-rational reasons, as the constructivist literature asserts) is of relevance.

against assuming that the staff's expressed preferences stand independently from the key member states' articulated preferences.[5]

Rising states and the multilateral system   The book's findings are also relevant for another strand in the International Relations literature – one that analyzes how the post-war multilateral system created by the USA and its allies will fare in the face of rising states (see Chapter 1). To begin with, an understanding of systemic adaptation to the rising states needs to include a dimension that differentiates across institutions. The book's finding that accommodation varies across institutions suggests that the system's adaptation to the rising states will be uneven – it will occur at different degrees in different institutions. At the very least, this uneven procession has so far been the case. In this regard, caution is warranted in discussing "system adaptability" in broad terms, as one needs a picture of what is happening in each institution (and across different issue areas) to assemble a larger sense of the system.

The book also reveals why institutional adaptation is likely to be a slow process, which could be problematic if rising states press for speedier institutional change that favors their preferences. The adjusted power approach suggests, and the empirical cases have shown, that the economically declining states that remain institutionally dominant in multilateral economic institutions will simultaneously face incentives for accommodation (giving more formal political power to the rising states) and limited accommodation (holding back as much formal political power for themselves as they can).[6] In addition to the tendency for limited accommodation, the book has also shown that existing institutional rules and conventions, by and large, create inertia against speedy change (Fioretos 2011; Pearson 2004).[7] In this context, it becomes crucial whether or not the rising states will continue to be patient with such incremental change. Chapter 5, for instance, emphasized that the rising states were content with fulfilling some, but not all of their key preferences regarding formal political asymmetries in the 2008–2010 shifts in the institutions.

---

[5] Some work that focuses on areas where greater delegation to the staff occurs, such as risk assessment, also note the importance of actors from member states, alongside the staff (e.g., Moschella 2010).

[6] This tendency for limited accommodation might explain some commentators' frustration with the USA not pulling its weight enough in adapting the system to changed times (e.g., Brooks et al. 2012).

[7] As Pierson notes, it is in the very nature of institutional rules, of the kind that exist in the IMF and the World Bank, to be difficult to overturn, as these rules need to assuage states' fears against volatility and instability in inter-state relations.

This point about slow change in favor of the rising states becomes even more pertinent when one considers that the most momentous crisis since the Great Depression – the 2008 global financial crisis – did not unseat existing institutional ways (Eichengreen and O'Rourke 2010). The book finds that the Great Recession accelerated some of the reforms (to member state representation, including formal political power) that previous institutional discussions had spelt out. Particularly, in the case of the upgrade of the G20 and the 2010 changes in the IMF and the World Bank, the 2008 crisis is important to understanding the timing of these changes. Yet, the role of the crisis in these changes should not be overestimated. For instance, in the case of the IMF, the members had already decided on the 2008 shifts in 2006 and had been envisioning them for nearly a decade (Chapter 5). In the case of the 2010 changes at the World Bank, someone without the knowledge of the Great Recession would have a hard time deducing that these changes followed a monumental crisis that not only increased the demands on the institution's resources but also put poor developing countries' commitment to reducing extreme poverty under significant pressure (World Bank 2010). The change in the Bank's shareholding was not unusual (in fact, just below the historical average increase in shares), and the subsequent shift in the distribution of formal political power among the members was modest judged by the institution's preceding discussions of change (Chapter 6).

Just as institutional settings adjusted the reflection of inter-state asymmetries in economic power, they also mediated the effects of the Great Recession, at least when the institutional alterations to formal political power are concerned. The Great Recession's effects across the institutions were uneven and hinged upon the factors the book highlighted. To be clear, these points do not suggest that the Great Recession had no impact. Nor do I suggest one can generalize the findings of the book to the relationship between crises and institutions.[8] Rather, the point is that existing paths on which institutions had set themselves and the existing institutional frameworks mediated the crisis' impact (e.g., Pierson 2004; Mahoney and Thelen 2010).

Overall, the understanding of how the multilateral system is changing in the face of rising states requires complementing the big picture with the smaller, detailed analysis of the extent of "accommodation" within each institution. Given institutions mediate the importance of the change in

[8] Relevant works here include Abdelal et al. (2010); Blyth (2002); Chwieroth (2010); Ikenberry (1992). Constructivist accounts do not suggest there is an automatic mechanism through which crises as material events translate into policy outcomes in institutions (see Moschella 2010, p. 3); rather, that crises provide windows of opportunity for ideational shifts.

the distribution of power, that distribution affects institutional dynamics unevenly.

Further explorations and future research

The book unearths a number of issues upon which future studies could expand.

Analyzing the complex relationship between formal and informal power provides an avenue of expansion to the book's discussions (e.g., Stone 2011). The study of formal political power remains fundamental and critical to understanding the design, the functioning, and the change in international institutions (Chapter 1). At the same time, the 2008–2010 institutional changes, which the book examines (the IMF, the World Bank, the G20), specifically aimed to alter formal political asymmetries, so centering the analysis on formal political power was important. The book has, however, also related its discussions to informal power. In Chapter 2, utilizing Stone's work (2011), I have suggested that in the current period, when the large advanced economies are experiencing relative decline, their informal power is reduced. This point, in turn, makes these states more sensitive to their formal political power, providing one of the rationales for "limited accommodation." In Chapter 3, I discussed how quota adjustments contain features of both formal and informal governance.

One relevant question here is whether the shifts in members' informal power over institutions explain the changes in members' formal political power in 2008–2010, particularly at the IMF and the World Bank. Stone's analysis of informal power argues informal power increases with structural power, which in turn permits the member states to be able to rely on alternative institutional platforms. No evidence suggests that the rising states in the IMF and the World Bank have differing outside (exit) options across the two institutions. As noted in the specific chapters on these two institutions, in both cases, the rising states have threatened to form their own clubs and have taken steps to do so. More importantly, despite the two institutions' differentiated purposes, both institutions concern inter-state financial relations. In this respect, why the rise of large emerging economies, with their enhanced importance for global trade and financial flows, would confer them higher structural power (namely informal influence, per Stone) in the case of one institution and not the other remains unclear (see Chapter 5). Also, the factors that this book emphasized – the institutionally dominant states' priorities and the state financing of the institution – plausibly affect which members have informal influence over the institution. For instance, the more the institution depends on upfront financing from member states, the more the rising states should formally and informally matter to the institution. Regardless, future studies could further focus on the inter-relationship between formal and informal power and governance.[9]

While the book has largely focused on state actors' international postures, it also raises a number of questions about the interaction between domestic politics-international relations that future studies could answer. Specifically, in Chapter 4, the book has shown that when the US officials were creating the post-war multilateral trading system and its corresponding institution, the International Trade Organization (ITO), they did not heed the demands of domestic audiences on the question of formal political asymmetries within the institution. While the US officials preferred formal voting equality in the institution, Congressional members as well as representatives from key domestic businesses expressed serious concern about formal equality. This point, as the Chapter emphasized, does not undermine the findings of the two-level game frameworks, which argue that the international position needs to incorporate the opinions of domestic groups that will approve (broadly and narrowly) the agreement. It does, however, question whether this kind of a domestic-international linkage should be merely assumed.

On a different point, the book's discussion on the dynamics between the declining states and the rising states invites further study on how domestic politics can interfere in this relationship. As the book has emphasized, *one of* the reasons for declining states' preference for limited accommodation could be the importance of formal political power from a domestic perspective, as the US Congressional sensitiveness to the US formal political power in multilateral economic institutions shows (Chapters 1, 2, and 3). In this context, the Congress's continued attention to US formal power in the institutions might create a future tendency for limited accommodation, or at the very least emerge as a key factor with which the US Executive officials, who delegate and oversee international negotiations at the IMF and the World Bank, need to increasingly contend.[10] At the same time, however, actors from declining states tend to be sensitive to the costs of international engagement, which create a rationale for increasing burden sharing on the international stage. In the case of the US Congress, for instance, this desire to burden share, which might inevitably translate into giving the rising states more formal

---

[9] At the same time, while there is no reason to expect a one-to-one correspondence between informal and formal political power, there is likely a strong association between the two.

[10] While the following point extends beyond the scope of the analysis, it is interesting to note that although the 2008 changes examined started under US President George W. Bush, they continued under President Obama. The ideological switch did not significantly affect the US position.

political power in the IMF and the World Bank, might counteract the eagerness to preserve formal political influence. How the rationales for accommodation, on the one hand, and preferences for limited accommodation, on the other, interact for key domestic actors could comprise fruitful future research.[11]

Moreover, for obvious reasons, the book has focused on the institutionally dominant states' preferences and the room they provide for accommodation, but in the future the rising states' preferences could be more thoroughly integrated into the analysis. The book has not dismissed the rising states' preferences, but has instead argued that the *expression* of their preferences, to a great extent, remains contingent upon the room for maneuver the declining states provide. For instance, in comparing the IMF and the World Bank, Chapter 6 argued that giving the rising states more formal political power in the latter institution would conflict with the declining states' priorities for that institution. While the declining states wish to see the IBRD (the non-concessional lending arm of the Bank) increasingly serve the non-rising states, particularly the poorest ones, both financially and otherwise, the rising states wish to continue their involvement with the IBRD and cater the institution more to their needs. In this case, because the rising states' position enhancement would not serve the declining states well, the rising states face limited opportunity to increase their formal political power. Such a focus on institutional context remains crucial to interpreting and unpacking the rising states' preferences because they are unlikely to put political capital into pushing for greater political power, when they know it is not the most politically feasible approach. In contrast, facing an opportunity for position enhancement in the IMF, the rising states capitalized on it. The upshot of these discussions for future studies is that as the rising states build more influence within and outside of the institutions, they will start contesting the space for accommodation the declining states provide.

This point becomes more pertinent if one also considers that the rising states will face lower costs to international engagement as they continue their rise and converge upon the declining states. The book cautioned against interpreting the rising states as "position maximizers" that grab all the institutional political power they can (Chapter 2). For instance, they might be cautious about increasing their financial commitments internationally. As Chapter 6 showed, the rising states do not wish to significantly increase their donations to the International Development Association,

---

[11] These points about domestic actors do not change the book's conclusions about how the inter-state distribution of economic power relates to the distribution of formal political power in multilateral economic institutions, as Chapter 4 shows.

the concessional lending arm of the Bank. They justify this lack of interest, partially, on their desire to focus on development within their own borders. If one takes this rationale at face value, as the rising states continue to grow, such rationale will subside. In turn, as they might wish to increase their financial contributions to the institution, they will demand more influence, including greater formal political power. Again, they might increasingly push the boundaries of the accommodation space provided by the rising states. At the same time, however, the book suggests that the rising states never face a clean slate in the institutions. Not just the declining states, but also the existing rules and conventions of institutions create a framework, albeit surmountable, with which the rising states need to contend. In this regard, one cannot ignore the kind of detailed institutional analysis this book provides to map out the rising states' future trajectory.

Finally, even though the book focuses on a range of multilateral economic institutions (IMF, World Bank, ITO, G20) at different periods in time, its discussions could nonetheless be expanded to other institutions. One line of future research could adapt the adjusted power approach to the security realm and explore the differences across the two spheres of international interactions. The variation in the way in which security institutions reflect the underlying asymmetries in economic and military power could be fruitful. The regional multilateral development banks could also be the focus of future research. Further, as Chapter 7 emphasized, one of the byproducts of the G20's shift from being a marginal forum for finance ministers to a central forum for heads of state has been the parallel shift in platforms, such as the Financial Stability Forum, which is a hybrid institution comprising both governments and non-state actors. Future studies could extend the book's discussions to beyond the central inter-governmental institutions that this book analyzed.

Implications of the book for global economic governance

Although the book has not claimed to provide insights into the totality of global economic governance, a number of its discussions on the 2008–2010 changes to three of the most central multilateral economic institutions (the IMF, WB, G20) reveal important aspects of the current state of global economic governance and its potential trajectory into the future.

Some scholars (e.g., Drezner 2012) have recently claimed that the multilateral economic institutions studied in this book have survived the test of the Great Recession impressively and have managed to coordinate inter-state action while facilitating the continuation of the openness of the global economy. I agree with these works regarding the centrality and perseverance of these multilateral economic institutions, and I also agree with the thrust of their analysis that the Great Recession's repercussions have not unleashed forces of institutional disintegration. At the same time, however, this book's detailed analysis of the 2008–2010 shifts in members' formal political power demonstrates institutional fragilities that the members will need to address going forward. It is unlikely that these potential sources of tension in the institutions are serious enough to threaten the survival of the institutions, but they nonetheless point to crucial issues with which the member states will have to contend going forward.

The remainder of this book, first, discusses why I agree with those that argue the recent period has brought with it renewal for these institutions. Second, I discuss why the examination of the 2008–2010 changes also reveals institutional fragilities.

Revival and change

The 2008–2010 shifts in the distribution of formal political power analyzed in this book harbor a sense of revival for the institutions and promise change in policy outcomes alongside shift in control over the institution. In addition to the changes outlined in the previous chapters, the IMF staff and member states also utilized both the 2008 global economic crisis and the reform process as opportunities to revamp the institution's lending facilities. In 2009, the IMF's Stand-By Agreements (SBA), under which most middle-income countries have borrowed from the IMF, was tweaked. The normal access limits were doubled under the new SBA to 600 percent of the member state's quota, and the IMF emphasized that normal access limits could be waived in exceptional circumstances, or for rapid disbursement, the Fund's emergency access guidelines could be invoked. Under the new SBA, high access precautionary arrangements (HAPAs) for countries that may not need the funds but still want access in case of an emergent need were expanded. Importantly, conditionality was simplified.[12] Under the new SBA access to resources can be frontloaded and the demand for structural conditionality (related to overall macroeconomic criteria) was eliminated in favor of specific conditions (e.g., a need to increase reserves) that were identified in the state's need to borrow.

Also, two new lending facilities were added for middle-income countries in 2009. The Precautionary Credit Line (PCL) and the Flexible Credit Line (FCL) both emphasize borrowing to prevent crises and both

---

[12] IMF conditionality has been under revision since 2002 with a view to simplifying it, though early evaluations are skeptical about significant substantive change (IMF 2007b).

target countries with strong economic performance, but the PCL is geared toward countries with relatively weaker economic performance than the FCL. Therefore, the FCL contains some ex post conditionality, under which the member state needs to meet the criteria identified at the time of accessing the fund. The FCL only contains ex ante conditionality in that the state accessing the fund needs to demonstrate high economic performance and sound macroeconomic policy governance. Importantly, the FCL has no access limit, and the PCL has higher limits than both previous facilities, with up to 500 percent of the quota available up front with access going up to 1,000 percent of the quota.

These new precautionary facilities aim to overcome problems associated with previous programs, but nonetheless remain limited in demand from the emerging markets. Previous programs included the Contingent Credit Line (CCL), for precautionary lending, created in 1999 and abolished in 2003 after never being used. Experts attribute the lack of reliance on this fund to the stigma associated with drawing on IMF funds. This stigma, in turn, was related partially to the asymmetric representation of states within the institution and the IMF's imposition of conditionality on the emerging economies (Chapter 5; Griffith-Jones and Ocampo 2011). In 2008, the short-term liquidity facility (SLF) was established for rapid disbursements to countries with sound economic policies that were facing liquidity needs, but no country borrowed from this facility either. In addition to the usual problems, the fact that the access-seeking country needed to have completed a positive Article IV (bilateral surveillance) report with the IMF further restricted access (Griffith-Jones and Ocampo).

Compared to the lack of demand for these facilities, the new PCL and FCL have done relatively better. By 2011, four countries had signed agreements under these facilities (Poland, Colombia, Mexico, and Montenegro). Nonetheless, two main questions beset these precautionary facilities – whether there is a continued stigma associated with access and whether countries need these facilities at all (if they have strong economic performance, they can access private funds). Presumably, the stigma is lower now that the countries that would qualify for the precautionary funds – the large emerging markets – have greater formal political power in the institution, signaling less asymmetry between them and the institution. However, the latter problem remains.

These shifts in lending facilities, despite the unknowns that beset their future, offer a number of implications related to this book. The book showed the rising states' position enhancement in the IMF was greater than their gains in the World Bank. These aforementioned changes in the lending facilities for the rising states, regardless of their level of utilization, compound the gains the rising states have made in 2008–2010. The shifts in loan programs represent the IMF's attempts to cater its services more to the emerging economies. Moreover, the reform of the lending facilities also underscores the book's earlier discussions about the declining states' (large advanced economies') efforts to dissuade the rising states from utilizing alternative platforms. While some of these states may never borrow from the IMF again, the more the IMF's loan programs can cater to the potential borrowers out of the group of the rising states, the greater the chances for these states to utilize the IMF. Further, the changes in loan programs also provide another manifestation of the shifting power dynamics within the institution. The rising states' overt discontent with the institution's lending, including its conditions, dates back at least to the Asian financial crisis. That the political environment within the institution has finally ripened to integrate the rising states' demands affirms as well as embodies the rising states' position enhancement in the IMF (Chapter 5). More generally, as these discussions suggest, the shifts in the distribution of formal political power within the multilateral economic institutions both confirm shifts that had long been in the making (in this case, the rising states' altered relationship with the institution) as well as facilitate further change.

Increases in the emerging economies' formal (and informal) political power position them well to push for more reform that reflects their preferences. One of these areas concerns additional changes to the IMF's quota formula. As the book discussed, the 2008–2010 shifts in members' formal political power in the IMF went farther than preceding reform discussions in the institution, but those changes nonetheless left some of the key preferences of the rising states unfulfilled. Particularly, the rising states disagreed with the inclusion of some key variables in the IMF quota formula as well as their weights (Chapter 5). As anticipated by those discussions, the large emerging economies have since pushed for a revision of the 2008 formula, which currently remains on the IMF's agenda (in 2013). During these discussions, for instance, some of the rising states have continued to push for increasing the weight of GDP PPP (relative to the weight of GDP at market exchange rates) (IMF 2013; Chapter 5). To the extent that the declining states are interested in keeping these rising states bound to the IMF, they might have to provide further room for accommodation.

Another important area of policy change concerns the IMF's policy against capital controls.[13] In reversing its policy, the institution has

---

[13] For a work that examines the debates within the IMF on capital account liberalization, see Chwieroth (2010).

recently moved to trying to establish multilateral guidelines for managing capital inflows. As previous work has shown (e.g., Abdelal 2007), the institution's policy on capital controls was, to a great extent, shaped by the influence of G7 countries as its core shareholders. The institution's shift in approach is similarly related to the changing nature of its core shareholders. As a key IMF paper (2011, p. 3) on this topic notes: "Emerging markets (EMs) are experiencing a surge in capital inflows, lifting asset prices and growth prospects. While inflows are typically beneficial for receiving countries, inflow surges can carry macroeconomic and financial stability risks." This statement is significant because it reflects that states that have all along disagreed with the IMF's stance on capital controls are in a strong enough position to have their perspectives be reflected in the IMF's policy approach. Moreover, these rising states are currently exercising their enhanced voice in the institution to challenge the use of multilateral guidelines to govern capital controls – they advocate that national autonomy, not multilateral guidance, should rule the appropriateness of capital controls. For instance, the Brazilian finance minister, Guido Mantega, has noted:

These measures of self-defense [capital controls] are a legitimate response to the effects of the monetary policies adopted by reserve currency-issuing countries . . . Ironically, some of the countries that are responsible for the deepest crisis since the Great Depression, and have yet to solve their own problems, are eager to prescribe codes of conduct to the rest of the world.[14]

As this crucial example demonstrates, the rise of the large emerging markets can lead to important changes in the policy advice the IMF disseminates. The example also suggests that the rising states' increasing formal political power will allow them to carve out more autonomy from the institutions' policies (see more on this below; Chapter 5).[15]

The rise of emerging economies has also been affecting discussions on the IMF's Special Drawing Right (SDR). Basically, the SDR is a reserve asset, and a basket of currencies determines its value. Currently, the basket comprises the US dollar, the UK pound, the Japanese yen, and the euro. A currency has to be "freely usable" to be included in the SDR, and the export shares of the country is the other important criterion for inclusion in the basket. Recent discussions at the IMF have centered on whether the Chinese currency (the renminbi) specifically and the

---

[14] Quoted in "Brazil Rejects IMF Line on Capital Controls," *The Financial Times*, April 15, 2011, online edition.

[15] The point here is not that these emerging markets will reverse the liberalization in their capital markets. In fact, some states, like China, will likely continue to relax restrictions in the movement of capital in and out of their countries. Rather, the point is the rising states will demand from the institutions the autonomy to impose capital controls.

currencies of emerging economies generally can be included in the SDR. The IMF's Executive Board has the authority to revise the currencies that make up the SDR, and to determine what constitutes a freely usable currency. In this respect, the decision to alter the composition of the SDR is governed as much by political considerations as technical deliberations.[16] As the IMF itself openly admits, whether the inclusion of an emerging economy's currency in the basket would increase the attractiveness of the SDR is only partially a technical matter (IMF 2011b). There are also ongoing discussions on widening the SDR's usage through increasing the allocation of SDRs members receive or having debt issued in SDR. So far, although the discussions fall short of the Chinese calls for a "super-sovereign reserve currency" (Xiaochuan 2009), they reveal that as the distribution of formal political power in the IMF changes, so will important features and policies of the institution.

Although the changes that the World Bank experienced, at least when judged by the shifts in formal political power, were relatively modest compared to the IMF, the Bank also experienced revitalization and change during 2008–2010. In the 2010 meetings, the Bank's member states agreed to about an $86 billion (approximately 30 percent) increase to the Bank's capital. As Chapter 6 discussed, whether this is a significant amount remains open to debate, but 2010 was the first time since 1988 that the Bank's member states agreed to a capital boost, and thus it constitutes a significant date in the Bank's history. Implicit to this capital increase was the Bank's role in addressing the repercussions of the Great Recession. At a time of global economic crisis, private flows especially into the non-emerging developing economies are reduced, increasing the need for public funds from multilateral economic institutions. Moreover, the global economic crisis will have long-term repercussions for the reduction of poverty in many developing countries (World Bank 2010). With millions more people stuck in (or relapsed back to) extreme poverty, the Bank's broad mission of global poverty reduction is re-emphasized, while its specific work in developing social safety nets is called upon.

At the same time, the 2010 changes to formal political power compelled the Bank to identify areas of key strategic focus. The Bank is a diffuse organization in the sense that it aims to tackle the challenge of global economic development from numerous angles, ranging from the environment, to infrastructure, to a focus on fragile states, to education, to health, and to immigration. This diffuse nature of the Bank, among other factors, detracts from the Bank's ability to claim success in tangible

---

[16] The same holds for the decision on how to reform quotas (and thus voting rights) at the IMF (Chapter 5).

development outcomes.[17] It also makes it difficult for member states to steer the actions of the Bank and make the institution accountable to them. Therefore, the members utilized the 2010 shifts as an opportunity to compel the Bank to declare strategic areas of focus. The Bank has defined these areas as: targeting the poor especially in Sub-Saharan Africa, creating opportunities for growth, acting on issues that require global collective action, good governance, and preparing for crises.[18] On the one hand, the generality of the list does not give much hope that the Bank, just through the identification of a handful of priorities, will become less diffused. On the other hand, more important than this list is the motivation behind the list: the Bank's recognition that it needs to step down from areas into which other international organizations or non-governmental organizations have stepped. As the Bank puts it, "[w]ithin these five priorities, we will continually assess where we can have the most impact ... We will be selective" (DC2010-0002/1, p. 5). The outcome of this recognition remains to be seen, and previous studies suggest that the Bank cannot easily match words and actions (Weaver 2008). Regardless, that change is underway is clear.[19]

The selection of the heads of the IMF and the World Bank is another area where future change is likely. In the IMF, scandals forced Dominique Strauss-Kahn out as Managing Director in 2011, and Christine Lagarde, another French national, replaced him. In the World Bank, the American Robert Zoellick stepped down as the president in 2012 to make way for another American, Jim Yong Kim. In this regard, the bargain struck in the beginning of these institutions seems to be upheld – with the Americans taking the Presidency of the World Bank and the Europeans taking the top management position in the IMF. To the extent that the Europeans and the Americans coalesce in voting at the Executive Board, their voting power will determine the outcome of these positions.

Yet, much has actually changed. Member states in both institutions have agreed to make the process of choosing the leadership more transparent, and the heads of these institutions now need to build support from

---

[17] See the discussions in IEG (2009) report. The factors that detract from the Bank's ability to claim results even in specific areas has to do with inadequate data collection and still ineffective means of monitoring and measuring the results of Bank-funded projects.

[18] As Chapter 6 emphasized, the USA in particular prefers the Bank to focus on the poorest countries.

[19] Even though leading officials have made references to the rising states' influence on the World Bank's economic development agenda (e.g., Zoellick 2010), particularly its adherence to Washington Consensus, I do not discuss that issue here because the actual adherence of the Bank to a straightforward agenda of privatization, deregulation, and liberalization is more complicated in reality than in popular discourse (Babb 2012; Naim 2000).

the large emerging markets. For instance, India and Russia supported Kim's Presidency. Moreover, President Obama's nomination of Kim, a Korean-American who is not a career civil servant in the US government, as Zoellick had been, but an academic is indicative. Even more importantly, during the competition for the Presidency, the developing countries considered themselves in enough of a position of strength to mount a serious challenge to the status quo. They nominated two candidates, Ngozi Okonjo-Iweala (Nigeria) and José Antonio Ocampo (Colombia) – the first candidates that are not nominated by the USA to be considered and interviewed by the Executive Board in the entire history of the World Bank. In this context, the G24, an inter-governmental platform for both emerging and low-income developing countries, has noted, "We recognize that for the first time in the history of the World Bank there was an open process for the selection of the President that involved a debate on the priorities and the future of the institution."[20] In short, the 2008–2010 shifts in members' formal political power in the Bank both affirm and, plausibly, foreshadow more change.

The same story of change affecting policy outcomes will likely continue in the G20. The G20's upgrade in 2008 has and will likely continue to affect global economic cooperation among states. For instance, the G20 has provided a platform for the most systemically important economies' discussions of the reform of the international financial institutions. At the same time, the G20 has delegated important tasks to the IMF, asking it to assess the G20 economies, to explore the external implications of their national policies and to make policy recommendations in accordance with these evaluations (Chapter 7). This is known as the G20 "mutual assessment process," and it aims to revive the IMF's multilateral surveillance function, through which the institution evaluates prospects for and threats to global financial and monetary stability. The G20 also facilitated relatively quick action on supplementing the international financial institutions' resources during the 2008 global financial crisis. For instance, it moved fast to triple the IMF's lending capacity in 2009. Overall, the upgrade of the G20 and its subsequent work, despite all its failings some of which are discussed below, indicates major economic powers' recognition that in an interdependent world, the resolution of shared problems, including an economic crisis, demand inter-state cooperation. This picture contrasts with the beggar-thy-neighbor policies of the 1930s.

The 2008–2010 period has witnessed important changes to the governance of the institutions, which this book analyzed in detail, but also to their policies, to which the preceding section alluded. And, these changes

---

[20] www.imf.org/external/np/cm/2012/041912.htm (Last accessed: April 27, 2012).

harbor the potential for more change. In this light, I agree with those scholars who emphasize the centrality and the resilience of existing multi-lateral economic institutions.

Sources of tension and weakness

Still, this book's detailed study of the 2008–2010 changes in the IMF, the World Bank, and the G20 also reveal sources of conflict among its key member states (shareholders) as well as spots of potential weakness in the eyes of outsiders (stakeholders). Specifically, the analysis that follows suggests that the multilateral economic institutions examined in this book remain internally divided; are on the whole used to serve the needs of the relatively rich; and increasingly face a leadership problem.[21]

Neglected but important: the poorest members in the IMF and the World Bank   First, the 2008–2010 shifts in the distribution of economic power have produced negligible gains for those with the least amount of voice in the institution, specifically the poorest states. And given the importance of these members for the institutions' core mandates, the neglected position of the poorest members raises questions about whether the institutions can generate effective policies without giving these members meaningful voice (Birdsall 2007). At the same time, because the poorest states remain the central concern for many international non-governmental organizations that work on economic development, their neglected position also raises questions about stakeholders' assessments of the institutions.[22]

The book has shown that the position of the low-income countries was a tangential aspect of the 2008–2010 shifts in the IMF and the World Bank. The 2008–2010 changes to members' formal political power did provide the low-income countries (LICs) with minuscule gains in voting power in both institutions, and in the World Bank the African states gained a third chair on the EB.[23] Still, the bulk of the gains from the 2008–2010 changes accrued to the rising states. For instance, in absolute terms, in the World Bank, the gains just the G20 emerging economies made in terms of voting power was ten times the gains the entire group of

---

[21] Here, the discussion refers to the relatively rich countries. For a work that discusses the relationship between individuals and countries vis-à-vis these institutions see Kaya and Keba (2011).

[22] Consider, for instance, Oxfam or Overseas Development Institute here.

[23] The discussions on LICs referenced the following categories of states: (1) Sub-Saharan states (minus South Africa), (2) the UN classification of Least Developed Countries, (3) the World Bank classification of LICs.

low-income countries made as a result of the reforms.[24] In terms of the rate of change in states' voting power, in the World Bank, the gains the G20 emerging economies made were about 18.6 percent; whereas, the gains by the Sub-Saharan African states, which the Bank considers central to its goal of economic development, were about 7.4 percent, again as a result of the 2008–2010 shifts (see also Chapter 6). As the book discussed, although the 2008 reforms in the Bank doubled the basic votes, which meant enhancing the voice of the poorest states compared to their pre-2008 standing, the 2010 shifts in members' formal political power undermined the gains the poorest members made by accruing gains primarily to the emerging economies.

Importantly, it remains debatable whether the poorest members have the access they need to these organizations' resources. In the case of the IMF, although the institution revamped its lending facilities for the LICs in 2008–2010, whether these changes are of significance is an open question. IMF lending to its poorest members, up until 2010, occurred through the Poverty Reduction and Growth Facility (PRGF, established in 1999), the Emergency Post-Conflict Assistance program (established in 1995), and through the Exogenous Shocks Facility (ESF, established in 2005).[25] In 2010, the IMF replaced the PRGF with the Extended Credit Facility (ECF), and the Standby Credit Facility (SCF) replaced the ESF. Additionally, the IMF instituted the Rapid Credit Facility (RCF) the same year, which provides outright disbursement of funds for emergency purposes, including external shocks and natural disasters with limited conditionality. The ECF provides longer-term lending than the SCF and is intended for economies that continue to face lasting balance of payment problems (as opposed to short-term ones due to an external shock, for instance). Qualifying members can access the SCF on a precautionary basis. The IMF claims to have streamlined conditionality in both the ECF and the SCF. This streamlined conditionality fits with the IMF's longer-term move toward targeted (to the goals of macroeconomic stability) and reduced conditionality.[26] The revamped Poverty Reduction and Growth Trust (PRGT) administers these new funds.

Despite these changes, it remains doubtful whether the alterations to the IMF's lending facilities for its poorest members ameliorate existing weaknesses in the IMF's lending. At the very least, more research is

---

[24] The discussions here compare pre-reform voting power to the post-2010 reform voting power.

[25] For a more extended discussion of these programs see Lombardi (2010b) and Boughton and Lombardi (2010).

[26] Additionally, in July 2009, the IMF's EB provided interest-relief on concessional loans through the end of 2011. This change, however, was not structural.

necessary before one can conclude they will have any positive impact. The amounts available through the new facilities remain modest. The amount available through the ECF is the typical 100 percent of the quota per year and 300 percent of the quota in the total lending; the same holds for the SCF. The RCF is also a limited resource because the most a country can access is 100 percent of its quota (cumulatively). In contrast, the Flexible Credit Line, which was discussed above, offers precautionary lending to countries with good economic performance (read emerging economies) with no access limits. As Lombardi (2010, p. 89) notes, the IMF's concessional lending has traditionally been "relatively modest in comparison to the overall resources lent out." This trend continues to hold. Further, the 2008–2010 shifts in formal political power decreased some low-income countries' quotas, which suggests that these members continue to face limitations in their access to IMF funds (Chapter 5).

For different reasons, the poorest members of the World Bank also face barriers to access from the institution. During 2008–2010, while the International Development Association (IDA) credits to members initially went up, they returned to their 2008 level in 2010 (see Figure 6.2). While the Bank's Independent Evaluation Group finds the IBRD response in a handful of emerging markets adequate, it finds that "the more modest [IDA] response reflected an inelastic funding envelope and performance-based resource allocation" (IEG 2011, p. x). In determining the IDA allocations, the Bank does not only examine how poor a country is, but also how the potential borrower country rates on the World Bank's Country Policy and Institutional Assessments (CIPA) and on measures of country performance on Bank loans. Thus, even though the IDA is supposed to give priority to the poorest countries, which would suggest Sub-Saharan African countries should receive a large portion of its resources, the performance criteria contributes to keeping the region's share of IDA resources to about half. Although the LICs, compared to other country groupings, are in greater need of the public funds provided through the international financial institutions, the institutions face increasing competition as loan/aid givers. Specifically, the Bank's concessional lending to the poorest states, which are those that are eligible to borrow from the IDA, dropped significantly since the 1990s. While the Bank's lending was about 17 percent of the external financing received by these countries in 1995, it dropped to less than 8 percent in 2005 (Birdsall and Subramanian 2007). In addition to the private sector, which fizzles out during severe crises, and other multilateral donors, the emerging economies provide loans to the poorest countries. Despite the emergence of serious competitors to its business, the institution has not significantly revised its approach to concessional lending. All in all, beyond the fact that the 2008–2010 shifts garnered them relatively little gains, the poorest states face obstacles in accessing the IMF's and the World Bank's resources.

Leaving aside any normative implications, the lopsided treatment of shareholders, where the poorest states continue to have an institutionally weak position, is problematic for the fulfillment of these institution's core functions. First, on the most basic level, the institutions fail to serve the interests of a large group of member states. In this regard, their legitimacy in the eyes of these states will remain an open question. Second, the LICs have relatively greater need for the technical advice these institutions disseminate. And, because the institutions have more sway over weaker states, the institutions have the greatest leverage over their poorest members. Thus, whether the institutions' policies are deemed as successes or failures will be primarily observed in the economic development of their low-income members. Along these lines, as mentioned, the international development community, including non-governmental organizations, tends to assess the policies of the international financial institutions based on their impact on the poorest members. This point again suggests the relatively neglected position of the LICs makes the institutions vulnerable to outside criticism.

Third, both the IMF's and the World Bank's policies and technical advice in LICs would likely be more effective if the institutions better integrate the opinions and experience of the poorest states (e.g., Birdsall 2007). Making more active participants out of LICs in both institutions, in turn, demands that these states have greater voice in the institutions (Birdsall and Subramanian 2007). For instance, greater voice can instigate the loan recipients' greater "ownership" of the loans programs (which include conditionality). Without ownership, the Bank has less information about how the domestic institutions work, and also less influence over how they should be reformed. For instance, the lack of adequate information about local conditions detracts from the Bank staff's understanding of inter-sectoral linkages in a country. Recent evaluations by the World Bank's independent evaluation office shows that the Bank is still struggling to engender ownership in these states, despite the fact that ownership is seen as key to the Bank's programs (IEG 2009). Similar discussions to these can be extended to the IMF's role in LICs.

Poorest states as key stakeholders to the G20   Since only emerging and advanced economies belong to the G20, LICs are an easily identifiable external stakeholder to the G20. At the same time, the issue of assistance to LICs is a self-declared goal of the G20, and the G20 states have cited the importance of serving the interests of LICs to facilitate the effectiveness and the legitimacy of the group. As the G20's Toronto Declaration (2010) indicates, the group has "committed [itself] to narrowing the development gap" and to "consider the impact of [their] policy actions on low-income countries." Moreover, the discussion on the LICs aids in the understanding of how the rise of emerging economies is changing the landscape of multilateral economic policy-making. After all, both emerging economies and the LICs continue to share poverty as a common problem.[27] In this context, whether the emerging economies can lead the G20 to fashion policies that benefit the LICs is an important question in assessing whether their rise will contribute to policies that benefit the so-called developing world as a whole.

Although large emerging economies in the G20 have successfully placed development issues on the group's agenda, this agenda largely consists of low-level commitment items by states and reflects emerging economies' development priorities as opposed to the LICs' concerns. The notion of low commitment here denotes issues that do not require G20 member states to adjust their policies. Consider the most expansive document on this subject – the Seoul Development Consensus. Table 8.1 summarizes the key points, the commitments made under the Multi-Year Action Plans, from this Consensus. The table groups the commitments the G20 has made under the Seoul Consensus in three different categories: data collection/surveillance, best practice identification, and positive duties. As the table demonstrates, most of the G20's commitments were under surveillance/data collection, where multilateral institutions need to gather and distribute data. Data collection denotes a low commitment area. So does the identification of best practices, where many other items under the Consensus fall. In contrast, few of the Consensus' provisions fall under positive duties, namely active policy provision or adjustment, by the G20 members. Positive duties, thus, denote the most demanding commitments.

Simultaneously, it remains unclear whether the G20's agenda meaningfully incorporates the LICs' priority concerns in development. For instance, the G20 has passed the opportunity to tackle duty-free access for LIC exports whether in or outside the context of the stalled Doha Development Agenda of the World Trade Organization (Qureshi 2010). In another example, the G20 states have not adequately addressed trade finance for LICs. Especially during crises, trade finance

---

[27] Emerging economies of the G20 contain 58 percent of the world's poorest based on the $2 a day poverty line (World Bank 2010).

Table 8.1 *The Seoul Consensus on development*

Type of item	Explanation
Surveillance/Data Collection	– calls on a host of multilateral organizations, including the ILO, OECD, World Bank, and UNESCO, to develop indicators for assessing skills and productivity in employment
	– monitor effects of multilateral initiatives on LICs, such as the Global Aid for Trade Review, 2011
	– G20 Trade Finance Expert Group and the WTO Experts Group on Trade Finance and OECD Export Credit Group are tasked with identifying the trade finance gap for LICs
	– World Bank and others to improve information on food stocks and production
	– "further implementation" of the UN Global Pulse Initiative, which reports poverty data
	– Global Partnership for Financial Inclusion (GPFI) to share information and monitor progress to ensure that small and medium-sized enterprises financing needs are better met
	– gather data on all multilateral efforts to develop tax systems in developing countries, identification of key constraints in developing countries' tax collection, development of a platform for South–South cooperation to build capacity on effective taxation, identification of ways to assist developing countries to tax multinational corporations effectively
Distributive (positive duties)	– creation of a High-Level Panel for Infrastructure Investment (HLP) to garner financial support for infrastructure financing
	– assist a select group of LICs in increasing their capacity for human capital, e.g., through a focus on training institutions
	– "progress towards" duty-free and quota-free market access for least-developed countries
	– maintain Aid-for-Trade levels beyond 2011 that reflect the average of 2006–2008
	– SME Finance Innovation Fund, multilateral fund for proposals that win the SME Finance challenge

Best Practice Identification

– calls on a host of multilateral organizations, including the ILO, OECD, World Bank, and UNDP, to identify the best practice of investment for creating job creation and maximizing value-added and make recommendations

– FAO and the World Bank are tasked with recommending "innovative results-based mechanisms" in agriculture

– overview and identification of best practices in social protection

– SME Finance Challenge – identification of winning proposals for getting private capital to SMEs

– identification of best practices in combating corruption

is a vital issue for LICs, as it has been in the 2008 global financial crisis. Traders in LICs often face liquidity constraints, and the various transactions involved in these countries are much higher than in other types of economies. For instance, while average prices for letters of credit in large emerging markets were 70–150 basis points in 2010 (reflecting the post-Recession risk concerns), the same numbers for even low-risk African economies were 200–320 basis points (Trade Finance Experts Group 2010). The higher the risk, the more expensive it becomes for traders to gain financing. In some cases, it is prohibitively expensive. Thus, public funds, such as those facilitated by the G20, are of great importance. Although trade finance, as acknowledged by the G20 is a critical issue for LICs, the group has covered little substantive ground on this matter. For instance, in the 2009 London Summit the G20 pledged $250 billion in trade finance to ease the costs of trading. Yet, it is unclear how much of this trade finance has gone to serve the needs of traders in LICs. More certainly, it is clear this amount was not enough to serve the needs of LICs. As the G20 states were getting ready to roll back on trade finance by the 2010 Toronto Summit, the then Director-General of the WTO, Pascal Lamy (2010), was drawing attention to gaps in recovery in trade finance, especially between emerging markets and LICs: "While our experts tell us that there is a large appetite for risk and ample liquidity to finance trade from China, India, Brazil and Korea, at the lower end of the market, there continues to be strong constraints. This is particularly true for Sub-Saharan Africa." While regional development banks had stepped in, to some extent, to address these gaps (Auboin 2010), the G20, by their own admission, had failed even in the collection of data to understand the needs for trade finance in LICs (Trade Finance Experts Group 2010).

Similarly, foreign aid remains under-addressed in the G20 summits and working groups (e.g., Kumar 2010). The lack of emphasis on foreign aid in the G20's development agenda was justified by the Korean Chair of the 2010 G20 summit, president of South Korea, Lee Myung-bak, as emulating non-aid-dependent growth in key middle-income countries (e.g., Myung-bak 2010a, 2010b). Lim (2011, p. 209) captures this point well: "advanced industrial nations regard their own development as an achievement of the past and tend to take an aid-centric approach to international development, leading developing countries ... tend to adopt a growth-centric approach." These comments should not be taken to suggest that leading developing economies skipped reliance on aid; rather, the comments highlight that these countries' leaders do not consider aid to have been an important facilitator of their growth. The emphasis on non-aid-related growth, such as on infrastructure and human capital, cannot be overlooked. And, foreign aid has well-known pitfalls. For instance, much aid can go to waste, or even worse into corruption, and aid can make countries excessively dependent on outside resources (e.g., Easterly 2006; Moyo 2009).

These potential hazards aside, from the perspective of LICs, the quantity and the quality of foreign aid are of critical importance to address. For starters, many of the LICs remain debt-ridden – therefore they need foreign aid in the form of debt-forgiveness – or they remain in need of aid to jumpstart the growth process (Collier 2006). Also, given that many LICs suffer from negative current account balances (they import more than they export), aid also plays an important role in the financing of their deficits (Golub et al. 2011). The 2008 ratio of aid to current expenditure in some LICs was at 90 percent or higher (e.g. Burundi and Rwanda) and for fourteen of the LICs, it exceeded 50 percent (IMF 2009, p. 23). Add to this the fact that these countries have little room for counter-cyclical policies (World Bank 2010), aid becomes even more important. Yet, aid flows to LICs declined relative to GDP in 2009 because of the Great Recession, and most of the funding that resulted from multilateral development banks was non-concessional in nature (World Bank 2010, p. 15), thereby raising concerns about debt-sustainability in LICs. For these reasons, it remains doubtful whether the G20's general exclusion of foreign aid from its agenda serves the LICs' interests.

In sum, the fact that the 2008–2010 changes in the institutions do not benefit the LICs in a significant manner confirms one of the implicit assertions in the book – it would be misleading to talk about the institutional rise of "developing countries" as a whole in the institutions given the divergence within the developing world between the emerging markets (particularly the large emerging markets) and the LICs (Chapter 5). This bifurcation within the developing world invokes questions about whether the newcomers to the institutions' core group of shareholders, the rising states, can re-fashion the institutions to serve the interests of the weakest members. The book's analysis offers a negative response to this question. On the whole, the institutions continue to serve the needs of the relatively rich as opposed to the relatively poor, with the difference that there are newcomers to the relatively rich group.

Divided houses? Tensions between rising and declining states   The discussions in the book reveal tensions between the rising states and the declining states. These tensions range in significance and intensity, but nonetheless they are all relevant in assessing the future of global economic governance through these institutions. In the G20, one of the main points of potential contention concerns the contents of the institution's agenda.

The large advanced economies would like to limit the group's discussions to financial and economic issues, sticking to the institution's original goal of facilitating international financial stability. In contrast, the emerging economies would like to, and in some instances have managed to, expand the group's focus to include other issues, ranging from climate change to global development. The rising states' desire for the expansion of the G20's agenda makes sense because the G20 has relatively egalitarian, non-hierarchal decision-making that permits the rising states to influence the group's work (Chapter 7). The large advanced economies' desire to restrain the agenda of the G20 also makes sense – the expansion of the agenda contributes to the deepening of their accommodation of the rising states. While the book has shown that the declining states' accommodation of the rising states was relatively less contentious in the context of the G20, it also demonstrated that this was not an immaterial accommodation. In this respect, the declining states' potential hesitation to deepen the accommodation even further makes sense. The potential expansion of the agenda also raises questions about the putative trade-off between effectiveness and scope. The more loaded the agenda, the harder it may become to reach decisions among the twenty or so participants. Regardless, an intensification of the disagreements regarding how to utilize the G20 can undermine the institution.

More importantly, the book identified important potential conflicts between the rising and the declining states at the IMF and the World Bank. To begin with, both the rising and the declining states have a greater interest in using the IMF as a platform to induce alterations in the other side's behavior, while shielding their own policies from change. For instance, in reforming the IMF, one of the large advanced economies' motivations has been to bring greater multilateral scrutiny to the rising states' policies, such as the USA's desire to pressure change in China's exchange rate policy (Chapter 5). Leaving aside the question of how this will be achieved in practice, even though the IMF on paper has the mandate to oversee states' monetary policies, the large emerging economies' position enhancement decreases the leverage the institution has over these rising states. As this chapter's discussions on capital controls and the SDR reveal, the rising states are looking to use their enhanced position to affect change in the institution's policies, or at the very least carve out more autonomy for their preferred policies. Yet, the large advanced economies reason that with greater formal power in the institutions, these rising states will assume increased responsibility. More realistically, however, the large emerging markets will do what large advanced economies have done for decades – use their formal political power to instill their own preferences into the institutions.

Another potential fracture might stem from the fact that while the rising states might prefer further change in the institution, shifting the distribution of formal political power in their favor may become increasingly politically difficult. As noted previously, even in the case of the IMF, where the large emerging economies fulfilled a number of their key preferences during the 2008–2010 changes, they nonetheless had other concerns that these reforms left unaddressed. Hence, their ongoing push for more change especially concerning the distribution of formal political power, for which the continuing discussions on additional modifications to the IMF's quota formula is an example (see above). In this respect, more change vis-à-vis formal political power may be necessary to maintain the institution's relevance and credibility from the perspective of these shareholders. Simultaneously, however, actualizing such further change may become increasingly difficult. The book discussed how within the group of declining states, the losses in formal political power were, expectedly, distributed unequally. For instance, in the IMF, the large European economies were among the largest losers; whereas, the USA experienced relatively less of an impact on its formal standing. Whether or not these within-group distributions of losses were justifiable is a discussion for another time. Here, the relevant point is that in further rounds of adjustments to members' formal political power, these within-group tensions might intensify. All in all, the rising states' demands for further position enhancement in the institutions may meet the reluctance of some declining states to suffer further losses as well as increasing efforts for "cost shifting" within this group (Chapters 2 and 5). In other words, while the rising states' demands for position enhancement will likely rise, the space for accommodation by the declining states will continue to be relatively narrow.

In the case of the World Bank, the tensions between the declining and the rising states also unearth divisions over key issues, such as how the Bank can best provide its intended global good of economic development (Chapter 6). The large advanced economies would prefer that the large emerging markets reduce their reliance on funds from the Bank's non-concessional lending arm, the IBRD. In contrast, the large emerging economies would like the IBRD to better tailor its lending instruments to emerging economies, including reducing the costs of borrowing from the IBRD. The rising states and the declining states also have disagreements regarding the IDA. The IDA is a donor-dependent institution with the large advanced economies serving as the primary donors. These states do not wish to lose their influence over the IDA, but they still want the large emerging markets to make greater financial contributions to it. Such a strategy may prove to be self-contradictory, given influence comes with being the largest donors. In other words, to incentivize the rising states to contribute more to the IDA, the declining states may need to agree to changes in accordance with the rising states' preferences (see Chapter 6). At the same time, the large emerging markets do not think they should be under the burden of further financing the IDA because they reason that they already adequately contribute to it. Directly, some of these states make contributions, albeit small, to the IDA. Indirectly, as borrowers from the IBRD, they contribute to the IDA because the IBRD transfers resources to it. These disagreements between the rising and the declining states, beyond quibbles over financial burden sharing, point to divisions over how to best utilize the Bank's resources for global economic development. They reveal tensions over where the Bank should go, whether its resources should predominantly serve the poorest states, or whether the Bank should also continue to serve the relatively well-off members of the developing world.

These points also raise broader questions regarding the Bank's purpose and functioning. There is the obvious issue of the financing of the Bank. The Bank will likely face financial difficulties if the IBRD stops lending to the largest emerging markets (Birdsall and Subramanian 2007). Additionally, the Bank's comparative advantage (relative to other multilateral economic institutions) as a global knowledge bank may be undermined if its relations with emerging markets remain a source of tension among its core shareholders. The loan relationship, as discussed in Chapter 6, creates a platform not just for the loan recipient to learn from the Bank's experience but also for the Bank to learn from the borrowers' experiences. In this regard, the Bank's accumulation of knowledge about different development experiences may be undercut, if it disengages from the middle-income world. Given that the Bank has to increasingly compete on its technical advice, its status as a global knowledge institution would be weakened with feebler links with the middle-income world (Birdsall and Subramanian).

These discussions also raise questions about institutional design. The way in which the two financial institutions were designed – as financial institutions that need to be repaid on the loans they make – limits the LICs' access to these institutions. Making loans to countries with better economic performance increases the chances of these institutions being repaid. For instance, because performance criteria govern access to IDA loans, the Bank cannot necessarily go where it is most needed. The Bank's reliance on the sale of its triple-A rated bonds in international financial markets necessitates such criteria, since the Bank needs to maintain its reputation by limiting country default on loans. In this respect, the Bank's financial model, which would be very difficult to revise, is a limitation on its pattern of lending.

At the same time, the state-oriented nature of the institutions leads to some conundrums. For instance, even though China and India are no longer poor as states, they still contain millions of poor individuals. The declining states are focusing on the rising states' increasing economic prowess in objecting to these states' further reliance on Bank loans. Yet, the rising states are claiming that their continued access to the public funds through the institutions is justified based on them containing a large percentage of poor individuals. This is a conundrum because even if there were political will in transforming these institutions, it would be extremely difficult in practice to re-fashion the IBRD and the IDA to deal with private individuals as primary clients. Such a re-fashioning would entail redesigning core, entrenched aspects of the Bank, including its finances. For instance, the Bank's creditworthiness in international markets is related closely to having sovereigns as clients that are not likely to default. In short, aspects of institutional design limit possibilities for further change, and these institutional restrictions, in turn, point to impenetrable ceilings that the institutions can hit in remaining appealing to a broad range of shareholders and stakeholders.

Leadership in doubt? Another potential source of tension or uncertainty for the institutions concerns the American role in the institutions. Previously, I have underscored that asymmetric US influence over these institutions had already been chipping away at the credibility and relevance of the institutions. In some ways, the reforms have reaffirmed US leadership. The USA led the increase in the position of the rising states because the results of inaction could have been devastating for the institutions. As discussed before, the USA prefers *within* system change (reform of the institutions) to a change *of* the system (the replacement of the institutions with new ones or the atrophy of the institutions), as the current multilateral economic structure continues to reflect its interests better than uncertain alternatives (Chapter 2). Additionally, these institutions help the USA achieve its aims more cheaply – consider that the funds deposited by states in the World Bank give more "bang for the buck" because the Bank is a cooperative arrangement among different states. Even when the USA contributes more than other states, all members' contributions are pooled together to serve ends that are more often than not aligned with US goals and preferences. And, at a time of relative decline, these institutions matter increasingly for the pursuit of US interests, not least because of the rationale of pooling resources, but also because increases in the USA's informal power enhances the importance of formal power (Chapter 2). In sum, the fact that the institutions recognized the rise of large emerging economies through some increases to their formal political power in 2008–2010 can be interpreted as the USA reasserting its leadership at a time when it remains unclear as to whether any other state, or group of states, is ready to assume the position of the USA.

From an alternative perspective, however, the 2008–2010 changes leave the USA in such a strong formal position in the institutions that this position creates a potential liability for the future acceptability of these institutions to a range of shareholders. As the book has shown, the USA has suffered fewer losses in voting power than other large advanced economies as a result of the 2008–2010 shifts in formal political power. For instance, the rate of change in the USA's voting power in the IMF was approximately negative 3 percent; whereas, the same number for the G20 European economies was about negative 11 percent. One could fathom a number of different rationales for this outcome, ranging from the USA's continued importance as the world's largest economy to the relatively greater decline of a number of European economies and the effects of the European debt crisis. Still, the outcome makes it likely that the USA's position will be a question, if not a point of tension, in future discussions of reform among the group of declining states.

Also, even after the reforms, the USA has retained its de facto veto power over decisions that require a supermajority, which is 85 percent of the voting shares (because the USA's voting power remains above 15 percent). Previous shifts in the distribution of formal political power had also protected the US veto. During the 1988 increase to the Bank's capital, the US contributions translated into the US voting power decreasing to 18.75 percent, thereby undercutting the USA's then veto power. To preserve the US veto, the Bank Board increased the supermajority requirement from 80 to 85 percent (Babb 2009, p. 137). The veto power potentially serves an important domestic purpose. The USA's engagement with multilateral economic institutions is closely related to the "power of the purse" that the Congress holds in the American system, and the need for US financial contributions to pass Congressional approval.[28] And, the veto power assures Congress that the USA's interests are well protected in the institutions (see US Senate 2010). Nonetheless, this de facto veto means that any constitutional reforms, such as further changes to the voting power, depend on the USA's consent, as these decisions require a supermajority. And, overall, the veto power potentially creates a liability for these institutions, given

---

[28] On the relationship between the Congress and the two international financial institutions, see, for instance, Broz (2008), Babb (2009), Lavalle (2011).

that it perpetuates (even if just symbolically) the very asymmetries that underlined the credibility of the institutions in the first place.[29]

This point becomes especially pertinent if one considers that the USA faces increasing costs in exercising leadership in the post-Great Recession world. As Martin Wolf (2009) put it: "the US is currently seen as the source of the problem rather than of the solution. The [2008 global economic] crisis is, therefore, a devastating blow to US credibility and legitimacy across the world." This skepticism about the US role in these institutions stems, partially, from the fact that the global economic crisis emanated from the USA, the heart of what was supposed to be the most mature financial market in the world. Also, the lightly regulated US markets were among the primary contributors to the crisis.[30] In this respect, the US model is seen as having been largely discredited and, plausibly, governments will increasingly look elsewhere for successful economic policy-making (e.g., Birdsall and Fukuyama 2011). The USA's ability to persuade (or cajole) others to alter their policies or have them play by international institutions' rulebooks will be relatively more circumscribed, at least in the short run.

Concluding thoughts

This book analyzed the relationship between the inter-state distribution of economic power and states' formal political power in institutions. It has shown that institutions manifest the underlying distribution of economic power at differing degrees depending on the institutionally dominant states' core preferences, the manner in which member states finance the institution, and existing institutional rules and conventions (on adjusting formal political power). Within this framework, it has demonstrated that the importance of the changes in inter-state economic power will hinge upon the specific institutional setting: while some institutional settings will enhance the rising states' formal political power, others will be less responsive. Through this analysis, it has also touched upon some under-explored issues in the study of international political economy, ranging from the failed International Trade Organization's endorsement of voting equality, to the study of IMF's quota shifts over time, to the 2008–2010 shifts' implications for global economic governance.

---

[29] *Financial Times*, "Germany asks US to give up its IMF veto," September 14, 2010.

[30] On the regulation of US markets and the 2008 crisis, see, for instance, Cassidy (2009), Roubini and Mihm (2010), and Stiglitz (2010a).

References

Books, articles, papers

Abbott, K. W. and Snidal, D. 2000. "Hard and soft law in international governance," *International Organization* 54(3): 421–56.

Abdelal, R. 2007. *Capital rules: the construction of global finance.* Cambridge: Harvard University Press.

Abdelal, R., Blyth, M., and Parsons, C. (eds.) 2010. *Constructing the international economy.* Ithaca, NY: Cornell University Press, Cornell Studies in Political Economy.

Acemoglu, D. and Robinson, J. 2013. *Why nations fail: the origins of power, prosperity, and poverty.* New York: Crown Business.

Aggarwal, V. 2010. "I don't get no respect: the travails of IPE," *International Studies Quarterly* 54(3): 893–5.

Alesina, A. and Dollar, D. 2000. "Who gives foreign aid to whom and why?" *Journal of Economic Growth* 5(1): 33–63.

Aslund, A. 2009. "The group of twenty must be stopped," *Financial Times,* November 26. www.ft.com/intl/cms/s/0/37deaeb4-dad0-11de-933d-00144 feabdc0.html#ax zz3RvTZc0d2.

Auboin, M. 2010. "The G20 mandate on fixing trade finance for low-income nations," *Vox,* November 25. www.voxeu.org/article/fixing-trade-finance-low-income-nations-g20-mandate.

Babb, S. L. 2009. *Behind the development banks: Washington politics, world poverty, and the wealth of nations.* Chicago: University of Chicago Press.

    2012. "The Washington consensus as transnational policy paradigm: its origins, trajectory, and likely successor," *Review of International Political Economy* 20(2): 268–97.

Baker, A. 2006. *The group of seven: finance ministries, central banks, and global financial governance.* New York: Routledge.

Barnett, M. and Finnemore, M. 1999. "The politics, power, and pathologies of international organizations," *International Organization* 53(4): 699–732.

Barro, R. J. and Lee, J. 2005. "IMF programs: who is chosen and what are the effects?" *Journal of Monetary Economics* 52: 1245–69.

Beeson, M. 2009. "Comment: trading places? China, the United States, and the evolution of the international political economy," *Review of International Political Economy* 16(4): 729–41.

Best, J. 2007. "Legitimacy dilemmas: the IMF's pursuit of country ownership," *Third World Quarterly* 28(3): 469–88.

Bidwell, P. and Diebold, W. 1949. *The United States and the International Trade Organization international conciliation.* New York: Carnegie Endowment for International Peace.

Bird, G. and Rowlands, D. 2006. "IMF quotas: constructing an international organization using inferior building blocks," *Review of International Organizations* 1(2): 153–71.

Birdsall, N. 2007. "Why it matters who runs the IMF and the World Bank," in Ranis, G., Vreeland, J. R., and Kosack, S. (eds.), *Globalization and the nation state: the impact of the IMF and the World Bank.* London, New York: Routledge Studies in the Modern World Economy, pp. 429–51.

Birdsall, N. and Fukuyama, F. 2011. "The post-Washington consensus: development after the crisis," *Foreign Affairs* (March/April): 45–53.

Birdsall, N. and Subramanian, A. 2007. "From World Bank to world development cooperative," Center for Global Development. www.cgdev.org/publica tion/world-bank-world-development-cooperative.

Blomberg, B. and Broz, L. 2006. "The political economy of IMF voting power," Working Paper. www.princeton.edu/~pcglobal/conferences/IPES/papers/ broz_blomberg_F1030_1.pdf.

Blyth, M. 2002. *Great transformations: economic ideas and institutional change in the twentieth century.* Cambridge, UK: Cambridge University Press.

Boughton, J. M. 2001. *Silent revolution: the International Monetary Fund, 1979–1989.* Washington, DC: International Monetary Fund.

Boughton, J. M. and Lombardi, D. (eds.) 2010. *Finance, development, and the IMF.* London: Oxford University Press.

Bradford, C. I. and Lim, W. 2011. "Conclusion: priority innovations and challenges for the G20," in Bradford, C. I. and Lim, W. (eds.), *Global leadership in transition: making the G20 more effective and responsive.* Seoul; Washington, DC: Korea Development Institute; Brookings Institution, pp. 324–32.

Bronz, G. 1949. "The international trade organization charter," *Harvard Law Review* 62: 1089–125.

Brooks, S. and Wohlforth, W. 2009. "Reshaping the world order how Washington should reform international institutions," *Foreign Affairs*, 88(2): 49–63.

Brooks, S., Wohlforth, W., and Ikenberry, G. J. 2012. "Don't come home America: the case against retrenchment," *International Security* 37(3): 7–51.

Brown, G. 2010. *Beyond the crash: overcoming the first crisis of globalization.* New York: Free Press.

Broz, J. L. 2005. "Changing IMF quotas: the role of the United States Congress," in Buira, A. (ed.), *Reforming the governance of the IMF and the World Bank.* New York: Anthem Press, pp. 283–328.

2008. "Congressional voting on funding the international financial institutions," *Review of International Organizations* 3: 351–74.

Broz, J. L. and Hawes, M. B. 2006. "Congressional politics of financing the International Monetary Fund," *International Organization* 60(2): 367–99.

Bryant, R. 2008. *Reform of quota and voting shares in the International Monetary Fund: "nothing" is temporarily preferable to an inadequate "something".* Washington, DC: The Brookings Institution.

Buchanan, A. and Keohane, R. O. 2006. "The legitimacy of global governance institutions," *Ethics and International Affairs* 20(4): 405–37.

Burnside, C. and Dollar, D. 2000. "Aid, policies, and growth," *American Economic Review* 90(4): 847–68.

Bush, G. W. 2010. *Decision points* (1st ed.). New York: Crown.

Canuto, O. and Lin, J. Y. 2010. "Introduction," in Nabil, M. K. (ed.), *The great recession and developing countries: economic impact and growth prospect.* Washington, DC: The World Bank, pp. 1–12.

Cassidy, J. 2009. *How markets fail: the logic of economic calamities.* London: Allen Lane.

Chin, G. 2010. "Remaking the architecture: the emerging powers, self-insuring, and regional insulation," *International Affairs* 83(3): 693–715.

Chwieroth, J. 2008. "Organizational change 'from within': exploring the World Bank's early lending practices," *Review of International Political Economy* 15(4): 481–505.

    2010. *Capital ideas: the IMF and the rise of financial liberalization.* Princeton: Princeton University Press.

Cohen, B. 2006. "The macrofoundations of monetary power," in Andrews, David M. (ed.), *International monetary power.* Ithaca: Cornell University Press, pp. 31–51.

    2008. *International political economy: an intellectual history.* Princeton: Princeton University Press.

    2010. "Are IPE journals becoming boring?" *International Studies Quarterly* 54(3): 887–91.

Collier, P. 2006. *The bottom billion: why the poorest countries are failing and what can be done about it.* Oxford; New York: Oxford University Press.

Cooper, A. 2010. "The G20 as an improvised crisis committee and/or a contested 'steering committee' for the world," *International Affairs* 86(3): 741–57.

    2012. "The G20 as the Global Focus Group: Beyond the Crisis Committee / Steering Committee Framework." G20 Information Center, G20 Research Group, University of Toronto. www.g20.utoronto.ca/analysis/120619-cooper-focusgroup.html.

Cooper, R. N. and Truman, E. M. 2007. "The IMF quota formula: linchpin of fund reform," *International Economics Policy Brief* No. PB07-1. Washington, DC: Peter G. Peterson Institute for International Economics. www.piie.com/publications/pb/pb07-1.pdf.

Copelovitch, M. S. 2010. *The International Monetary Fund in the global economy: banks, bonds, and bailouts.* Cambridge; New York: Cambridge University Press.

Cox, R. W. 1992. "Multilateralism and world order," *Review of International Studies* 18(2): 161–80.

Cox, G. W. 2004. "Lies, damned lies, and rational choice analyses," in Shapiro, I., Smith, R. M., and Masoud, T. E. (eds.), *Problems and methods in the study of politics.* New York: Cambridge University Press, pp. 167–85.

Darling, A. 2011. *Back from the brink: 1,000 days at Number 11.* London: Atlantic Books.

Diebold, W. 1952. *The end of the I.T.O.* Princeton: Princeton University Department of Economics and Social Institutions, International Finance Section.

Dollar, D. 2007. "Globalization, poverty and inequality since 1980," in Held, D. and Kaya, A. (eds.), *Global inequality: patterns and explanations*. Cambridge: Polity, pp. 73–103.

Dreher, A., Sturm, J., and Vreeland, J. R. 2009. "Development aid and international politics: does membership on the UN security council influence World Bank decisions?" *Journal of Development Economics* 88: 1–18.

2009. "Global horse trading: IMF loans for votes in the United Nations security council," *European Economic Review* 53: 742–57.

Drezner, D. W. 2007. *All politics is global: explaining international regulatory regimes*. Princeton: Princeton University Press.

2008. "The realist tradition in American public opinion," *Perspectives on Politics* 6(1): 51–70.

2012. "The irony of global economic governance: the system worked," CFR Working Paper. www.cfr.org/international-organizations-and-alliances/irony-global-economic-governance-system-worked/p29101.

Drezner, D. W. and McNamara, K. R. 2013. "International political economy, global financial orders and the 2008 financial crisis," *Perspectives on Politics* 11(1): 155–66.

Dryden, S. 1995. *Trade warriors: USTR and the American crusade for free trade*. New York: Oxford University Press.

Duffield, J. S. 2003. "The limits of 'Rational Design,'" *International Organization* 57(2): 411–30.

Easterly, W. R. 2006. *The white man's burden: why the west's efforts to aid the rest have done so much ill and so little good*. New York: Penguin Press.

The Economist. 2009. "The IMF assessed: a good war," September 17. www.economist.com/node/14456879.

Eichengreen, B. 1987. "Hegemonic stability theories of the International Monetary System," NBER Working Paper No. 2193, March. www.nber.org/papers/w2193.pdf.

2007a. "A blueprint for IMF reform: more than just a lender," *International Finance* 10(2): 153–75.

2007b. "Hegemonic stability theories of the International Monetary System," in *Can nations agree? Issues in international economic cooperation*. Washington, DC: The Brookings Institution, pp. 255–86.

2009a. "Can Asia free itself from the IMF?," *Project Syndicate*. www.project-syndicate.org/commentary/can-asia-free-itself-from-the-imf-.

2009b. "The G20 and the Crisis," *Voxeu*, March 2. www.voxeu.org/article/g20-global-governance-and-missing-vision.

Eichengreen, B. and O'Rourke, K. H. 2010. "What do the new data tell us?" *Voxeu*, March 8. www.voxeu.org/article/tale-two-depressions-what-do-new-data-tell-us-february– 192010-update.

Einhorn, J. 2006. "Reforming the World Bank – creative destruction," *Foreign Affairs* 85(1): 17–22.

Elster, J. 1989. *Nuts and bolts for the social sciences*. Cambridge: Cambridge University Press.

2000. "Rational choice history: a case of excessive ambition," *The American Political Science Review* 94(3): 685–95.

Evans, P., and Finnemore, M. 2001. "Organizational reform and the expansion of the South's voice at the Fund," Vol. G-24 Discussion Papers Series, United Nations Conference on Trade and Development. http://unctad.org/en/Docs/pogdsmdpbg24d15.en.pdf.

Feis, H. 1948. "The Geneva proposals for an international trade charter," *International Organization* 2(1): 39–52.

Ferejohn, J. 2004. "External and internal explanation," in Shapiro, I., Smith, R. M., and Masoud, T. E. (eds.), *Problems and methods in the study of politics*. New York: Cambridge University Press, pp. 144–64.

Finnemore, M. 1996. *National interests in international society*. Ithaca: Cornell University Press.

Fioretos, O. 2011. "Historical institutionalism in international relations," *International Organization* 65(2): 367–99.

Fleck, R. and Kilby, C. 2006. "How do political changes influence US bilateral aid allocations? Evidence from panel data," *Review of Development Economics* 10(2): 210–23.

Foot, R., MacFarlane, S. N., and Mastanduno, M. 2003. *US hegemony and international organizations: the United States and multilateral institutions*. Oxford; New York: Oxford University Press.

Frankel, J. and Saravelos, G. 2010. "Reserves and other early warning indicators work in crisis after all," *Voxeu*, July 1. www.voxeu.org/article/early-warning-indicators-and–192008–09-crisis-new-evidence.

   2012. "Can leading indicators assess country vulnerability? Evidence from the 2008–09 global financial crisis," *Journal of International Economics* (87): 216–31.

Fues, T. and Wolff, P. 2010. "The G-20 and global development: which road to take?" *Think tank 20: global perspectives on the Seoul G-20 summit*. November. Washington, DC: The Brookings Institution, pp. 21–3.

Fukuyama, F. 1992. *The end of history and the last man*. New York: Maxwell MacMillan.

Gardner, R. N. 1980. *Sterling-dollar diplomacy, the origins and the prospects of our international economic order* (New, expanded ed.). New York: McGraw-Hill.

Gilpin, R. 1981. *War and change in world politics*. Cambridge; New York: Cambridge University Press.

Gold, J. 1972. *Voting and decisions in the International Monetary Fund; an essay on the law and practice of the fund*. Washington, DC: International Monetary Fund.

   1974. *Membership and nonmembership in the International Monetary Fund: A study in international law and organization*. Washington, DC: International Monetary Fund.

   1981. "The origins of weighted voting power in the Fund," *Finance and Development* 18(1): 25–8.

Goldstein, J. 1988. "Ideas, institutions, and American trade policy," *International Organization* 42(1): 179–217.

   1993. "Creating GATT rules: ideas, institutions and American politics," in Ruggie, John (ed.), *Multilateralism matters*. New York: Columbia University Press, pp. 201–32.

Goldstein, J. and Gowa, J. 2002. "US national power and the post-war trading regime," *World Trade Review* 1(2): 153–70.

Golub, S., Bernhardt, A., and Michelle, L. 2011. "Development and trade strategies for LDCs. 2001–2010 and looking ahead," Paper Prepared for UNCTAD, March.

Grant, R. and Keohane, R. 2005. "Accountability and abuses of power in world politics," *American Political Science Review* 99(1): 29–43.

Green, D. P. and Shapiro, I. 1994. *Pathologies of rational choice theory: a critique of applications in political science.* New Haven: Yale University Press.

Grieco, J. M. 1990. *Cooperation among nations: Europe, America and nontariff barriers to trade.* Ithaca: Cornell University Press.

1995. "The Maastricht Treaty, economic and monetary union and the neo-realist research programme," *Review of International Studies* 21(1): 21–40.

Griffith-Jones, S., Helleiner, E., and Woods, N. (eds.) 2010. "Financial Stability Board: an effective fourth pillar of global economic governance?" Center for International Governance Innovation. www.cigionline.org/sites/default/files/FSB%20special%20report_2.pdf.

Griffith-Jones, S., and Ocampo, J. A. 2011. *Global governance for financial stability and development.* New York: Initiative for Policy Dialogue, Columbia University. http://policydialogue.org/files/publications/Griffith-Jones_Ocampo1.pdf.

Hawkins, D., Lake, D., Nielson, D., and Tierney, M. (eds.) 2006. *Delegation and agency in international organizations.* London: Cambridge University Press.

Helleiner, E. 2012. "The limits of incrementalism: the G20, the FSB and the international regulatory agenda," *Journal of Globalization and Development*, 2(2): 1–19.

Helleiner, E. and Pagliari, S. 2011. "The end of an era in international financial regulation? A postcrisis research agenda," *International Organization* 65(1): 169–200.

Hoekman, B. M. and Kostecki, M. M. 2001. *The political economy of the world trading system: the WTO and beyond.* Oxford: Oxford University Press.

Hopf, T. 2010. "The logic of habit in international relations," *European Journal of International Relations* 16(4): 539–61.

Horsefield, J. K. 1969. *The International Monetary Fund, 1945–1965: twenty years of international monetary cooperation.* Washington, DC: International Monetary Fund.

Hudec, R. 1998. "The GATT legal system: a diplomat's jurisprudence," in Howse, R. (ed.), *The world trading system: critical perspectives on the world economy.* New York: Routledge, pp. 8–59.

Huntington, S. 1993. "The clash of civilizations: the debate," *Foreign Affairs*, Summer. www.foreignaffairs.com/articles/48950/samuel-p-huntington/the-clash-of-civilizations.

Hurd, I. 1999. "Legitimacy and authority in international politics," *International Organization* 53(2): 379–408.

2007. *After anarchy: legitimacy and power in the United Nations security council.* Princeton: Princeton University Press.

Hurrell, A. 2008. "Lula's Brazil: a rising power, but going where?," *Current History* 107(706): 51–7.

Ikenberry, G. J. 1992. "A world economy restored: expert consensus and the Anglo-American postwar settlement," *International Organization* 46(1): 289–321.

2000. *After victory: institutions, strategic restraint, and the rebuilding of order after major wars*. Princeton: Princeton University Press.

2008. "The rise of China and the future of the west: can the liberal system survive?" *Foreign Affairs* 87(1): 23–37.

2009. "Liberal internationalism 3.0: America and the dilemmas of liberal world order," *Perspectives on Politics* 7(1): 71–87.

2012. *Liberal leviathan: the origins, crisis, and transformation of the American world order*. Princeton: Princeton University Press.

Ikenberry, G. J. and Wright, T. 2008. Rising powers and global institutions. A Century Foundation Report. http://72.32.39.237:8080/Plone/publications/pdfs/pb635/ikenberry.pdf.

International Affairs. 2013. Special Issue, "Negotiating the Rise of New Powers," 89(3): 561–792.

Irwin, D. A., Mavroidis, P. C., and Sykes, A. O. 2008. *The genesis of the GATT*. New York: Cambridge University Press.

Jackson, J. H. 2000. *The jurisprudence of GATT and the WTO: insights on treaty law and economic relations*. Cambridge: Cambridge University Press.

Jervis, R. 1999. "Realism, neoliberalism and cooperation: understanding the debate," *International Security* 24(1): 42–63.

Johnston, A. I. 2008. *Social states: China in international institutions 1980–2000*. Princeton: Princeton University Press.

Kahler, M. 1998. "Rationality in international relations," *International Organization* 52(4): 919–41.

2013. "Rising powers and global governance: negotiating change in a resilient status quo," *International Affairs* 89(3): 711–29.

Kapur, D. 2002. "The common pool dilemma of global public goods: lessons from the World Bank's net income and reserves," *World Development* 30(3): 337–54.

Kapur, D., Lewis, J. P., and Webb, R. (eds.) 1997. *The World Bank: its first half century*. Washington, DC: The Brookings Institution.

Kastner, S. L. 2007. "When do conflicting political relations affect international trade?" *Journal of Conflict Resolution* 51(4): 664–88.

Kaya, A. 2012. "Conflicted principles, uncertain agency: The International Monetary Fund and the Great Recession," *Global Policy* 3(1): 24–34.

2012b. "Revival of multilateralism and the challenges ahead," *Global Economy and Development Working Paper No. 49*. Washington, DC: The Brookings Institution.

Kaya, A. and Keba, A. 2011. "Why global inequality matters: derivative global egalitarianism," *Journal of International Political Theory* 7(2): 140–65.

Kennedy, P. 1989. *The rise and fall of the great powers: economic change and military conflict from 1500 to 2000*. New York: Vintage Books.

Keohane, R. 1984. *After hegemony: cooperation and discord in the world political economy*. Princeton: Princeton University Press.

1998. "International institutions: can interdependence work?" *Foreign Policy* 110: 82–96.

2003. "Global governance and democratic accountability," in Held, D. and Koenig-Archibugi, M. (eds.), *Taming globalization: frontiers of governance*, London: Polity Press, pp. 130–59.

2009. "The old IPE and the new," *Review of International Political Economy* 16(1): 34–46.

Keohane, R. O. and Buchanan, A. 2006. "Precommitment regimes for intervention: supplementing the security council," *Ethics & International Affairs* 25(1): 41–63.

Keohane, R. O. and Nye, J. S. 1977. *Power and interdependence: world politics in transition*. Boston: Little, Brown.

Keohane, R. O., Nye, J. S., and Hoffmann, S. 1993. *After the Cold War / international institutions and state strategies in Europe, 1989–1991*. Cambridge: Harvard University Press.

Kharas, H. and Lombardi, D. 2012. *The group of twenty: origins, prospects and challenges for global governance*. Washington, DC: The Brookings Institution.

Kilby, C. 2013. "The political economy of project preparation: an empirical analysis of World Bank projects," *Journal of Development Economics* 105: 211–25.

King, M. 2006. Speech to the Indian council for research on international economic relations (ICRIER), New Delhi, India, February 20. www.bankofengland.co.uk/archive/Documents/historicpubs/speeches/2006/speech267.pdf.

Kirshner, J. 2010. "The tragedy of offensive realism: classical realism and the rise of China," *European Journal of International Relations* 18(1), 53–75.

Kirton, J. 2011. "The G8: legacy, limitations and lessons," in Bradford, C. I. and Lim, W. (eds.), *Global leadership in transition: making the G-20 more effective and responsive*. Washington, DC: Brookings Institution and Korean Development Institute.

Koremenos, B. 2005. "Contracting around international uncertainty," *American Political Science Review* 99(4): 549–65.

Koremenos, B., Lipson, C., and Snidal, D. 2001a. "The rational design of international institutions," *International Organization* 55(4): 761–99.

2001b. "Rational design: looking back to move forward," *International Organization* 55(4): 1051–82.

Krasner, S. 1983. *International regimes*. Ithaca: Cornell University Press.

1985. *Structural conflict: the third world against global liberalism*. Berkeley: University of California Press.

1991. "Global communications and national power: life on the Pareto frontier," *World Politics* 43(3): 336–66.

Kumar, R. 2010. "IMF reforms bode well for the G-20 Seoul summit, but more tangible gains are needed," *Think Tank 20: Global Perspectives on the Seoul G-20 Summit*. Washington, DC: Brookings Institution.

Kuziemko, I. and Werker, E. 2006. "How much is a seat on the security council worth? Foreign aid and bribery at the United Nations," *Journal of Political Economy* 114(5): 905–30.

Lake, D. A. 1993. "Leadership, hegemony, and the international economy: naked emperor or tattered monarch with potential?" *International Studies Quarterly* 37(4): 459–89.

2010. "Making America safe for the world: multilateralism and the rehabilitation of US authority," *Global Governance* 16(4): 471–84.

2013. "Great power hierarchies and strategies in twenty-first century world politics," in Carlsnaes, W., Risse T., and Simmons, B. (eds.), *The handbook of international relations* (2nd ed.). Newbury Park: Sage, pp. 555–77.

Lamy, P. 2010. "The importance and availability of commodity finance lines in the global trade system," Global Commodities Finance Conference, Geneva, Switzerland, June 9. www.wto.org/english/news_e/sppl_e/sppl158_e.htm.

Lancaster, C. 2007. *Foreign aid: diplomacy, development, domestic politics*. Chicago: University of Chicago Press.

Lavelle, K. C. 2011. *Legislating international organization: The US congress, the IMF and the World Bank*. New York: Oxford University Press.

Layne, C. 2009. "The waning of U.S. hegemony – myth or reality? a review essay," *International Security* 34(1): 147–72.

2012. "This time it's real: the end of unipolarity and the Pax Americana," *International Studies Quarterly* 56(1): 203–13.

Leech, D. 2002. "Voting power in the governance of the international monetary fund," *Annals of Operations Research* 109(1–4): 375–97.

Lerrick, A. 2007. "All eyes on the World Bank," *Statement presented to the Subcommittee of Security and International Trade and Finance of the Committee on Banking, Housing and Urban Affairs of the United States Senate*. Washington, DC: American Enterprise Institute.

Lesage, D., Debaere, P., Dierckx, S., and Vermeiren, M. 2013. "IMF reform after the crisis," *International Politics* 50(4): 553–78.

Lesage, D. and Kacar, Y. 2010. "Turkey's profile in the G20: emerging economy, middle power and bridge-builder," *Studia Diplomatica* 63(2): 125–40.

Lim, W. 2011. "Sharing knowledge for development," in Bradford, C. I. and Lim, W. (eds.), pp. 209–18.

Lipscy, P. 2003. "Japan's Asian monetary fund proposal," *Stanford Journal of East Asian Affairs* 3(Spring): 93–104.

Lipson, C. 1991. "Why are some international agreements informal?" *International Organization* 45(4): 495–538.

Lister, F. K. 1984. *Decision-making strategies for international organizations: the IMF model*. Denver: Graduate School of International Studies, University of Denver.

Lombardi, D. 2010a. "An unexpected agenda item at the next IMF annual meetings." www.brookings.edu/research/opinions/2010/09/07-imf-lombardi.

2010b. "The role of the IMF in low-income countries: an institutional approach," in Boughton, J. M. and Lombardi, D. (eds.), pp. 3–14.

2011. *The governance of the financial stability board*. Washington, DC: The Brookings Institution.

Lombardi, D. and Woods, N. 2008. "The politics of influence: an analysis of IMF surveillance," *Review of International Political Economy* 15(5): 711–39.

Loree, R. F. 1950. *Position of the national foreign trade council with respect to the Havana charter for an international trade organization*. New York: National Foreign Trade Council.

MacDonald, P. K. and Parent, J. M. 2011. "Graceful decline?: The surprising success of great power retrenchment," *International Security* 35(4): 7–44.

Mahoney, J., and Schensul, D. 2006. "Historical context and path dependence," in Goodin, R. E. and Tilly, C. (eds.), *Oxford Handbook of Contextual Political Analysis*. Oxford: Oxford University Press, pp. 454–71.

Mansfield, E. D. and Pevehouse, J. C. 2000. "Trade blocs, trade flows, and international conflict," *International Organization* 54(4): 775–808.

Martinez-Diaz, L. 2007. *The G20 after eight years: how effective a vehicle for developing-country influence?* Washington, DC: The Brookings Institution.

Mason, E. S. and Asher, R. E. 1973. *The World Bank since Bretton Woods: the origins, policies, operations, and impact of the International Bank for reconstruction*. Washington, DC: Brookings Institution.

McIntyre, E. 1954. "Weighted voting in international organizations," *International Organization* 8(4): 484–97.

Mearsheimer, J. 1994/1995. "The false promise of international institutions," *International Security* 19(3): 5–49.

2001. *The tragedy of great power politics*. New York: W. W. Norton & Company, Inc.

Mikesell, R. F. 1994. *The Bretton Woods debates: a memoir. Essays in International Finance No. 192*. Princeton, NJ: Princeton University.

Milner, H. V. 1997. *Interests, institutions, and information: domestic politics and international relations*. Princeton: Princeton University Press.

2005. "Globalization, development and international institutions: normative and positive perspectives," *Perspectives on Politics* 3(4): 833–54.

Mohammed, A. A. 2004. "Who pays for the World Bank?" G24 Research Paper. http://g24.org/wp-content/uploads/2014/03/Mohammed-2.pdf.

Momani, B. 2004. "American politicization of the International Monetary Fund," *Review of International Political Economy* 11(5): 880–904.

Moravcsik, A. 1997. "Taking preferences seriously: a liberal theory of international politics," *International Organization* 51(4): 513–53.

2000. "The origins of human rights regimes: democratic delegation in postwar Europe," *International Organization* 54(2): 217–52.

Morrow, J. D., Siverson, R. M., and Tabares, T. E. 1998. "The political determinants of international trade: the major powers, 1907–90," *American Political Science Review* 92(3): 649–61.

Moschella, M. 2010. *Governing risk: The IMF and global financial crises*. New York: Palgrave Macmillan.

Mosley, L. and Singer, D. A. 2009. "The global financial crisis: lessons and opportunities for international political economy," *International Interactions* 35(4): 420–29.

Moss, T., Staats, S. J., and Barmeler, J. 2010. "Billions more for international institutions? The ABCs of the General Capital Increases (GCI)," *Center for Global Development Brief*. www.cgdev.org/publication/billions-more-interna tional-institutions-abcs-general-capital-increases-gci.

Moyo, D. 2009. *Dead aid: why aid is not working and how there is a better way for Africa*. New York: Farrar, Straus and Giroux.

Myung-bak, L. 2010a. "G20 summit shouldn't overlook the poorest countries," *The Washington Post*, November 10. www.washingtonpost.com/wp-dyn/con tent/article/2010/11/09/AR2010110 905009.html.

2010b. "Seoul G20 summit: priorities and challenges," Paper presented at the World Economic Forum, Davos, Switzerland, January 28. www.g20.utoronto.ca/summits/2010seoul.html.

Naim, M. 2000. "Fads and fashions in economic reforms: Washington consensus or Washington confusion?" *Third World Quarterly* 21(3): 505–28.

Nelson, R. M., Weiss, M. A., Belkin, P., and Mix, D. E. 2012. "The eurozone crisis: overview and issues for congress," Congressional Research Service, September 26. www.fas.org/sgp/crs/row/R42377.pdf.

Neumayer, E. 2003. "Do human rights matter in bilateral aid allocation? A quantitative analysis of 21 donor countries," *Social Science Quarterly* 84(3): 650–66.

Odell, J. 2001. "Case study methods in international political economy," *International Studies Perspectives* 2(2): 161–76.

2009. "Breaking deadlocks in international institutional negotiations: The WTO, Seattle, and Doha," *International Studies Quarterly* 53(2): 273–99.

Odell, J. and Eichengreen, B. 1998. "The United States, the ITO, and the WTO: exit options, agent slack, and presidential leadership," in *The WTO as an International Organization*. Chicago: University of Chicago Press.

Ostrom, E. 1991. "Rational choice theory and institutional analysis: toward complementarity," *The American Political Science Review* 85(1): 237–43.

Patrick, S. 2011. "The G20: shifting coalitions of consensus rather than blocs," in Bradford, C. I. and Lim, W. (eds.), pp. 257–64.

Pauly, L. 1997. *Who elected the bankers?: surveillance and control in the world economy*. Cambridge: Cambridge University Press.

2008. "The institutional legacy of Bretton Woods IMF surveillance, 1973–2007," in Andrew, D. (ed.), *Orderly change: International Monetary relations since Bretton Woods*. Ithaca, NY: Cornell University Press, pp. 189–210.

Pierson, P. 2004. *Politics in time: history, institutions, and social analysis*. Princeton: Princeton University Press.

Pincus, J. R. and Winters, J. A. 2002. "Reinventing the World Bank," in Pincus, J. and Winters, J. A. (eds.), *Reinventing the World Bank*. Ithaca: Cornell University Press.

Porter, R. 1947. "Weighted ITO vote abandoned by U.S.; one voice per nation accepted if we receive a permanent seat on executive board," *New York Times*, December 16. http://query.nytimes.com/gst/abstract.html?res=940CE2DF1E 3BEF3ABC4E52DFB467838C659EDE.

Powell, W. W. and DiMaggio, P. J. 1991. *The new institutionalism in organizational analysis*. Chicago: University of Chicago Press.

Putnam, R. 1988. "Diplomacy and domestic politics: The Logic of Two-Level Games," *International Organization* 42(3): 427–46.

Qureshi, Z. 2010. "The G-20 and global development," in Fardoust, S., Kim, Y., and Paz Sepúlveda, C. (eds.), *Postcrisis growth and development: a development agenda for the G-20*. Washington, DC: The World Bank, pp. 119–71.

Radelet, S. and Sachs, J. 1998. "The onset of the East Asian financial crisis," NBER Working Paper Series 6680. www.nber.org/papers/w6680.pdf.

Rajan, R. 2008. "The future of the IMF and the world bank," *American Economic Review* 98(2): 110–15.

Rapkin, D., Elston, J., and Strand, J. 1997. "Institutional adjustment to changed power distributions: Japan and the United States in the IMF," *Global Governance* 3(2): 171–95.

Rapkin, D. P. and Strand, J. R. 2005. "Developing country representation and governance of the International Monetary Fund," *World Development* 33(12): 1993–2011.

Reinhardt, E. and Kucik, J. 2008. "Does flexibility promote cooperation? An application to the global trade regime," *International Organization* 62(3): 477–505.

Reus-Smit, C. 2007. "Human rights and the social construction of sovereignty," *Review of International Studies* 27(4): 519–38.

Rodrik, D. 2008. *One economics, many recipes: globalization, institutions, and economic growth*. Princeton: Princeton University Press.

Rogoff, K. 2003. "The IMF strikes back," *Foreign Policy* 134(January–February): 38–46.

Rosendorff, B. P. and Milner, H. V. 2001. "The optimal design of international trade institutions: uncertainty and escape," *International Organization* 55(4): 829–57.

Roubini, N. and Mihm, S. 2010. *Crisis economics: a crash course in the future of finance*. New York: Penguin Press.

Ruggie, J. G. 1982. "International regimes, transactions, and change: embedded liberalism in the post-war economic order," *International Organization* 36(2): 379–415.

Sanford, J. E. and Weiss, M. A. 2009. "The global financial crisis: increasing IMF resources and the role of congress," *Congressional Research Service*, May 14. http://fpc.state.gov/documents/organization/125510.pdf.

Scharpf, F. W. 1999. *Governing in Europe: effective and democratic?* Oxford: Oxford University Press.

Schirm, S. A. 2011. "Global politics are domestic politics: how societal interests and ideas shape ad hoc groupings in the G20 which supersede international alliances," Paper presented at the International Studies Association (ISA) Convention, Montreal, Canada.

Schneider, H. and Wilson, S. 2010. "The 'G-2,' U.S. and China, will be the center of the G-20 debates in Seoul," November 10, *The Washington Post*. www.washingtonpost.com/wp-dyn/content/article/2010/11/10/AR20101110 04254.html.

Schuler, K. and Rosenberg, A. 2012. *The Bretton Woods transcripts*. New York: Center for Financial Stability.

Schweller, R. 2001. "The problem of international order revisited – a review essay," *International Security* 26(1): 161–86.

Schweller, R. L. and Priess, D. 1997. "A tale of two realisms: expanding the institutions debate," *Mershon International Studies Review* 41(1): 1–32.

Schweller, R. L. and Pu, X. 2011. "After unipolarity: China's visions of international order in an era of U.S. decline," *International Security* 36(1): 41–72.

Seabrooke, L. 2007. "Everyday legitimacy and international financial orders: the social sources of imperialism and hegemony in global finance," *New Political Economy* 12(1): 1–18.

Shepsle, K. A. 2006. "Rational choice institutionalism," in Binder, S., Rhodes, R., and Rockman, B. (eds.), *The Oxford Handbook of Political Institutions*. London: Oxford University Press.

Shorr, D. and Wright, T. 2010. "The G20 and global governance: an exchange," *Survival: Global Politics and Strategy* 52(2): 191–98.

Simmons, B. A. and Martin, L. L. 2002. "International organizations and institutions," in Carlsnaes, T. R. and Simmons, B. A. (eds.), *Handbook of International Relations*. Thousand Oaks: Sage Publications, pp.192–211.

Steffek, J. 2003. "The legitimation of international governance: a discourse approach," *European Journal of International Relations* 9(2): 249–75.

Steinberg, R. H. 2002. "In the shadow of law or power? Consensus-based bargaining and outcomes in the GATT/WTO," *International Organization* 56(2): 339–74.

Stiglitz, J. E. 2002. *Globalization and its discontents* (1st ed.). New York: W.W. Norton.

    2010a. *Freefall: America, free markets, and the sinking of the world economy* (1st ed.). New York: W.W. Norton & Co.

    2010b. "Towards a new global reserve system," in Sachs, J. D., Kawai, M., Lee, J., and Woo, W. T. (eds.), *Future of the Global Reserve System – An Asian Perspective*. Asian Development Bank. http://aric.adb.org/ grs/report.php?p=Stiglitz.

Stone, R. W. 2008. "The scope of IMF conditionality," *International Organization* 62(4): 589–620.

    2011. *Controlling institutions: international organizations and the global economy*. New York: Cambridge University Press.

Store, J. G. 2010. "G20 sorely lacking in legitimacy," *New Straits Times*, March 29.

Strezhnev, A. and Voeten, E. 2013. United Nations General Assembly Voting Data. http://hdl.handle.net/1902.1/12379.

Thacker, S. 1999. "The high politics of IMF lending," *World Politics* 52(October): 38–75.

Thelen, K. and Mahoney, J. 2010. *Explaining institutional change: ambiguity, agency, and power*. Cambridge: Cambridge University Press.

Thompson, A. 2010. "Rational design in motion: uncertainty and flexibility in the global climate regime," *European Journal of International Relations* 16(2): 269–96.

Truman, E. M. 2013. "The Congress should support IMF governance reform to help stabilize the world economy," Peterson Institute for International Economics. Policy Brief, March. www.iie.com/publications/pb/pb13–7.pdf.

Van Houten, L. 2002. "Governance of the IMF: decision making, institutional oversight, transparency and accountability," International Monetary Fund, Pamphlet Series 53.

Vaubel, R. 1991. "The political economy of the International Monetary Fund: a public choice analysis," in Vaubel, R. and Willett, T. D. (eds.), *The political economy of international organizations*. Boulder: Westview Press.

Vestergaard, J. 2011. "The World Bank and the emerging world order: adjusting to multipolarity at the second decimal point," *DIIS Report 2011:05*. Copenhagen: Danish Institute for International Studies. www.academia.edu/5575568/The_World_Bank_and_the_emerging_world_order_Adjusting_to_multipolarity_at_the_second_decimal_point.

Viner, J. 1948. "Power versus plenty as objectives of foreign policy in the seventeenth and eighteenth centuries," *World Politics* 1(1): 1–29.

Virmani, A. 2011. "Global economic governance: IMF quota reform," IMF Working Paper No. 11/208.

Voeten, E. 2005. "The political origins of the UN Security Council's ability to legitimize the use of force," *International Organization* 59(3): 527–57.

2004. "Resisting the lonely superpower: responses of states in the United Nations to US dominance," *Journal of Politics* 66(3): 729–54.

Vreeland, J. R. 2007. *The International Monetary Fund: politics of conditional lending*. London; New York: Routledge.

Wade, R. 2011. "Emerging world order? From multipolarity to multilateralism in the G20, the World Bank, and the IMF," *Politics & Society* 39(3): 347–77.

Weaver, C. 2008. *Hypocrisy trap: the World Bank and the poverty of reform*. Princeton: Princeton University Press.

Weingast, B., and Katznelson, I. 2005. *Preferences and situations: points of intersection between historical and rational choice institutionalism*. New York: Russell Sage Foundation.

Wilcox, C. 1947. "The London draft of a charter for an international trade organization," *The American Economic Review* 37(2): 529–41.

1949a. *A charter for world trade*. New York: Macmillan.

1949b. "Why the International Trade Organization?" *Annals of the American Academy of Political and Social Science* 264(1): 67–74.

Wilkinson, R. and Scott, J. 2008. "Developing country participation in the GATT: a reassessment," *World Trade Review* 7(3): 473–510.

Winters, M. 2010. "Choosing to target: what types of countries get different types of World Bank projects," *World Politics* 62(3): 422–58.

Wolf, M. 2004. *Why globalization works*. New Haven: Yale University Press.

Woods, N. 2000. "The challenge of good governance for the IMF and the World Bank themselves," *World Development* 28(5): 823–41.

2005. "A note of decision-making reform in the IMF," Paper presented at the G24 Technical Meeting, Manila, Philippines. http://g24.org/wp-content/uploads/2014/03/Woods-3.pdf.

2006. *The globalizers: the IMF, the World Bank, and their borrowers*. Ithaca: Cornell University Press.

2008. "Whose aid? Whose influence? China, emerging donors and the silent revolution in development assistance," *International Affairs* 84(6): 1205–21.

2010. "Global governance after the financial crisis: a new multilateralism of the last gasp of the great powers?" *Global Policy* 1(1): 51–63.

2011. "The impact of the G-20 on global governance: a history and prospective," in Bradford, C. I. and Lim, W. (eds.), pp. 36–47.

Woods, N. and Lombardi, D. 2006. "Uneven patterns of governance: how developing countries are represented in the IMF," *Review of International Political Economy* 13(3): 480–515.

Wooldridge, J. 2002. *Econometric analysis of cross section and panel data*. Cambridge: MIT Press.

Zedillo, E. 2009. "Repowering the World Bank for the 21st century: report of the high-level commission on modernization of World Bank group governance." http://siteresources.worldbank.org/NEWS/Resources/WBGovernanceCOM MISSIONREPORT.pdf.

Zeiler, T. 1999. *Free trade, free world: the advent of GATT.* Chapel Hill: University of North Carolina Press.

Zoellick, R. 2010a. "Democratizing development economics," Speech delivered at Georgetown University, September 29. http://web.worldbank.org/WBSITE/ EXTERNAL/NEWS/0,,contentMDK:22716997~pagePK:34370~piPK:427 70~theSitePK:4607,00.html?cid=EXT_TWBN_D_EXT.

  2010b. *The end of the third world? Modernizing multilateralism for a multipolar world.* Woodrow Wilson Center for International Scholars, April 14. http:// web.worldbank.org/WBSITE/EXTERNAL/NEWS/0,,contentMDK:22541 126~pagePK:34370~piPK:42770~theSitePK:4607,00.html.

Documents from Multilateral Institutions

Al-Assaf, I. 2009. *Statement to the Development Committee Seventy-Ninth Meeting,* Washington, DC, April 26.

Boudou, A. 2010. *Statement to the Development Committee Eighty-Second Meeting,* Washington, DC, October 9.

Chawla, A. 2009. *Statement to the Development Committee Seventy-Ninth Meeting,* Washington, DC, April 26.

  2010. *Statement to the Development Committee Eighty-First Meeting,* Washington, DC, April 25.

Chidambaram, P. 2007. *Statement to the Development Committee Seventy-Sixth Meeting,* Washington, DC, October 21.

  2008. *Statement to the Development Committee Seventy-Seventh Meeting,* Washington, DC, April 13.

Dos Santos, T. 2007. *Statement to the IMFC Sixteenth Meeting,* Washington, DC, October 20.

E/CONF.2/7. 1948. *Final Act of the United Nations Conference on Trade and Employment: Havana Charter for an International Trade Organization.* United Nations Conference on Trade and Employment, March 24.

E/PC/T/33. 1946. *Report of the First Session of the Preparatory Committee.*

E/PC/T/C.V/14. 1946. *Voting in the International Trade Organization – Memorandum by the United Kingdom Delegation for Committee V,* November 5.

E/PC/T/C.V/21. 1946. *The Question of Voting in the International Trade Organization – Memorandum Submitted by the Delegations of the Netherlands and the Belgo-Luxembourg Economic Union,* November 9.

E/PC/T/C.6/25. 1947. *Summary Record of the Fourth Meeting of the Drafting Committee of the Preparatory Committee of the United Nations Conference on Trade and Development,* January 30.

E/PC/T/C.6/62. 1947. *First Report of the Administrative Sub-Committee (Report on Executive Board Membership and Voting,* February 10.

E/PC/T/C.6/W.3. 1947. *Formula for Weighted Voting – Proposed by the United Kingdom Representative,* January 21.

E/PC/T/C.6/W.6/Add.1. 1947. *United States Suggestion Addition to E/PC/T/C.6/W.6 Concerning Weighted Voting*, January 27.

E/PC/T/W/221. 1947. *Second Session of the Preparatory Committee of the United Nations Conference on Trade and Employment – Chapter VIII*, June 23.

Flaherty, J. 2006. Statement to the IMF/World Bank Board Annual Meetings, Press Release No. 25. Washington, DC, September 19–20.

G20. 2005. Communiqué. Finance Ministers and Central Bank Governors Meeting. October 15–16.

2005. Communiqué. The G-20 Statement on Global Development Issues.

2008. "Declaration," Summit on Financial Markets and the World Economy, November 15.

2008. The Group of Twenty: A History.

2009. The Global Plan for Recovery and Reform. G20 Statement. April 2.

[Pittsburgh]. 2009. G20 Statement. Leaders' Statement The Pittsburgh Summit, September 24–25.

[Toronto]. 2010. Declaration. Toronto Summit, June 27.

[Progress Report]. 2010. Progress Report On The Economic And Financial Actions Of The London, Washington and Pittsburgh G20 Summits Prepared By Korea, Chair Of The G20. July 20.

[Seoul]. 2010. Declaration. Seoul Summit, November 11–12.

[Seoul Summit Document]. 2010. G20 Seoul Summit Document. November 12.

[Trade Finance Experts]. 2010. Trade Finance Experts Group April Report.

2011. Communiqué. *Meeting of the Finance Ministers and Central Bank Governors*, Paris, February 18–19.

2011. Declaration. "Action plan on food price volatility and agriculture." *Paper presented at the Meeting of G20 Agriculture Ministers*, Paris, France, June 22–23.

[Interagency Report]. 2011. Price Volatility in Food and Agricultural Markets: Policy Responses. Interagency Policy Report to the G20.

G24. 2012. Intergovernmental Group of Twenty-Four on International Monetary Affairs and Development. G24 Communiqué.

Geithner, T. 2009. Hearing before the Committee on Foreign Relations of the United States Senate, One Hundred Eleventh Congress, First Session, November 17. Washington, DC.

2010a. Statement to the International Monetary and Financial Committee Twenty-Second Meeting, October 9. Washington, DC.

2010b. Statement to the Development Committee Eighty-Second Meeting, October 9. Washington, DC.

2010c. Statement to the Development Committee Eighty-Second Meeting, Washington, DC, October 9.

2011. Written Testimony Before the House Committee on Appropriations Subcommittee on State, Foreign Operations, and Related Programs. One Hundred Eleventh Congress, First Session, March 9. Washington, DC.

IMF EBD/69/165. 1969. *"Incremental Approach"* to Quota Calculations, October 16.

EBM. 2000a. Staff Commentary on the External Review of Quota Formulas, June 6.

2000b. Report to the IMF Executive Board of the Quota Formula Review Group, April 28.

2001. Alternative Quota Formulas: Considerations, September 27.

2003. Quota Distribution – Selected Issues, July 17.

2005. Quotas and Voice – Further Considerations, September 2.

2006a. Quotas and Voice: Further Thoughts on Approaches to Reform, June 23.

2006b. Quotas and Voice – A Possible Package of Reforms, and the Chairman's Concluding Remarks, August 4.

2006c. Quotas – Further Thoughts on a New Quota Formula, and Statistical Appendices I and II, November 22.

2007a. Committee to Study Sustainable Long-Term Financing of the IMF: Final Report, January 31.

2007b. Structural Conditionality in IMF-Supported Programs. Independent Evaluation Office.

2009. The Implications of the Global Financial Crisis for Low-Income Countries.

2010a. IMF Quota and Governance Reform – Elements of an Agreement, October 31.

2010b. Executive Board Report to the IMFC on Quota and Governance Reforms, September 22.

2010c. IMF Governance Reform, July 7.

2011a. Criteria for Broadening the SDR Currency Basket, September 23.

2011b. Enhancing Monetary Financial Stability – A Role for the SDR?, January 7.

2011. Recent Experiences in Managing Capital Inflows – Cross-Cutting Themes and Possible Policy Framework.

2012. Quota Formula Review – Initial Considerations, February 10.

2013. Report of the Executive Board to the Board of Governors on the Outcome of the Quota Formula Review, January 30.

EBM/89/154. 1989. *Ninth General Review of Quotas – Report to the Board of Governors and Proposed Resolution*, November 28.

EBM/90/79. 1990. *Minutes of the Executive Board Meeting*, May 21.

EBM/97/97. 1997. *Minutes of the Executive Board Meeting*, November 18.

EBS/58/59. 1958. *Enlarging Fund Resources through Increases in Quotas.*

SM/59/6. 1959. *Special Quota Increases*, January 26.

SM/78/221. 1978. September 15. *Report of the Executive Directors to the Interim Committee on the Seventh General Review of Quotas.*

SM/81. 1981. February 24. *Economic Criteria Entering Quota Calculations, Supplement 1.*

SM/81/91. 1981. April 23. *Present and Calculated Quotas.*

1987. Committee of the Whole on Review of Quotas, September 17.

SM/95/152. 1995. *The Evolution of the Shares in Fund Quotas of Developing Countries*, June 22.

Indrawati, S.M. 2009. Statement to the Development Committee Eightieth Meeting, October 5. Washington, DC.

Kudrin, A. 2007. Statement to the Development Committee Seventy-Sixth Meeting, October 21. Washington, DC.

2009. Statement to the Development Committee Eightieth Meeting, October 5. Washington, DC.

2011. Statement to the Development Committee Eighty-Third Meeting, April 16. Washington, DC.

Lagarde, C. 2008. Statement to the Development Committee Seventy-Seventh Meeting. Washington, DC, April 13.

2009. Statement to the Development Committee Eightieth Meeting, Washington, DC, October 5.

Lousteau, M. 2008. Statement to the IMFC Seventeenth Meeting, April 12.

Mantega, G. 2007. Statement to the IMFC Sixteenth Meeting, October 20. Washington, DC.

2007b. Statement to the Development Committee Seventy-Sixth Meeting, October 21. Washington, DC.

2008. Statement to the Development Committee Seventy-Eighth Meeting, October 12. Washington, DC.

2009. Statement to the Development Committee Eightieth Meeting, October 5. Washington, DC.

2011a. Statement to the IMFC Twenty-Fourth Meeting, September 24. Washington, DC.

2011b. Statement to the Development Committee Eighty-Fourth Meeting, September 24. Washington, DC.

Miceli, F. 2007. Statement to the IMFC Fifteenth Meeting, April 14. Washington, DC.

Minezaki, N. 2009. Statement to the Development Committee Eightieth Meeting. October 5. Istanbul, Turkey.

Mukherjee, P. 2009. Statement to the Development Committee Eightieth Meeting, October 5. Washington, DC.

2011. Statement to the Development Committee Eighty-Fourth Meeting, September 24. Washington, DC.

Pado-Schioppa, T. 2008. Statement to the IMFC Seventeenth Meeting, April 18. Washington, DC.

Polak, J. 1981. "Economic criteria entering quota calculations," Statement to the Executive Board Meeting 81/29, February 27.

Saldago, E. 2010. Statement to the IMFC Twentieth Meeting, April 24. Washington, DC.

Shinohara, N. 2008. Statement to the Development Committee Seventy-Eighth Meeting, October 12. Washington, DC.

Strauss-Kahn, D. 2007. Statement to the IMF Executive Board, September 20. Washington, DC.

Subbarao, D. 2010. Statement to the IMFC Twentieth Meeting, April 24. Washington, DC

Wieczorek-Zeul, H. 2009. Statement to the Development Committee Eightieth Meeting, October 5. Istanbul, Turkey.

World Bank. 1975. *Review of IBRD Capital Structure*, November 4. Board Report 77884.

1995. *Note to Executive Directors on Possible Increases in IBRD Shareholding of Certain Members*. Board Report 76701. Nov. 10.

1998. *IBRD Share Allocation Review: Report to IDA Deputies*, January 16. Board Report 68804.

2005–2011. *Annual Report.* http://go.worldbank.org/VLWFADE5O0.

2008. *Committee on Governance and Executive Directors' Administrative Matters (COGAM): Report of the Working Group on Internal Governance*, September 5. Board Report 45382.

2010. Report prepared by Staff of the World Bank for G20 Growth Framework and Mutual Assessment Process, June 26–27.

DC 192007-0009/1. Option Paper on Voice and Participation: Final Update Report. Background Report for D.C. Meeting, April 6.

DC2007–0024. Voice and Participation of Developing and Transition Countries at the World Bank Group: Options Paper. Background Report for D.C. Meeting, October 11.

DC2008–0013. Enhancing Voice and Participation of Developing and Transition Countries in the World Bank Group: Options for Reform. Background Report for D.C. Meeting, October 12.

DC2008. Enhancing Voice and Participation of Developing and Transition Countries in the World Bank Group: Implementation of Reforms, November 25.

DC2009–0011. Enhancing Voice and Participation of Developing and Transition Countries in the World Bank Group: Update and Proposals for Discussion, September 29.

DC 192010-0002/1. Synthesis Paper: New World, New World Bank Group.

DC 192010-0006/1. World Bank Group Voice Reform: Enhancing Voice and Participation of Developing and Transition Countries in 2010 and Beyond. Background Report for D.C. Meeting, April 19.

DC2010–0006. World Bank Group Voice Reform: Enhancing Voice and Participation of Developing and Transition Countries in 2010 and Beyond. Background Report for D.C. Meeting, April 25.

IEG. 2009. Annual Review Of Development Effectiveness 2009: Achieving Sustainable Development. Independent Evaluation Group Report.

IEG. 2011. World Bank Group's Response to the Global Economic Crisis. Independent Evaluation Group Report.

Multiple Years. The World Development Indicators Data Set. http://data.worldbank.org/data-catalog/world-development-indicators.

Xiaochuan, Z. 2009. Reform the International Monetary System.

Xiaoling, W. 2007. Statement to the IMFC Sixteenth Meeting, October 20.

Xuren, X. 2009. Statement to the Development Committee Eightieth Meeting, October 5. Washington, DC.

2011. Statement to the Development Committee Eighty-fourth Meeting, September 23. Washington, DC.

Yong, L. 2007a. Statement to the Development Committee Seventy-Fifth Meeting, April 15. Washington, DC.

2007b. Statement to the Development Committee Seventy-Sixth Meeting, October 21. Washington, DC.

2008. Statement to the Development Committee Seventy-Eighth Meeting, October 12. Washington, DC.

2009. Statement to the Development Committee Seventy-Ninth Meeting, April 26. Washington, DC.

US Official Documents[1]

Acheson, D. 1945. In US House of Representatives Committee on Banking and Currency. *Bretton Woods agreements act hearings before the Committee on Banking and Currency.* 79th Cong., 1st session.

Clayton, W. and Wilcox, C. 1947. *Issues at Havana Conference*, September 30. US National Archives, College Park.

Congressional Budget Office. 2009. Budget implications of US contributions to the International Monetary Fund, May 19. www.cbo.gov/publication/24901.

ECEFP D-41/46. 1946. "The Subcommittee on Balance-of-Payments Restrictions," April 7.

ECEFP D-43/47. 1947. Draft Report of the Drafting Committee of the Preparatory Committee of the United Nations Conference on Trade and Employment, March 18.

ECEFP D-45/46. 1946. "Draft Charter of the International Organization of the United Nations," May 27.

ECEFP D-47/45. 1945. "Outline of Proposed International Trade Organization," April 3.

ECEFP D-54/47. 1947. Suggested United States Position with Regard to Weighted Voting and Other Provisions to Protect the Interests of the United States in the ITO Charter, March 31.

ECEFP D-62/47. 1947. Suggested United States Position with Regard to Weighted Voting and Other Provisions to Protect the Interests of the United States in the ITO Charter, April 16.

ECEFP D-63/44. 1945. "Proposed Multilateral Convention on Commercial Policy, Draft Text of Articles of Agreement," February.

ECEFP D-64/44. 1944. "Analysis of the Draft Text of the Proposed Multilateral Convention on Commercial Policy," October.

ECEFP D-72/45. 1945. "Outline of Proposed International Trade Organization," April 27.

ECEFP D-102/48. 1948. "The Development of the Charter for an International Trade Organization," August 16.

ECEFP D 218-/47. 1947. "Preliminary Summary of Geneva Draft of ITO Charter," October 13.

ECEFP M-20/46. 1946. The Minutes of the Meeting of the ECEFP, June 28.

ECEFP M-20/47. 1947. Minutes of the Meeting of the ECEFP, November 7.

Memorandum. 1947. Memorandum from Wilcox to Messieurs Kellogg, Leddy, Bronz, July 11. US National Archives, College Park.

Memorandum. 1948. Memorandum for Mr. Wilcox, February 26. US National Archives, College Park.

Morgenthau, H. 1944. "Bretton Woods Decisions: Closing Address by Secretary of the Treasury Henry Morgenthau," in *Pamphlet no. 4, pillars of peace:*

---

[1] All documents that begin with "ECEFP" are from the US National Archives, College Park, Maryland, USA.

documents pertaining to American interest in establishing a lasting world peace: January 1941-February 1946. Carlisle Barracks: Book Department, Army Information School.

Office Memorandum. 1947. "US Position on Voting Under the ITO Charter," October 20. US National Archives, College Park.

Office Memorandum Letters. 1946. Letter between Ed Kellogg and John Tomlinson, November 19. US National Archives, College Park.

Paper on Organizational Chapters. 1947. Geneva Draft Charter, December 19. US National Archives, College Park.

Truman, H. 1949. Special Message to the Congress Transmitting the Charter for the International Trade Organization. Washington, DC: United States Government Printing Office, 1966.

United States Delegation. 1947a. "The United Nations Conference on Trade and Employment . . . Havana." DS/9, November 21. US National Archives, College Park.

United States Delegation. 1947b. Speeches Made at the Plenary Sessions of ITO Conference, *SD/15*, December 6. US National Archives, College Park.

US Department of State 1946a. *Suggested Charter for an International Trade Organization of the United Nations*. Document No. 2598. Washington, DC: Department of State.

1946b. *Foreign Relations of the United States*. Document No. AL/12–3046. Washington, DC: Department of State Office of the Historian.

US House of Representatives. 1945. Committee on Banking and Currency. *Bretton Woods Agreements Act: Hearings before the Committee on Banking and Currency*. 79th Cong., 1st session, June, 12–25.

2013. Committee on Financial Services. *Evaluating U.S. Contributions to the International Monetary Fund*. 113th Cong., 1st session, April 24.

US Senate. 1947. Committee on Finance. *Hearings Before the Committee on Finance: First Session on Trade Agreements System and Proposed International Trade Organization Charter*. 80th Cong., 1st session.

2010. Committee on Foreign Relations. *The International Financial Institutions: A Call For Change*. 111th Cong., 2nd session, 10 March.

US Treasury. 1944a. *Joint Statement by Experts on the Establishment of an International Monetary Fund of the United States and Associated Nations*. Washington, DC: Department of the Treasury, April, 21.

1944b. *Questions and Answers on the Bank for Reconstruction and Development*. Washington, DC: Department of the Treasury, June 10.

White, H. D. 1945. Quoted in US House of Representatives Committee on Banking and Currency. *Bretton Woods Agreements Act Hearings before the Committee on Banking and Currency*. 79th Cong., 1st session.

Wilcox, C. 1947b. Department of State, Division of Central Services, Washington DC, Meeting Transcript, October 1. US National Archives, College Park.

Index